TSULTRIM ALLIONE

WOMEN OF
WISDOM

ARKANA
LONDON AND NEW YORK

This book is dedicated to
all women on a spiritual quest,
and especially to my mother,
Ruth Dewing Ewing,
and my daughters, Sherab and Aloka

First published in 1984
ARKANA edition 1986
ARKANA PAPERBACKS is an imprint of
Routledge & Kegan Paul Ltd

11 New Fetter Lane, London EC4P 4EE

Published in the USA by
Routledge and Kegan Paul Inc.
in association with Methuen Inc.
29 West 35th Street, New York, NY 10001

Set in Palatino, 10 on 12pt
and printed and bound in Great Britain
by The Guernsey Press Co Ltd,
Guernsey, Channel Islands

Library of Congress Cataloging in Publication Data

Women of wisdom.
Bibliography: p.
Includes index.
1. Women, Buddhist – China – Tibet – Biography.
I. Allione, Tsultrim, 1947-
BQ7920.W65   1984   294.3'923'0922[B]   84-11440

British Library CIP Data available

ISBN 1–85063–044–5

ARKANA

WOMEN OF
WISDOM

Tsultrim Allione was born in Maine and grew up in New Hampshire as Joan Rousmanière Ewing. From a young age she became interested in Buddhism through her grandmother. She travelled to India and Nepal in 1967 and then returned in 1969 and was shortly thereafter ordained as a Buddhist nun by H. H. Karmapa in Bodhgaya and was given the name Karma Tsultrim Chodron. As a nun she went on extensive solitary retreats, studied Tibetan language and religion, and made pilgrimages around Nepal and India. After three and a half years as a Buddhist nun she decided she wanted to follow the Tibetan Buddhist path without the external support of the monastic life and she returned to the United States and married and began her family. She has had four children, one of whom died, and has been married twice. She has continued to study and practice meditation under several great teachers for the past seventeen years. She has also taught Buddhist meditation, made numerous trips to India and Nepal, and now lives in Italy.

CONTENTS

Contents

ILLUSTRATIONS

Plates

Between pages 90 and 91

Line drawings

vii

FOREWORD

Contrary to popular opinion which holds that the Vajrayana tradition of Buddhism has been practiced primarily by men, many of the great contemplative teachers and practitioners have been women. In Tibet we found that women practitioners were frequently more diligent and dedicated than men. I am very pleased to see the publication of *Women of Wisdom*, which provides ample evidence to that effect. Tsultrim Allione's work should not be regarded as mere feminism. This collection of stories is a great contribution to spreading the understanding of Tibetan Buddhism in the West.

With blessings,

VAJRACARYA, THE VENERABLE CHÖGYAM TRUNGPA, RINPOCHE

ACKNOWLEDGMENTS

This book could not have come into being without the guidance and blessings of my precious teachers: His Holiness Gyalwa Karmapa, who ordained me and whose blessings are ever-present; Abo Rinpoche, who guided me in my retreats and whose humor and confidence gave me the courage to return to "worldly life"; Chögyam Trungpa Rinpoche, who has helped me in many transitions, always encouraging me to take the next step with trust in myself, he taught me to pull forth the essence of the teachings from their cultural framework; Namkhai Norbu Rinpoche, who introduced me to the Dzog Chen teachings and Machig Lapdron, and showed me that the principle of the teachings is the naked primordial state of awareness beyond ritual and hierarchy. He also patiently helped me with this book from beginning to end. I would also like to thank all the other lamas from whom I have received teachings over the years: His Holiness Dudjom Rinpoche, His Holiness the Dalai Lama, Kalu Rinpoche, Dingo Khentse Rinpoche, Sapchu Rinpoche, Khamtrul Rinpoche, Chatrul Rinpoche, Deshung Rinpoche, Sogyal Tulku, Nichang Rinpoche, Lama Thupten Yeshe and Thupten Zopa Rinpoche. I would also like to acknowledge Thinley Norbu Rinpoche, whom I have not yet met, but whose teachings have been illuminating.

I want to express special thanks to my parents, who have provided a platform of generous love and support over the years of my search and who did their best to understand my process and give me the space to find my own way. My mother, Ruth, gave me her love of spiritual and intellectual exploration and openness to alternative ways of seeing life, and my father, James, gave me his grounded and practical advice along the way and also helped with the writing of the book, based on his years of experience in journalism.

I would also like to acknowledge my sister, Carolyn Rousmaniere, who has been a soul sister as well as a blood sister. I give special thanks to Costanzo Allione, with whom I have been through so much we are like "war buddies," and who has encouraged me to keep going in moments of confusion and doubt. I also want to thank my magical children, Sherab Crystal, Aloka, and Costanzo Kunzang "Neen," who have put up with the hours of "Mummy working" and have inspired me and taught me so much by their fresh presence.

I especially wish to thank my friends, who have spanned continents and endured over years of separation. They have given me support of inestimable value. Sometimes just knowing that they were out there somewhere has helped, and at other times they have been nearby sharing their thoughts and insights: Dale Drasil, Sierra Satya Crawford, Pema Young, Nancy Scott Winker, Sue Hatfield Stone, Kris Ellis and the rest of the women from the Vashon Island women's group, Louise Putnam Finnegan whom I grew up with and who accompanied me on my last trip to Nepal, Elizabeth and Tim Olmstead who put me up in Kathmandu, Victress Hitchcock with whom I first went East; more recently in Rome, Mara and Andrea Sertoli, Constance Soehnlen, Charlene Spretnak, Marie Axler, Paola Carducci, Laura Albini, Dr Renzulli, Nancy and Barrie Simmons and Nancy Mehagian; my old friend June Campbell who acted as assistant when I was in a long retreat in India and with whom I travelled around India when I was a nun.

I would also like to thank friends in London: Noel and Fay Cobb, Dodo Von Greiff, Jill Purce, who acted as agent for the book, and Eileen Wood, my editor. Also thanks to friends in New York: Allen Ginsberg, who always had some kind of faith in me; Anne Waldman and Reed Bye, Sarah Kapp and Jack Niland; and to ex-New Yorkers Terry Clifford and Michal Abrams, who are now in a three-year Dzog Chen retreat in France and will surely be glad to have this book.

In the beginning stages of this book I was given amazing support and encouragement from Christine Sarfaty, Penny

Acknowledgments

Bernstein and Jim Rousmaniere. This was followed up by help from Gene Smith, Barbara Azziz, Jan Willis and Reginald Ray, Kenniard Lipman, Paula Spier, and Connie Bauer at Antioch International.

I would like to thank Eva van Dam for her painting for the cover, and Nigel Wellings for the line drawings.

I also really want to thank two women who kept my family functioning while I was writing this book – Terena Doughty and Julie West: without them it would not have been possible. I also want to thank Claire Warburton for typing and assistance in the hot sweaty summer. Thanks to James Low for his critical reading and response to the book.

I would also like to express my appreciation to those who helped me in Kathmandu: Yudron, Phuntsog Tobjhor, Lama Ralu, Lama Tsewang Gyurme, Keith and Meryl Dowman and my Dharma brother and heart friend Gyalwa in Swayambhu and the stupas with all their blessings. I also want to thank those who helped me in Manali: the wife of the late Abo Rinpoche and my Dharma sister, Urgyen Chodron, and her children who helped with the translation; Thinley Chodron and Gelek Namgyel, as well as Phoebe Harper and Gegyen Khentse, a true saint. My gratitude goes to Harish Budhraj, whom I call "the bodhisattva of Delhi" and who helped me in difficult moments.

I would like to extend my humble thanks and respects to the Buddhas, Dakinis and Dharma Protectors who made my travels go smoothly, brought me the right people and the right books at the right time and provided me with energy and perseverance while this book was being born. May they continue to guide this work to those whom it will benefit!

May any mistakes or omissions be forgiven and may all beings abide in a natural state of luminosity and wisdom without limits!

PREFACE

The roots of this book go back to my maternal grandmother, Frances Rousmaniere Dewing, who gave me a book of Zen Buddhist poetry when I was fifteen. She was a woman of wisdom in her own way, in her own time. She was the fourth woman in history to receive a doctorate from Radcliffe College. Her field was philosophy and she was a friend of William James and Kahlil Gibran, who greatly admired her and drew a portrait of her.

She was a free thinker and did not plan to marry, having decided to devote herself to an intellectual life. She taught at Wellesley, Mount Holyoke and Smith Colleges and was so dearly loved by her students that they still came to visit her when she was in her eighties. She met my grandfather, Arthur Stone Dewing, at a philosophy seminar when they were both doing their doctoral research, but it was not until six years later, at the age of thirty-five, that she made the difficult decision to give up her teaching career and marry him. In those days, women had to choose between marriage and a career. My grandfather was also a philosopher, a financial genius and a very eccentric person. He used to answer the telephone by crowing like a rooster. He kept snakes in his pockets, alligators in the bath-tub, tortoises in the back yard of their home, and he gave my mother a bear for a pet.

They had three daughters, Mary, Abigail, and Ruth. My mother, the youngest daughter, Ruth, shared her mother's love of ideas and her independent spirit. She walked all over southern Russia with a girlfriend when she was nineteen and got her pilot's license a few years later and then worked as a labor mediator.

She gave up a fascinating career in labor relations to marry my father, a small-town newspaper publisher, and have children. She did, however, imbue in my sister, my brother and myself a love of intellectual exploration and artistic and aesthetic beauty. I do not think her decision to marry was easy for her, either. I remember her desperate pleas at our chaotic dinner table for an "elevated conversation." Although at the time we all laughed at her, I realize now that this plea was a longing for food for her spirit.

I suppose with these women in my "lineage" it is not surprising that when I was nineteen I left my university studies and began an uncharted spiritual quest which eventually led me to write this book.

In June 1967, when I was nineteen, my friend from the University of Colorado and spiritual sister, Victress Hitchcock, and I flew from San Francisco to Hong Kong to join her parents, who were in the diplomatic corps in Calcutta. We traveled by boat from Hong Kong to Bombay, and there we were taken ashore by small boats, which left us at the bottom of a long flight of wide stone steps. As I walked up these steps I felt that I had finally arrived in a place where I could find true wisdom.

We stayed with Victress's parents in Calcutta for the monsoon. Her father was the Consul General in Calcutta, and his wife, Maxine, arranged for us to work as volunteers at Mother Teresa's "Orphanage and Home for Unwed Mothers." They hoped that this kind of work would get the fantasies of the "Mystic East" out of our heads and set us on a more acceptable path, but then they sent us to Kathmandu to work with Tibetan refugees.

One day, as we were exploring the upper stories of a house in Kathmandu, we went out onto a balcony, and in the distance I saw a small hill at the top of which was a white dome topped by a golden spire. It looked like something from a fairy tale, glittering invitingly in the bright sunlight. We were told that this was called "The Monkey Temple" as it was inhabited by wild monkeys; but its real name was Swayambhu, which means "self-sprung."[1] This small hill topped with a cluster of temples and a huge Tibetan stupa is sacred to both the Nepalese and the Tibetans. We were told that during the summer there were predawn processions from Kathmandu to Swayambhu and we decided to try to get up early enough to join one of these.

We rose the next day long before dawn and, when we stumbled bleary-eyed into the streets, we joined in a very bizarre parade consisting of Nepalese of all ages screaming songs and making noise with anything they had on hand from battered trumpets to tin drums. We were told that all this noise was to wake up the gods so that they would not forget to make the rice grow. We walked through the narrow stone and dirt streets of the city over a bridge and then up to the base of the hill, where we began a steep ascent.

We staggered up the hundreds of stone steps hardly aware of the ancient stone Buddhas, prayer flags and wild monkeys that surrounded us. It was beginning to get hot even at that hour. We were breathless and sweating as we stumbled up the last steep steps and practically fell upon the biggest vajra (thunderbolt scepter) that I have ever seen. Behind this vajra was the vast, round, white dome of the stupa, like a full solid skirt, at the top of which were two giant Buddha eyes wisely looking out over the peaceful valley which was just beginning to come alive. We wandered around this stupa amidst the singing, banging Nepalese and the humming Tibetans who were circumambulating the stupa spinning the prayer wheels which line the lower portion of the round dome.

We were just catching our breath when several six-foot-long horns emerged from the adjacent Tibetan monastery and started to make an unbelievable sound. It is a long, deep, whirring, haunting wail that takes you out somewhere beyond the highest Himalayan peaks and at the same time back into your mother's womb.

I was so moved by this place that I took a small hut on the neighboring hill, Kimdol,[2] and began to rise very early in the morning and make the rounds of the Tibetan monasteries on Swayambhu hill as they were chanting their morning rituals and having their first cups of Tibetan tea. There was one monastery which attracted me particularly. It was the one right near the stupa, and I used to linger there, sitting in an out-of-the-way corner at the back of the temple. One day I arrived early in the morning as usual and found they had left a little carpet there for me to sit on and a cup of the morning tea. From that day onward the little carpet was always waiting for me, and one of the monks, Gyalwa, who became my friend, always made sure I had tea.

It was as if the monks understood my bond with the place and the irresistible pull I felt from the stupa. As I sat there I felt as though part of myself, which had up until then remained empty, was being filled. A joyful sense of being in the blessings which were almost tangibly present began to steal over me. Although I had no intellectual reference points for this experience, later, after years of formal training in meditation, I realized that this was "beginner's mind"[3] and that the direct connection with the "bliss waves"[4] sent forth by great lamas held the secret of my search.

One cannot force or grasp a spiritual experience, because it is as delicate as the whisper of the wind. But one can purify one's motivation, one's body, and train oneself to cultivate it. Because we come from a culture which teaches us that there is always something external to be obtained which will lead us to fulfillment, we lose contact with our innate wisdom. As the Indian Tantric Buddhist saint Saraha says in one of his dohas (poems expressing the essence of his understanding):

> Though the house-lamps have been lit,
> The blind live on in the dark.
> Though spontaneity is all-encompassing
> and close, to the deluded it remains
> always far away.[5]

Beyond the profound impressions of the land and the sacred power places I visited, I also met several significant people who made profound impressions on me. After moving to Kimdol I met a Japanese traveler, Sawamura, who had been living with the Tibetans. He was traveling to northwestern India to see the Dalai Lama and invited me to go with him. So we traveled third class without tickets and hitch-hiked all the way across northern India, stopping at various Tibetan refugee camps or staying with hospitable Indians on our way.

When we arrived in Dharamsala, the Dalai Lama's head-quarters, he went to stay in a monastery with two lamas, Geshe Rabten and Gonsar Tulku. I, as a woman, had to stay down in the town. I had almost no money, so I stayed in a room made out of flattened kerosene tins papered with old newspapers. I had no sleeping bag, and since it was November it was already freezing at night in the mountains. I bought a blanket and a piece of cloth of equal size, sewed them together and stuffed the middle with newspaper. But the wind still whistled through the walls, and the rats who shared my room chose to move around at night, so I began to get up at four in the morning to circumambulate the Dalai Lama's residence with the devoted Tibetans who did this before beginning their work day. I had never been happier in my life.

After several weeks, Sawamura came and told me that there was a fasting ceremony beginning the next day which we could attend. I decided to do this, not realizing that we would not only fast, eating only once every two days, but we would also be doing thousands of prostrations on the freezing floor every few hours and hardly sleeping at all.

After five days I was called for an appointment with a high lama whom I had requested to see about studying mandala painting. He told me it would take at least a year to learn one mandala, and then at the end of my interview he said to me that the time I spent doing spiritual practice was the only time which would have any lasting value. This now seems obvious to me, but as I had no understanding of the path at that time, this statement struck me and I thought about it for a long time. Someone else said to me during this period: "Cut off your hair, hang it on the wall and contemplate impermanence." As I was only nineteen and had lived all of my life in America, I had never thought much about death, but had rather lived as though I was immortal. These two statements planted the seeds for what was to follow and I contemplated them when I returned to the West.

With the Tibetans I found a living esoteric tradition which had been carefully transmitted from teacher to disciple, without interruption, for centuries. The Tibetans also had an intelligence and a sense of joy and humor that I had never encountered before. After six months in India we returned to

Nepal, and as my parents had sent me a ticket I decided to return to the West. When I was on my way to the airport, Gyalwa, my friend from the Swayambhu monastery, appeared at a crossroads in Kathmandu. He pressed a string of mantra beads made of bodhi seeds and a picture of Swayambhu hill into my hands. It was as if he knew that these would help to bring me back to what I had discovered there.

When I was back in the United States I recited the mantras I had learned from the Tibetans using this string of beads. This helped me to keep in contact with the blessings of the Tibetan lamas, but I was still homesick for "my mountain." Though I tried to fulfill my parents' wishes and go back to school, I was miserable.

After a year I managed to get to a Tibetan meditation center called Samye Ling in Scotland. The day I arrived I heard that the abbot of the place, Chögyam Trungpa Rinpoche,[6] was to return from the hospital where he had been recovering from a car accident. I had imagined he would be a wise-looking old man, so when I saw him I was shocked to see a youthful, handsome Tibetan, who was still badly paralyzed from his accident.

I did not have any contact with Trungpa Rinpoche for several months, because he was still too weak to receive people and he was surrounded by a group of very possessive disciples. When I finally did meet him, it was quite funny and wonderful.

I was scheduled for an official "interview," which was something I had never experienced before. I told the people organizing the interviews that I had no idea what to say to him, but they assured me that I need not worry, for he would start the conversation. So I went into the room and sat timidly on the floor in front of his chair and looked at him. He did not say anything; nor did I. We stayed like that for about forty-five minutes.

Now I realize that what happened was some kind of mind-to-mind transmission, but at the time I only knew that I had experienced something that was completely beyond words and form. It reminded me of some of the experiences I had had sitting near the stupa at Swayambhu. It was an experience of space that extended outward without any reference back. This space was luminous and bliss-provoking, a release, similar to, but beyond, sexual orgasm. When I emerged everyone was eager to know what he had said and I had to respond, "Nothing!"

Trungpa Rinpoche was still not teaching formally, nor was Akong Rinpoche, the other lama there, so, when I heard of a Volkswagen bus which would be taking passengers from London to Kathmandu for a minimal fee, I leapt at the chance. Before I left, Trungpa Rinpoche gave me permission to take a copy of "The Sadhana of All the Siddhis," a Tantric practice he had written in Bhutan in 1968 while in retreat in the cave of Tatsang. This sadhana[7] was the most evocative and poetic piece of writing I had ever read. Part of it was an invocation to various incarnations of the great Karmapa, the leader of the Kagyu sect[8] of Tibetan Buddhism.

I read this sadhana as often as possible during my overland journey from London to Kathmandu. The trip was tortuous. In Afghanistan there were days and days of dirt roads so dusty that even when we closed all the windows and wrapped clothes around our faces, the dust penetrated. There were eight people of five different nationalities in the bus, which during the trip had two completely new engines, numerous repairs, and had to be towed two hundred miles at night over icy roads in the mountains of Turkey. We pulled into Kathmandu just before Christmas in 1969, after six weeks of continuous travel.

I went to Swayambhu and immediately noticed a hubbub of activity and an incredible assortment of monks, yogis with long matted hair, and Tibetans in an assortment of regional costumes. I learned that this was because His Holiness Karmapa had come to Kathmandu for the first time in thirteen years. He was staying at the monastery near the stupa which I had visited every morning during my first visit to Nepal. I was a bit put off by all the pomp and pageantry and the pushy Tibetan crowds, but then something inexplicable started to happen to me. I started to feel very agitated and was unable to eat or sleep much. I knew I had to make a connection with someone there. Of course the obvious person was the Karmapa, but perversely I was sure it was someone else. I went around for several days looking for signs, becoming more and more agitated. Then one day I was reading through the sadhana Trungpa Rinpoche had given me and noticed the continual references to Karmapa. Suddenly it dawned on me that it was obviously an auspicious coincidence that I had arrived in Kathmandu at the same time as his visit and that he was there in "my monastery." At the same time I came across a line in the sadhana which said: "The only offering I can make is to follow your example." Since he was a monk it was clear to me that I should follow his example and take the robes.

I went directly to the monastery on Swayambhu and, disregarding all the usual prostrations and formalities, walked in, offered him some flowers and indicated that I wanted to cut off my hair.[9] He laughed and then gave me a look I shall never forget. It was as though he was seeing everything: the past, the present and the future. Then he nodded his head and asked me to sit down. Through a primitive translation it was decided that I was to be ordained a week later in Bodhgaya, where the Buddha had reached full illumination under the bodhi tree.

I was given my ordination on the day of the full moon in January 1970, by Karmapa in the presence of the four major tulkus[10] in the Kagyu lineage. I was told by the Karmapa's translator that before I had come to him in Kathmandu he had seen me in a crowd and had said that I would become a nun and that I had been his disciple in a previous lifetime. He had therefore waived the usual preliminary stages and had given me the full ordination[11] immediately. It was at this time that I was given the name Karma Tsultrim Chodron, which means "Discipline Torch of Dharma in the Lineage of Karmapa." I began to be called this by the Tibetans, and when I eventually returned to the West, although I could have changed back to my Western name, I decided to carry on using my Tibetan name. I wanted to be continually reminded of the change that had taken place in my life and to be connected to the blessings of the Karmapa. Now, fourteen years later, my previous name, Joan Rousmaniere Ewing, sounds foreign to me, and I feel more comfortable with the name Tsultrim, even though it sounds a bit odd to Western ears and I often have to explain it.

After my ordination I returned to Kathmandu. There I discovered that I had a serious case of hepatitis and had to go to bed immediately. Two American friends, Pamela Crawford and John Travis, took me in to their house, and as I was lying there very light-headed from the fever, my Tibetan friend Gyalwa appeared and gave me some Tibetan medicine which made me feel better almost immediately. A few days later an American woman, Zena Rachevsky, who had taken the robes from His Holiness the Dalai Lama, arrived and insisted that I go to stay in her house on Kopan hill, near the Baudha Stupa. I stayed there for six months and was helped and supported by Lama Thupten Yeshe and the young Sherpa Lama Thupten Zopa. At that time there were only three Westerners and these lamas at Kopan. Since that time it has become an international meditation center and these lamas teach all over the world.

When I was strong enough I went up into the mountains with them and spent six weeks near Lama Zopa's cave, from which we had a view of Mount Everest. We were actually living in the clouds at 16,000 feet. We used to dig out little U-shaped places in which to meditate in the side of the mountain and pass our days there.

When I returned to Kathmandu I decided to move to Swayambhu and to begin to study Tibetan. Gyalwa found me a room right next to the stupa which was so small that I could sit in the middle and touch all the walls. Here I cooked, studied, slept and meditated. My lessons started at 6.30 a.m. I was taught by two other nuns, who had a rigorous meditation schedule and had only this time to teach me.

My room was like a little tree house. The windows opened onto some huge old trees. Living so near the stupa I came to know its life, day and night and through the seasons. What happened around the stupa was a condensation of the magical religious life and festivals of both the Nepalese and the Tibetans.

After a year in Nepal I went to India and went to see Karmapa in Sikkim. He said he had been watching me, and I felt so close to him that when it came time to leave I cried for a whole day. I had never felt this kind of grief before and I was inconsolable. But when I did leave and went to Bodhgaya, and to Sarnath where the Buddha first turned the wheel of the Dharma, and then on to Tashi Jong and Manali, I felt his presence constantly.

In Manali I decided to enter a long retreat in order to

complete the nungdro (preliminary practices)[12] and began formal training under the guidance of the great married yogi Abo Rinpoche. Previously I had been relating to my meditation in a rather unorthodox way. I had had several initiations and had done these practices, but mostly I had been reading "The Song of Mahamudra" by Tilopa and trying to practice in this way:

> Do nought with the body but relax,
> Shut firm the mouth and silent remain,
> Empty your mind and think of nought.
> Like a hollow bamboo
> Rest at ease your body.
> Giving not nor taking.
> Put your mind at rest.
> Mahamudra is like a mind that clings to nought.
> Thus practicing, in time you will reach Buddhahood.[13]

While I was doing this practice I met another Western nun, and when she asked me what practices I did, I said mostly Mahamudra. She was horrified as this is supposed to be a very advanced practice, and she told me I must do all the preliminaries first. I was swayed by her and I began with the preliminary practices and then continued with various Tantric visualization practices with mantra recitation and so on for the next eight years. Up until then I had had my own personal way of approaching the teachings, and at this point I entered into "the system," so to speak. Previously I had had direct contacts with Karmapa in dreams and visions in which he gave me specific teachings and initiations. After this it became harder and more forced, and my dreams and visions became fewer and fewer over the years; but I acquired a better knowledge of Buddhism and went through some rigorous mind training.

My favorite thing to study was the biographies of the great teachers of Tibetan Buddhism. Since I was trying to follow the same path I found the stories of their struggles and the ensuing realizations that they gained tremendously helpful and inspiring. I found tidbits of stories of women here and there and I reread them many times, but there was nothing very substantial. Now it is obvious to me why I longed for stories of women and amazing that I did not consciously wonder about the lack of women's biographies. I guess it was part of my conditioning to accept that all the important saints were men, but I think that unconsciously the roots of the research for this book began at that time.

After two and a half years in India I decided to return to the United States to see my family, and also Trungpa Rinpoche who had moved there from Scotland. I stayed in the United States for a year, studying with Trungpa Rinpoche, but found that wearing the robes there became more of a hindrance than a blessing. I think I was the only Tibetan Buddhist nun in America at that time. To me the point of the robes was to simplify one's external appearance so that one could concentrate on one's inner development. The novelty of the Tibetan robes in America seemed to have the opposite effect. I felt that I wanted to live in America as staying in India had been very draining on my health; but I was in a quandary as to whether I should continue as a nun or give back my vows.

Trungpa Rinpoche suggested that I return to India to see Karmapa and invite him to the States, and to make my decision there. When I got to India there was a war in Sikkim and I could not go to see Karmapa. I had to send him the invitation, and I went to Tashi Jong where Dingo Khentse Rinpoche was giving a series of initiations which could last up to three months. Here I met again my meditation teacher from Manali, Abo Rinpoche, who had come from Manali to take these initiations. I also met a man I had known in Holland four and a half years before, with whom I had been corresponding.

Abo Rinpoche had four children and a wonderful wife, and he had a great sense of humor. When I told him I was having repeated dreams about a baby he laughed so hard he almost fell off his seat, and then he said: "All nuns should have babies." I didn't know quite how he meant this, and I continued to struggle with my decision until one day I told him I was having a lot of sexual thoughts and feelings and that I really felt I could not continue as a nun. I asked him when he thought I should give back my vows.[14] He said: "It depends how much longer you can wait!" Then he laughed so hard that tears were running down his face. I also saw the absurdity of the situation and that I was holding on to something that wasn't appropriate anymore. He also assured me I would be able to continue my meditation practice as a lay person.

I returned my vows the next day to Khamtrul Rinpoche, who was a monk. Rather than making me feel guilty, he just quietly said that I should dedicate the merit I had gained by being a nun for the benefit of all sentient beings, do some purification practices and continue on the path.

I now see the time I spent as a nun as an invaluable experience. I think it is important for women to have the experience of living a "virgin" existence. I mean virgin in its true sense: a maiden alone, complete in herself, belonging to no man.

"The virgin forest is not barren or unfertilized but rather a place that is especially fruitful and has multiplied because it has taken life into itself and transformed it, giving birth naturally and taking dead things back to be recycled. It is virgin because it is unexploited, not in man's control."[15]

This time gave me a chance to develop myself without the inevitable drain which comes with relationships. As I was only twenty-two at the time of my ordination, I was not formed enough myself to resist being swept away whenever I fell in love. The robes and the celibacy that went with the ordination served as a protective shell in which I could grow and find myself. But once this process had been established, holding on to this form would have become repressive for me. One of the most important things to realize is that during this time, although I had my vows, I was not obligated to ask permission to anyone to travel or study where I wished. I lived alone, but usually near a lama who could teach me, and I was free and independent. Some Tibetan nuns choose to live within a monastic situation where one has obligations, but others live and travel freely as I did.

Shortly after I disrobed I married the Dutchman, Paul Kloppenburg, with whom I had been corresponding and whom I met again in Tashi Jong. He had been studying with the Tibetans for four years also. Within a year I went from being a solitary nun to being a mother.

The internal changes and adjustments were enormous. I realized that the physical demands of pregnancy and nursing a baby were going to make it impossible to continue my meditation practice with the same intensity as before. I had made a decision which could never be reversed and I was suddenly under the power of forces from within my body that were stronger than I had ever experienced before. We got married in India and then moved to Vashon Island in the Puget Sound near Seattle where we made a small meditation center. I became pregnant again with Aloka, my second daughter, nine months after the birth of Sherab, my oldest daughter. We lived very simply, growing our food and living in one room with a separate meditation room and retreat hut. We would take turns with the babies so we could meditate. During this time, I appreciated sharing information with other women in similar situations. When I was in my second pregnancy a group of island women decided to meet and discuss their babies and breastfeeding problems. After one meeting we decided we did not want to talk about our babies but we wanted to explore our own interior lives and to hear each other's stories. Through these meetings I began to be aware of the female experience and to cherish the company of women.

In India, being a woman had been something I had hoped would not get in the way. Through this group I realized that being a woman was not a liability, but rather that women had an ability to heal, to hear and support without judging and to have direct insight into situations. I began to love being a woman, being with women, and wanted to understand women more. I then realized that Tibetan Buddhist women's stories had not been told. I longed to join my spiritual path with my awareness of myself as a woman, and began thinking about this book.

Though my first husband was kind and helpful, after three years I felt constrained by the relationship and wanted to move out on my own for a while. We moved to Boulder with the children in 1976. I began teaching at Naropa Institute and within the Buddhist community in Boulder, and lived separately from my husband. I also did some lecture tours around the States during the following three years.

Although I enjoyed living in a Buddhist community, after several years I felt unhappy with the patriarchal, hierarchical, structured organization there. I also felt I was often parroting the words of Trungpa Rinpoche and losing touch with my own experience. I was becoming an expert rather than a beginner.

Although I could appreciate the benefits of this structure I felt the ever-increasing forms and rituals and my attempts to fit into the organization were creating an inner conflict and my practice was not progressing.

As I was experiencing this crisis I met my second husband, Costanzo Allione. He came to Naropa Institute to film the poets. Allen Ginsberg, who was the co-director of the Naropa poetry project, introduced us at a party. Allen and I had been friends since I had been in the States as a nun and had traveled around the western part of the States together with Ram Dass (Richard Alpert) raising money for a retreat center. When I came back to Boulder Allen had asked me to act as his meditation instructor, so it was in this capacity that I was introduced to Costanzo. After a year of traveling back and forth from Italy we got married in Boulder and moved to Rome.

Within a few months I was pregnant again, and almost immediately the doctor began to question the date of conception. When I was six months pregnant we discovered I was having twins.

This period was my own personal "descent" experience. I had left all my friends and my work behind. I had been teaching and lecturing around the States and had many good friends with whom I could share my spiritual path and who understood the world within the context of the Buddhist teachings.

Suddenly I realized that I had left more than I thought. My husband was gone most of the time, working in Rome or traveling. Our villa, which was an hour from Rome, was isolated and very cold. I was practically immobilized by the pregnancy and depression. I had nothing except my two small daughters and my giant womb. I had gone from being very independent, to feeling extremely dependent and powerless. It was as though my whole path had been diverted into a whirlpool of emptiness. I felt alienated from everything and everyone and could not motivate myself to meditate. I was uncomfortable standing up and lying down. The last two months I had to stay in bed so that the twins would not be born too early. I could foresee nothing except years of babies, fatigue, and loneliness.

The birth experience was traumatic. I had had my daughters at home with the assistance of a homebirth clinic from Seattle, but there were no such facilities in Italy, and since I was having twins I had to go to the hospital anyway.

Italy is very behind the times in terms of childbirth and postpartum care. The worst thing was that after the twins (a boy, Costanzo Kunzang, and a girl, Chiara Osel) were born, they put them into incubators and would not allow me to touch them for two weeks. Even though they both weighed over five pounds, I could only see them from a distance of twelve feet through two glass walls that were usually fogged over. Once I sneaked in to get a look at them and was harshly reprimanded by the nurse. I only saw their weight chart, which was going down everyday. The pediatrician kept assuring me this was normal and could not understand my floods of tears. I knew that they needed me as much as I needed them, and that they had almost as much need to feel the loving body of their mother as they needed food. I felt they needed to be touched or they would not survive. I would cry for hours on end, expressing my milk with a breast pump with such vigor that I was feeding three babies in the nursery and injured my thumb joint. I also realized concretely at this time how the natural domain of women, the birthing of babies, has been completely taken over by the patriarchy. There was an "expert" telling me every day that everything was fine and the babies only needed a few more weeks in the incubator before I could hold them and feed them. I felt completely impotent, weak from the pregnancy and birth, and intimidated by the hospital's authority. I do not think I have ever cried as much as in those two weeks of separation from my babies. If I had really believed they needed the incubator it would have been different, but I was not at all convinced.

Finally, through an American friend, I got in touch with an American pediatrician Dr Renzulli, who asked me why I wasn't nursing my babies. When I told him the hospital would not let me try, he said I must try and if they could nurse I should get them out as soon as possible. He really helped me and compromised his reputation by going against the advice of the hospital. I shall be forever grateful for his intercession at a point when I was too weak to assert myself.

When I did finally get to nurse the twins they sucked strongly and each took in a very substantial amount. We took them out the following day, against the hospital's recommendation. Although the following weeks were exhausting and my eyes were always red and burning, I was so happy I did not mind.

Everything was going well and they were passing their pediatric check-ups with flying colours until, at two and a half months, the little girl died of "Sudden Infant Death Syndrome."[16] I found her dead in her little bed one morning.

This death proved to be a turning point for me. It was the bottom of my descent, and having hit the bottom I had a springboard to push myself back to the surface. Namkhai Norbu Rinpoche, a Tibetan lama who lives in Italy, came to do the funeral. When I asked him why this had happened, ready to believe the worst of myself and my karma in my guilt-ridden state, he just said very softly: "It was for her own reasons." Then I told him I had lost faith in everything and he just looked at me and did not say anything. He quietly set about making a protection bracelet for the remaining twin and gave me a special practice for my own protection and for the rest of the family. I felt that he was releasing us from a strange curse.

Since I had left Boulder and all that it represented to me, I had been in a state of inner turmoil and depression. This state left me open to negative forces, and the weaker I became the more oppressed I felt by strange negativities. We were living in a huge spooky old villa, and from the moment we had arrived there things had become worse and worse. The furnace did not function, most of the time, there were hurricanes and earthquakes and many disturbances. When the baby died we decided to leave immediately, but Norbu's visit already alleviated a lot of the strange feelings I had been experiencing. Then when we went to the hospital where Chiara's body was, he did something which made me begin to understand that he is a very great lama, even though he is not surrounded by an entourage and dresses and acts like an ordinary person.

I had called him as soon as I had found her dead and he had performed the transference of consciousness (powa) from a distance. A few days later he and a group of his students came to do a funeral practice at our villa, and afterwards we went to the hospital morgue. He put a paper mandala on Chiara's navel and some sacred sand on the crown of her head. Then we went outside and I went to him and threw my arms around his neck and started to weep uncontrollably. Instead of hugging me and comforting me, he just stood there very relaxed. I do not know if it was my surprise at his lack of reaction or what, but I suddenly felt the pain draining out of my tight body and my mind fell into a state of vastness, like a broad, peaceful lake. I simultaneously realized that I was charging myself up and making it worse by clinging to her. I realized that thousands of babies die every day and that I had just been protected from this reality by living in an affluent country.

Since the death of Chiara everything has been uphill. I have been re-emerging from my descent. This has not been easy. I have had to reassess every aspect of myself. The death of the baby put my relationship with my husband, which was already strained, into a crisis. Many people think that this kind of tragedy brings couples closer together, but, actually, ninety per cent of the time it works the other way. We had to work with our relationship in many different ways. My contact with Norbu Rinpoche helped me to find my way back to the spiritual path. As he is a Dzog Chen teacher and works with each individual, the direct transmission of energy he connected me to brought me back to the "beginner's mind" I had experienced in my first year in Nepal.

In a way I have traveled a full circle on my spiritual path, but I also realize that through all the various disciplines and life experiences I have changed and am now integrating these experiences with what I am beginning to understand as women's spirituality and Dzog Chen. I do not feel my search for my path as a woman conflicts with practices I have done before but, rather, it is bringing forth other kinds of awareness.

I realize now that, for me, spirituality is connected to a delicate, playful spacious part of myself which closes up in militantly regimented situations. The more I try to limit my mind in outward forms, the more this subtle energy escapes like a shy young girl. It is as if I need to trust the vastness of my mind and let go, let my shoulders drop, not try to control situations, and yet not follow rampant discursive thoughts or hold on when my mind gets fixated.

I think that this luminous, subtle spiritual energy is what is meant by the dakini principle.[17] She is the key, the gate opener, and the guardian of the unconditioned primordial state which is innate in everyone. If I am not willing to play with her, or if I try to force her, or if I do not invoke her, the gate remains closed and I remain in darkness and ignorance.

I met the dakini in another way about a year after Chiara's death when I was in California at a group retreat given by Namkhai Norbu Rinpoche. One night we were doing the Chod practice,[18] and at a certain point, when we were invoking the presence of Machig, visualizing her as a youthful white dakini, a wild-looking old woman suddenly appeared very close to me. She had grey hair streaming up from her head, and she was naked, with dark golden-brown skin. Her breasts hung pendulously and she was dancing. She was coming out of a dark cemetery. The most impressive thing about her was the look in her eyes. They were very bright, and the expression was one of challenging invitation mixed with mischievous joy, uncompromising strength and compassion. She was inviting me to join her dance.

Afterwards I realized that this was a form of Machig Lapdron. She was a woman who really embodied the wisdom of the feminine. She had fed babies with those breasts, yet she was undomesticated. She was fearless yet compassionate, ecstatic yet grounded, and above all she was inviting me with her confidence and her joy.

A few days later I started to have a series of repetitive dreams. Every morning just before I woke up, I dreamt that I must go to the Swayambhu, but that there would be many obstacles. In each dream the obstacles varied but the theme was the same. Each morning I awoke with an urgent feeling that I must go back to "my mountain." Since I had had similar dreams over the years, and had come to understand Swayambhu as a symbol of my spiritual center, at first I understood these dreams symbolically. But these dreams were more insistent and had a different quality from the others I had dreamed before, and I felt perhaps I really had to go back to my mountain; I discussed it with my husband and we decided to go to Nepal that winter so I could go to Swayambhu Stupa.

Although the idea of collecting the life stories of great Tibetan women teachers had been with me for some time, because of all that had happened I had postponed this project. I had also decided that I wanted to get a degree which would encompass the study I had done up to that point. I combined all of these ideas and found that Antioch International would accept my idea of going to Nepal and collecting the biographies of these women as a Master's thesis based on the years of study I had already done.

Although we had planned to go as a family to spend a year in Nepal while I did my research, in the end we decided this would be too stressful and that I should go alone for a much shorter period and then return if necessary. So In March 1982 I set forth for Kathmandu, fifteen years after my first visit there.

When I arrived, I left my luggage at my hotel and set off by foot to Swayambhu. I noticed that though I had tried to bring my children and husband with me, I was returning alone by the same path I had originally taken. I had the peculiar sensation of the unification of my inner psychic space with the external landscape as I walked up the stone steps towards the stupa.

It was hot in the midday sun and I stopped to catch my breath half way up and chatted to some Nepalese women who were also on a pilgrimage. When I got to the top I went into the Kagyu Gompa, where I had originally met Karmapa, and asked for my old friend Gyalwa, hoping he would still be there. When he appeared he beamed at me and took me down into his dank room and started offering me endless cups of Tibetan tea and Nepalese glucose biscuits. I explained my mission to him and then went down the mountain again.

When I returned to Swayambhu a few days later, Gyalwa told me that he had found the biography of Machig Lapdron and that the lama of the Kagyu monastery had agreed to begin to translate it the next day. Suddenly the connection between the repetitive dreams that I had had about returning to Swayambhu and the vision of Machig Lapdron dawned on me. From sunrise to sunset for the next three days, Lama Tsewang Gyurme, Phuntsog Tobjhor and I translated the biography of Machig Lapdron.

In the days between these two trips up Swayambhu I had gone to Baudha, another great stupa and active Tibetan community in the Kathmandu valley. Here I was introduced to a Tibetan woman called Yudron. Yudron (Plate 7) had been a disciple of the most famous recent woman master in Tibet, Shug Sep Jetsun Rinpoche. She had been a nun in Shug Sep Jetsun's nunnery when she was young and then had become the consort of a lama, but had been separated from him when the Chinese invaded Tibet. She had then married a Tibetan businessman and had had two sons, Jigme Kunzang and Phuntsog Tobjhor.

She remembered meeting me years before at the big initiation which the Dingo Khentse Rinpoche had given in Tashi Jong when I was a nun. She immediately understood the need for the stories of women gurus, and when she began to talk about her teacher tears ran down her face. She sent her youngest son, Phuntsog Tobjhor, with me to translate the Machig Lapdron text, and when it was finished she took me out of Kathmandu to Parping,[19] where her eldest son, Jigme, was in the three-year retreat. We walked up to the Asura Cave by way of the self-originated Tara, a lovely little relief figure of the goddess of compassion which has magically appeared on an out-of-the-way rock above Parping. It started to appear about ten years ago and is now quite distinct. Most Westerners are sceptical about this and say someone probably comes in the night and works on it, but this is unlikely because no one is profiting by it. The lama who lives near the Asura Cave, Lama Ralu, gave me the biography of Jomo Memo, and Phuntsog Tobjhor translated it on the spot.

As I was about to leave Kathmandu, a friend of Yudron's, who had also been in the Shug Sep Jetsun's nunnery as a child, gave me the biography of Nangsa Obum. I took this with me to Manali, where I wanted to visit the widow of Abo Rinpoche (Plate 5) who had died shortly after the birth of my eldest daughter. She had been a close friend of mine when I was there as a nun. She has helped many people who have come there to study Dharma and everyone lovingly calls her Amala, which means "mother" in Tibetan, though her real name is Urgyen Chodron.

In Manali, her eldest son, Gelek Namgyel, and Phoebe

Harper (an Australian woman who has been studying Tibetan yoga for years) translated the biography of Nangsa Obum under the guidance of Gegyen Khentse, who now teaches Abo Rinpoche's disciples.

I returned to Italy with these three biographies, and having made a rough draft went over them with Namkhai Norbu Rinpoche to check the translation.

Then I returned to Nepal and India with my daughter Sherab in November of 1982 and received the biographies of Drenchen Rema and Machig Ongjo in Manali. These were translated by Abo Rinpoche's daughter Trinlay Chodron and I, again under the guidance of Gegyen Khentse. Yudron also gave me the biography of Shug Sep Jetsun at this time, but it is too long to include here.

After I returned from India I went to hear Namkhai Norbu teach in Conway, Massachusetts. One evening he took out the text of the biography of A-Yu Khadro, which he had told me about and showed me before, and began to translate it spontaneously into Italian, and the Italian was then translated into English by Barrie Simmons. I tape-recorded this translation and then on my return to Rome transcribed, edited and went over it with Namkhai Norbu Rinpoche to make sure it was correct.

At this point I had all the biographies included here and had discovered that there were several, perhaps many, other great women whose biographies could not be included because of their excessive length or unavailability. When I began the research for the book I knew of only a few great women yoginis in Tibet. It is encouraging and inspiring to discover that there are many more than I had originally thought. I see this book as a first step, not a final statement about these courageous and powerful women. May their blessings spread widely and benefit all sentient beings!

Tsultrim Allione
Tibetan New Year
March 1984
Rome, Italy

Notes

1 Swayambhu Nath is called 'Phags.pa Shing.kun ("Sublime Trees")
by the Tibetans. There are various legends connected with this
place, and it is difficult to ascertain the true origins of the stupa.
However, the whole hill is considered one of the most, if not the
most, sacred power places in the Kathmandu valley and over 120
medicinal herbs grow wild on it. One of these herbs which is
found only there cures the hepatitis that is rampant in Kathmandu.
The Tibetan name Shing.kun comes from the story that 21,000
arhats came from Vulture Peak, piled up the earth beneath the
dome of the stupa, and then Nagajuna (who gave the original
Prajna Paramita Sutra teachings) cut off his hair and scattered it
around the area praying that all kinds of trees would grow around
the stupa. After this many species of trees grew giving it the name
'Phags.pa Shing.kun. But it may be that Shing.kun is a corruption
of the Newari (language of the natives of Kathmandu) Singgu
meaning "self-sprung."

Another legend says that in very ancient times when Kathmandu was a lake, the Buddha Vipswi threw a seed of a thousand-
petaled lotus into the lake, and when this lotus grew there was a
ruby in the center which spread light over the whole world and the
primordial Buddha, Vajradhara, manifested as the stupa over this
lotus.

At the center of a stupa is a tree, called the "tree of life," and it is
said that beneath the Swayambhu stupa is a giant tree forty-two
feet in circumference. This could account for the connection to
sacred trees in the name. There are also tales that under the stupa
there is a palace of nagas (serpentine magical beings). It is
interesting to note that these nagas were said to have lived around
and below the central tree of the stupa. Serpents are often
guardians of thresholds, temples, treasures, esoteric knowledge
and lunar deities. J.C. Cooper in *An Illustrated Encyclopedia of
Traditional Symbols* describes the relationship of the serpent to the
tree like this: "Coiled round the Tree or any axial symbol, it [the
serpent] is the awakening of dynamic force; the genius of all
growing things; the anima mundi; cyclic existence. Associated with
the Tree of Life its aspect is beneficent, with the Tree of
Knowledge it is malefic" (p. 148).

A stupa is a three-dimensional mandala representing enlightenment. It has a square or cube base representing the element earth,
and the various levels represent the elements and the process of
illumination. The spire at the top represents the ten stages of

the bodhisattva path (sometimes there are thirteen). The stupa is related to as a body of enlightenment which emanates great blessings. By circumbulating or practicing near a great stupa one's mind is tremendously benefited and the merit of the practice is multiplied a thousandfold. The most important thing about a stupa is the strength of the blessings of the relics and mantras that it contains. Some stupas have such powers that they produce relics themselves. After the visit of Karmapa to Swayambhu stupa in 1969 the stupa produced thousands of ringsel (little pearl-like objects) which were found all around the front of the stupa. I was present and witnessed this phenomenon. For further information about Swayambhu see Keith Dowman's article "A buddhist guide to the power places of the Kathmandu Valley", in *Kailash, A Journal of Himalayan Studies*, vol. VIII, no. 3, 1981, pp. 208–13.

2 Kimdol: a hill near Swayambhu hill, smaller in size, which has on it various temples and viharas (abodes for pilgrims). The Tibetans call it Vulture Peak and the Nepalese call Kimdol "Heap of Rice". Many lamas from Tibet have stayed here, including the Thirteen Karmapa, the Tenth Shamarpa, the Sixth Drukpa Rinpoche, the Eighth Situ, etc. For further information see Keith Dowman's article mentioned in n. 1 above (pp. 205–8).

3 Beginner's mind is a term used by Shunryu Suzuki in his book *Zen Mind, Beginner's Mind*.

4 The Tibetan for these splendor waves or waves of divine grace is Jin Lab (byin labs); the Sanskrit is adhishtana. They are a very important part of the transmission received from one's guru and lineage.

5 H.V. Guenther (ed. and trans.), *The Royal Song of Saraha*, pp. 63–4.

6 Rinpoche is a title for a Tibetan teacher. It means "precious jewel." Chögyam Trungpa Rinpoche is a Tibetan lama (spiritual teacher) and author of numerous books and articles.

7 A sadhana is a complete Tantric practice involving the invocation of and visualization of a particular Tantric deity or deities, the recitation of a mantra, etc.

8 There are four major sects in Tibetan Buddhism: the Gelukpa (dGe.lugs.pa), the Kagyupa (bK'.brgyud.pa), the Sakyapa (Sa.skya.pa) and the Nyingmapa (rNying.ma.pa).

9 The shaving of one's hair is symbolic of the renunciation of worldly life and becoming a monk or a nun. When the Buddha left his princely life he shaved his head to symbolize this renunciation.

10 A tulku (sprul.sku) is an incarnation of a lama who has died and taken a new body in order to benefit sentient beings. Originally, this concept came from the teachings of the rNying.ma.pa school

with the predicted reappearance of particular teachers or assistants of Padma Sambhava, who originally brought the teachings of Tantric Buddhism to Tibet. These incarnations were reborn at certain intervals in order to rediscover hidden texts or to re-establish the correct meaning of the texts he had taught. They were known as Terton (gTer.ston). These incarnations were somewhat discontinuous in nature, as opposed to the later tulku system which is the basis for the succession of abbatial or monastic office. In this case, as soon as one abbot died the search would begin for the incarnation of that abbot (tulku) who before dying would have left prophecies in a letter as to his next incarnation's birthplace. Most of the great monasteries in Tibet operate with a succession of tulkus, and even now when the Tibetans are in exile, the system continues and new tulkus are being found. Some have recently been born in Occidental families.

11 Actually the full ordination for women, the Gelongma (dGe.slong.ma) is no longer given in Tibet – the line had been discontinued. What I was given was the Getsul (dGe.tsul) ordination, which was the most complete ordination available to women at that time. Recently there have been attempts to revive the Gelongma ordination by some Western nuns who traveled to Taiwan to receive it from Chinese Gelongmas. Basically, the life is the same for a getsul or a gelong, except that the gelong has many more minor vows to observe. The getsul and gelong must both observe ten basic vows: not to kill, not to steal, to practice celibacy, not to lie, not to use intoxicants, not to eat at a time when it is not permitted, not to take part in dance, song, music or theatrical spectacles, not to use garlands, perfume or ornaments, not to sleep on a high bed and not to receive gold or silver. For an analysis of why the lines of nuns disappeared, see Nancy A. Falk's essay "The Case of the Vanishing Nuns: The Fruits of Ambivalence in Ordination in Ancient Indian Buddhism" in *Unspoken Worlds: Women's Religious Lives in non-Western Cultures*.

12 For a complete description of the preliminary practices see *The Mahamudra: Eliminating the Darkness of Ignorance* by the Ninth Karmapa, Wang-Chung Dorje, translated by Alexander Berzin with a commentary by Beru Khyentze Rinpoche.

13 This is part of the "Song of Mahamudra" which can be found in C.C. Chang's *Teachings of Tibetan Yoga*, pp. 25–30.

14 Although the vows of a nun or monk are supposed to be kept for life, if one breaks one's vows one can either take them again or give them back to someone who is themselves keeping the vows, stating that one can no longer keep them. Although this is frowned

upon and afterwards one is considered to be a "fallen" monk or nun, in my experience the Tibetans understand that if one still has the intention to continue practicing the Dharma it is not so bad and doesn't really matter. There is also a whole tradition of Nagpa (Ngag.pa), who are full-time practitioners of Tantra but who may or may not be celibate. Tibetans recognize that since politics are often mixed with religion, a monastic life may not be the most conducive to meditation.

15 Nor Hall, *The Moon and the Virgin*, p. 11.

16 The true cause of this kind of death is not yet known. There are many theories about SIDS, and many doctors are working to discover the cause and to try to be able to predict when a baby is susceptible to this syndrome. What they do know is that it happens to babies who are apparently in the best of health and it happens during sleep, probably during the time of REM (rapid eye movement), the light sleep between waking and deep slumber. More babies under one year die of SIDS than of any other cause in the United States. It can happen within five minutes and has even happened when a baby is in the mother's arms. If she is lucky enough to notice the baby changing color and she wakes it up, the baby can be saved, but most commonly it happens at night or during a nap when no one is watching the baby. It rarely happens when the baby is under two months or over a year. The time of greatest risk is between two months and four and a half months. The medical establishment thinks this has to do with the maturation of the brain function controlling the breathing which takes place at this time.

17 See Introduction, pp. 25–42 for an explanation of the dakini.

18 See the prologue to the biography of Machig Lapdron, pp. 143–9, for an explanation of the Chod practice.

19 See notes 38, 39, 40, to the biography of A-Yu Khadro for an explanation of this place.

A NOTE ON THE TRANSLATIONS

In all cases the translations were done primarily by Tibetans, with a lama present for clarifying difficult passages; I helped with my more limited knowledge when there was a question of the meaning of a word or phrase. The Machig Lapdron text was translated by Phuntsog Tobjhor under Lama Tsewang Gyurme, the Nangsa Obum biography was translated by Gelek Namgyel and Phoebe Harper under Gegyen Khentse's guidance, the Drenchen Rema and Machig Ongjo ones were translated by Thrinley Chodron under Gegyen Khentse, the Jomo Memo text was translated by Phuntsog Tobjhor under Lama Ralu, and the A-Yu Khadro biography was translated from Tibetan to Italian by Namkhai Norbu and from Italian to English by Barrie Simmons. I edited, annotated and checked all the translations against the written original whenever possible.

My aim while translating these texts was to convey the meaning and rhythm of the story, rather than to make a word-for-word translation. First a rough translation was made with various Tibetans in Nepal and India, always under the guidance of a lama who could clarify obscure passages. Then when I returned to Italy I went over everything with Namkhai Norbu Rinpoche to make sure there were no mistakes.

The transliteration of Tibetan is always problematic because words frequently are not written as they are pronounced. So I decided to give a phonetic representation in the text and the correct transliteration in a glossary at the end of the book.

The Tibetan transliteration is done according to the Wylie system (T.V. Wylie, "A Standard System of Tibetan Transcription", *Harvard Journal of Asiatic Studies*, vol. 22, 1959, pp. 261–7). This system uses no diacritical marks, so the words are complete as they appear. It should be noted that ' represents the short *a* letter in the Wylie transliteration. The complete alphabet is as follows: k, kh, g, ng, c, ch, j, ny, t, th, d, n, p, ph, b, m, ts, tsh, dz, w, zh, z, ', y, r, l, sh, s, h, a.

In the transliteration I have capitalized the first pronounced letter in each word, in order to clarify the pronunciation of the words. In general I have tried to eliminate as many Tibetan terms from the text as possible and have put transliterations of the Tibetan in the notes in the case of long lists of teachings and so on, so as not to intimidate readers who are not familiar with the Tibetan language. I have also often substituted the Sanskrit for the Tibetan, both in order to make the text easier to pronounce, and because many of these terms are coming into common usage as Tibetan scholars often employ Sanskrit technical terms such as Dharmakaya, Sambogakaya and Nirmanakaya, when no comprehensive English equivalent can be found.

Rather than use an incomplete English translation I think it is better to use the Sanskrit term with a definition; for the concepts expressed often have no Western equivalent, and so, even if an English word were to be used, it would have to be totally redefined.

My hope in doing the translations was to make the teachings and meaning as accessible to the reader as possible, without sacrificing the integrity of the philosophical and spiritual tradition from which the biographies come.

INTRODUCTION

It is difficult to imagine our lives without the life stories of others. We learn in infancy how to be human by imitation. Without the examples of others a child cannot grow up normally. As children begin to grow up they begin to ask those around them for stories from their lives.

My own children take endless delight in tales of the most mundane events of my childhood. This tireless interest comes from a deep-seated need to have some reference points. From my stories they glean important information which helps them to understand their own lives and, as they grow older, to make decisions.

All cultures provide biographies in one form or another, be it tales of ancestral heroes, stories of relatives and friends, or formal biographies of cultural and religious figures. However, our culture provides very few life stories for women who are on a spiritual quest:

> Women's stories have not been told. And without stories there is no articulation of experience. Without stories a woman is lost when she comes to make important decisions in her life. She does not learn to value her struggles, to celebrate her strengths, to comprehend her pain. Without stories she is alienated from those deeper experiences of self and world that have been called spiritual or religious. She is closed in silence.[1]

Through this book, in answer to my own personal needs and those expressed by those around me, I seek to begin to fill this

[1]

gap with these stories of women who were not only on a spiritual quest but who reached great spiritual depths, and were able to help others.

All of these stories come from the high and remote land of Tibet. They are stories of women practicing the path of Tibetan Buddhism, a practice full of mystery and methods very remote from the Judeo-Christian framework most of us grew up in. However, there are fundamental themes in these stories which transcend cultural boundaries completely and make them useful and inspirational in the West.

These women had to deal with cultural and religious prejudices against women on a spiritual path which were very similar to those we encounter. Carol Christ states these conditions in her book *Diving Deep and Surfacing: Women Writers on a Spiritual Quest*:

> It begins in an *experience of nothingness*. Women experience emptiness in their own lives in self-hatred, in self-negation, and in being a victim; in relationships with men; and in the values that have shaped their lives. Experiencing nothingness women reject conventional solutions and question the meaning of their lives, thus opening themselves to the revaluation of deeper sources of power and value. The experience of nothingness often precedes an *awakening*, similar to a conversion experience, in which the powers of being are revealed. A woman's awakening to great powers, grounds her in a new sense of self and a new orientation in the world. Through the awakening to new powers, women overcome self-negation and self-hatred and refuse to be victims.[2]

This "dark night of the soul," or descent into darkness, is experienced by Nangsa Obum when she is beaten to death by her husband; by Jomo Memo when she loses consciousness and enters the initiatory cave; by Drenchen Rema when she defies her mother's statement that "girls cannot practice the Dharma!" and spends years in retreat living on water and mineral essences.

However, it is not only through negative experiences that women seek out the spiritual path. There is much documentation of the innate spiritual longing and capacity of women who have continued to seek the spiritual path even within religions which are oriented toward and defined by men's understanding of the realities of the universe. Women have applied the inspiration of male saints' biographies to themselves or identified with the roles of women in men's stories such as Mary in Christianity, Damema or Yeshe Tsogyel in the Tibetan tradition, or Mahapajapati, Sujata, and several others in the story of the Buddha.

The strength of women's spiritual inclination is demonstrated within the Christian tradition. It is rare to see men in Christian churches actually praying, whereas it is so common it is hardly notable to see a church full of women seeking union with God. In Italy, for example, it is usually the women who actually go to pray, whereas the men back up the church with words and money.

In the Jain religion, which created the precedence for the formation of an order of nuns by the Buddha, the number of nuns was twice that of monks even though women were considered to have a lesser spiritual capacity and were banned from the highest order of Jains, as being incapable of reaching liberation (moksha).[3]

The tenacity of women seeking spiritual depths is also demonstrated in Buddhism, where nuns were again given a second-rate status and therefore received less alms than monks and less esteem. Yet they have continued to take ordination and strive for liberation within a system which taught them they were less likely to reach this goal than men.

The point is that women under patriarchal systems have continued to prove that their spiritual needs and capacity are as great as men's, maybe even greater; however, they have been relating to religious systems created by men and intended to fulfil male needs. Though women have found ways of circumventing this situation, they have lacked stories of women's experiences to relate to their own understanding and experiences. Though one might say that when one deals with the development of the mind, there is obviously a transcendence of the differences between men and women, we must still realize that our experience is largely conditioned by the stories we hear. We try to relate our experience to the stories of others and thereby edit our perceptions according to what fits in:

> Women have lived in the interstices between inchoate experiences and the shapings given to experience by the stories of men. In a very real sense, women have not experienced their own experience. There is a dialectic between stories and experience. Stories shape experience; experience shapes stories.[4]

The current flood of books and biographies of women on spiritual quests has come from the recognition of women's experience. Women have begun to break away from the ways that men have taught them to perceive their experience. Women began really talking together in consciousness-raising groups and in conversation because of a general breakdown in the rigidity of social relationships in the past twenty years. Women experienced the shock of recognition when they heard other women describe their lives. We have been released from silence and are now exploring aspects of our experience that were previously either devalued by the patriarchal value systems or were never even consciously experienced or spoken of because of lack of stories and genuine communication. The whole area of women's spirituality is wide open, and many of us are seeking within and with each other to discover what our spiritual paths really are. There is a tremendous sense of excitement and at the same time a floundering for handles and stories which we can identify with. One of the things that has become clear to me is that this process of discovery is something communal, it is fed by communication and conversation. The stories of women in this book can provide us with fuel for our search. The strength and determination of these women working within a patriarchal system can help us to articulate our own struggles, to see some choices and possibilities that are open to us. We can evaluate the psychology and philosophy of these teachings and their effectiveness for women.

In supporting the re-emergence of the sacred feminine and women as influential forces in religious thought, I am not advocating that women become the defining factor of religious experience. But the values which women hold sacred and the female experience of spirituality should be revaluated and respected. These holistic values have become so atrophied that we have nearly destroyed our planet:

Women must become spokesmen for a new humanity arising out of the reconciliation of spirit and body. . . . Women should not buy into the masculine ethic of competitiveness that sees the triumph of the self as predicated upon the subjugation of the other. Unlike men, women have traditionally cultivated communal personhood that could participate in the successes of others rather than seeing these as merely a threat to one's own success.[5]

The first tenet of Buddhism is that all experience is tinged with suffering – birth, death and impermanence being the most obvious culprits creating this situation. Though it is obvious that there is an element of pain in all of these experiences, there are other ways this pain can be approached than by searching for its annihilation.

Starhawk clearly contrasts the differences between Buddhism and Witchcraft thus:

Witchcraft does not maintain, like the First Truth of Buddhism, that "All life is suffering." On the contrary, life is a thing of wonder. The Buddha is said to have gained this insight after his encounter with old age, disease and death. In the Craft, old age is a natural and highly valued part of the cycle of life, the time of greatest wisdom and understanding. Disease, of course, causes misery, but it is not something to be inevitably suffered: The practice of the Craft was always connected with the healing arts, with herbalism and midwifery. Nor is death fearful: It is simply the dissolution of the physical form that allows the spirit to prepare for a new life. Suffering certainly exists in life – it is part of learning. But escape from the Wheel of Birth and Death is not the optimal cure, any more than hara kiri is the best cure for menstrual cramps. When suffering is the result of the social order or human injustice, the Craft encourages active work to relieve it. Where suffering is a natural part of

[5]

the cycle of birth and decay, it is relieved by understanding and acceptance, by a willing giving over to both the dark and the light in turn.[6]

It is as though the Buddha wanted to be rid of the dark and the painful and only to experience the light and the blissful, nirvana. There is a tremendous emphasis on going beyond, leaving the world, the ideal state which transcends the patterns of light and dark. Women's religions tend to incorporate this duality and to hold it sacred. When this duality appears in men's religions we usually find that the male is associated with the sky, the spirit and transcendence, and the female nature with worldliness and murky complications.

This approach is described in *Womanspirit Rising*:

> . . . dualistic mentality opposes soul, spirit, rationality and transcendence to body, flesh, matter, nature and immanence. . . . Classical dualism also became the model for the oppression of women when the culture-creating males identified the negative sides with women over whom they claimed the right to rule.[7]

Buddhism is probably still less patriarchal than theistic religions which have a male father God. Buddhism teaches that we must work with our own minds to reach a state of liberation. The Buddha is the guide for this process, but it is not union with Buddha which is sought. In any case, a very similar social view of women was perpetuated and the ideal form for the practicing of this religion was the body of a man. In the "Sutra on Changing the Female Sex" the Buddha makes this clear:

> The female's defects – greed, hate and delusion and other defilements – are greater than the male's. . . . You [women] should have such an intention. . . . Because I wish to be freed from the impurities of the woman's body, I will acquire the beautiful and fresh body of a man.[8]

When the Buddha's aunt, Mahaprajapati, who had nursed him in his childhood when his mother died, approached him asking that women be admitted to the Buddhist monastic order, the Sangha, he refused her.

Then she and a group of other women shaved their heads and followed him to another town, and with the intercession of the monk Ananda he finally, with reluctance, admitted women to the order, on condition that they take eight extra vows. These vows were all oriented towards keeping women under the control of the male monastic community. For example, the first of these vows is that any nun, no matter what degree of knowledge or realization she possesses, must treat any monk, even the rudest novice, as if he were her senior.[9]

By admitting women into the monastic community, creating a community of nuns, the Buddha said that the life of the Sangha would be shortened by five hundred years. The women were thought to have an uncontrolled sexuality and longing for motherhood.

There has been much discussion amongst Buddhist scholars as to which statements attributed to the Buddha were actually the words of the Buddha and which should be attributed to the monks (some of whom were obviously misogynists) who followed and wrote down what the Buddha is supposed to have said hundreds of years after his death. I.B. Horner in her scholarly book *Women under Primitive Buddhism* makes an extensive study of the relationship between Buddhism and women. According to her research on the subject of women's acceptance into the monastic order, it seems that the Buddha was torn between his cultural conditioning and the Hindu social system, which clearly and unequivocally considered that women should be primarily child-bearers and servants to their family, and his conviction that women were as capable as men of attaining enlightenment. Although there was the precedence of Jain nuns, the idea of women living a religious life outside of the family was still thought to threaten social stability. The subordination of nuns to monks was most likely a compromise allowing women to pursue the spiritual path ascribed by the Buddha without completely disregarding the conventions of Hindu society of the day.

Women's strong desire to follow a spiritual path and the positive alternative offered by Buddhism, is indicated by the insistence of Mahapajapati and the others that followed her in

[7]

requesting admission to the order. Women were provided under Buddhism with an alternative to female servitude; although they were still subject to males, they were no longer chattels of their fathers and husbands. The life of a Buddhist nun also provided a positive alternative for unmarried and widowed women, who were considered to have little status in Hindu society.

Nuns still suffered from male distrust because of their relatively emancipated position and for this reason Buddhist laywomen were often presented much more positively than nuns in Buddhist stories. The Buddhist laywoman was still in her correct slot according to the Hindu social system while nuns held the ambivalent position of having been accepted but with great reservations, including the statement that their acceptance to the order would lead to an earlier demise for the monastic community. This ambivalence and its results are admirably analyzed by Nancy Ayer Falk in her essay "The Case of the Vanishing Nuns" in *Unspoken Worlds: Women's Religious Lives in Non-Western Cultures*.[10]

Buddhist nuns have always had to strive towards liberation against this background, retaining at best an uneasy status within the Buddhist community. For this reason they viewed their birth as women as something which they could overcome through faithfully adhering to their spiritual disciplines and seeking to realize the state in which such distinctions as male or female become irrelevant.

The Buddha protected nuns from exploitation by monks by saying that the nuns should not be called upon to sew, dye, or weave for the monks. Neither could the monks take for themselves donations made to the nuns. The mother of the famous monk Sumangala stated her freedom as a nun in this way:

> O woman well set free! How free am I,
> How thoroughly free from kitchen drudgery!
> Me stained and squalid 'mong my cooking pots
> My brutal husband ranked as even less
> Than the sunshades he sits and weaves away.
> Purged now of all my former lust and hate,

> I dwell, musing at ease beneath the shade
> of spreading boughs . . . O, but 'tis well with me![11]

When Buddhism spread to Tibet, starting in the seventh century AD, this ambiguity was carried over and the popular folklore of Tibet reflects these attitudes. Women have internalized these values, as we see here in a song sung by a woman in *The One Hundred Thousand Songs of Milarepa*:

> Because of my sinful karma I was given this inferior
>   [female] body,
> Through the evil-hindrance of this world,
> I never realized the identity of self and Buddha.
> Lacking the necessary diligence,
> I seldom thought of the Buddha's teaching,
> Though I desired the Dharma,
> Lazy and inert, I frittered time away.
> . . . .
> To a woman, a prosperous birth means bondage
>   and non freedom.
> To a woman, a wretched birth means the loss
>   of companionship.
> To our husbands we sometimes talk of suicide;
> We set aside and leave our gracious parents;
> Great is our ambition, but our perseverance is small.[12]

When looking at the stories of Tibetan women we must not fail to recognize that the Buddhist outlook was a strong influence on them, but it was not the only spiritual tradition practiced in Tibet.

Tibetan Buddhism is a complex combination of various religious traditions coming from the native Tibetan religion called Bon, various schools of Indian Buddhism and some Chinese influences. From India came both the fundamental Buddhist teachings called the Sutras (rDo in Tibetan) and the Tantras (rGyud in Tibetan). The Sutras emphasized the resolution of the problem of human suffering through the taming of the mind which controls the emotions and passions which produce suffering. The end result of the Sutric teachings

[9]

is cessation of suffering (nirvana). In the Sutric tradition both men and women attempted to eliminate the rampant persistent passions by following certain rules of conduct. As Sutric Buddhism was dominated by monks, often this literature disparages women, who were obviously temptations of men trying to subdue their passions.

When Buddhism was accepted as the national religion of Tibet in the latter part of the eighth century, the Tibetans embraced both Sutric Buddhism and the Buddhist Tantric tradition which was being propagated in Bengal and north-western India.

The origins of the Buddhist Tantras probably go back to the pre-Aryan stratum of Indian culture, which had strong matriarchal and erotic traditions. There is a notable difference in the way the feminine is seen in Buddhist and Hindu Tantras. In Hindu Tantric iconography the Great Mother, or Sakti, is the active principle and the creative principle which often sits or dances upon the horizontal Shiva, who represents the static male principle. This polarity existed within the Tibetan Buddhist Tantras as well, but the attributes of the male and female were reversed. The Tibetan system attributes the dynamic aspect to the male (upaya), and the female is associated with emptiness (sunyata) and profound knowledge (prajna). The reason for this could well be that the Tibetan society was already strongly patriarchal at the time of the arrival of the Buddhist Tantras from India, and therefore the attributes of the masculine and feminine were reversed to fit into Tibetan cultural predilections. This could be ascertained by viewing the native Bon deities, but because Bon was so much influenced by the advent of Buddhism in Tibet it is difficult to find purely Bon iconography which would prove this supposition.

Even the Tibetan division of the masculine and feminine is not as clear-cut as it might at first appear. Although the primary images of the union of masculine and feminine appear as a male embracing a smaller female figure who has her back to the viewer, there also exist other female images: the dakinis, who often are wrathful and dancing upon male figures; and static peaceful female figures such as Tara and Prajna Paramita. Agehananda Bharati in his book *The Tantric Tradition* makes a fascinating analysis of the question of the male–female polarity in the Tantric tradition. He suggests that there was a combination of forces absorbed in the Tibetan tradition:

> I think that the Vajrayana Buddhists created or absorbed two types of deities, chiefly female, i.e. genuine "Shaktis" in Indian sense female "energies" which retain their purely dynamic function in Tibetan Vajrayana (e.g. rdorje phag mo – Vajravarahi, "the Vajra-Sow"); and also, goddesses who embody the theologically genuine Vajrayana concept of the static yum (cosmic mother) who is also śes.rab (prajna, total wisdom), viz. the quiescent apothesized Prajñā-pārāmitā.[13]

So, it seems that there are primarily three images of the feminine presented in Tibetan Tantra: the dynamic, often wrathful, figure of the dakini, who is usually in a dancing or standing position; the seated female figure who represents a philosophical concept from Indian Buddhism such as Prajna Paramita; and the female figure who is embracing a larger male figure in sexual union (yab yum). The active dakini and the female figure representing a philosophical concept are most likely wholesale imports from India, and the yab yum figure seems to be found primarily in Tibetan and Nepalese images. Bharati states: "There are scores of variants in the erotic symbol sculpture of India, but the one typical of the yab yum is not found anywhere to my knowledge, in Indian sculpture proper."[14]

The only sexual images in Tibetan Vajrayana are the seated and the standing yab yum. I have heard of rare cases where the female is the primary figure, but these are very exceptional. This either indicates that the yab yum image was a pre-existing iconographical image present in the native Tibetan Bon, or it was absorbed from Nepal, or it appealed to the Tibetan cultural notions of feminine and masculine and was therefore adopted. In any case we can see from the Tibetan iconography that both the dynamic feminine, the dakini, and the static feminine, were present in Tibet. We can assume that the dynamic feminine was absorbed from the pre-Aryan matriarchal Indian religion and that the passive feminine was absorbed from later Indian and native Tibetan and Nepalese sources. The latter influences came from a patriarchal cultural base in both India and Tibet. All of this is mere conjecture at this point, but the important thing is the variety of feminine images available in Tibetan Buddhism.

Considering all of these factors we can see that, with the joining of the Buddhist teachings with the Tantric teachings in Tibet, the feminine took on a profoundly more important role than it had in primitive Buddhism. The feminine became an essential counterpart of the sexual polarity which provided the dynamics to reach a state of non-duality, the goal of the path. Feminine divinities also existed as important figures when they stood alone either as the fierce activation force of the dakini or the essentially gentle force of Tara, Prajna Paramita, etc.

In Tantric practice the female and male principles are understood as currents running through the bodies of both men and women. Males may visualize themselves as female deities and vice versa. We are all made up of both male and female principles, and the Tantric practices activate and integrate both forces within the individual. These forces may also be polarized through sexual intercourse.

Though in Tantra a vast assortment of images of the feminine were propagated, Western culture splits the feminine between the prostitute and the madonna, whom we see passively adoring her male offspring. In Tantra, we see the emergence of female images which are sexual *and* spiritual, ecstatic *and* intelligent, wrathful *and* peaceful. How refreshing not to have to be chaste and peaceful with downcast eyes, in order to be spiritual. We can be sharp and insightful, even angry, and still celebrate our womanhood. We can activate all parts of ourselves and increase our feminine and masculine energies, tuning them rather than denying and suppressing them, as we are taught to do in patriarchal religions. The naked, wrathful, dancing dakini creates a different effect on the psyche than the sweetly smiling madonna. However, the Tibetans did not fail to absorb the kindness and sympathetic female divinities from India. One of the most universally worshiped goddesses in Tibet is Tara, who is seen with one foot slightly extended ready to step down to help those in need. When women are not allowed to incorporate all these aspects of the feminine into themselves they become distorted and alienated from their own energies:

> Constricted, the joy of the feminine has been denigrated as mere frivolity; her joyful lust demeaned as whorishness, or sentimentalized and maternalized; her vitality bound into duty and obedience. This devaluation produced ungrounded daughters of the patriarchy, their feminine strength and passion split off, their dreams and ideals in the unobtainable heavens, maintained grandly with a spirit false to the instinctual pattern symbolised by the queen of heaven and earth. It also produced frustrated furies.[15]

The Dzog Chen (Maha Ati) teachings, the most ancient school of meditation in Tibet, also held the feminine in high esteem. Dzog Chen teaching is based on the idea that we are fundamentally already enlightened. Through transmission from an empowered teacher, and working directly with our energy, luminosity and vision are reawakened and the primordial state of illumination shines through. Passions are experienced "as they are" and without transformation; they are liberated on the spot like snow falling into water.

These teachings come from Orgyen, a land which existed in ancient times northwest of India, which was known as "the land of the dakinis," dakinis being mystical female beings who may appear in dreams, visions or human form. Another form of Dzog Chen came from a very ancient pre-Buddhist Bon tradition, which originated around Mount Kailash, between Western Tibet and India. This kingdom, called Shang-Shung, was the source of the Bonpo tradition, which was later discredited by the Buddhists in somewhat the same way as the Native American Indian teachings were disparaged by the Christians. However, recent research on the part of such scholars as Namkhai Norbu Rinpoche has revealed a potent Bonpo Dzog Chen tradition. In Dzog Chen traditions dakinis, female spiritual forces, are an absolutely integral part of the teachings. The teachings are often originally written in the mysterious cipher called the language of the dakini, "the twilight language." These teachings are transmitted, concealed and protected by dakinis. Without a deep connection with the dakini, the texts cannot be deciphered.

According to Namkhai Norbu Rinpoche, Garab Dorje, (dGa.rab rDo.rje),[16] the founder of the Dzog Chen tradition, who transmitted it to Padma Sambhava who brought it to Tibet, went so far as to say that the majority of those who could reach the ultimate level of the Dzog Chen teachings, the manifestation of the body of light, or the rainbow body, would be women. The rainbow body manifests at the time of death. The physical body completely disappears except for the hair and the fingernails, and a body of light is formed from the essence of the elements. This body can be perceived by those in very open states of mind. Namkhai Norbu Rinpoche explains that the reason for the predominance of women achieving the rainbow body is that women have a natural affinity for working with energy and vision, and the Dzog Chen practices leading toward the body of light are connected to working directly with energy and vision, rather than logic and intellectual studies.

In both Tantrism and Dzog Chen the practitioner must always maintain a positive relationship to the feminine or the development of the practice will be blocked. It is fascinating to see that the Dzog Chen tradition shows many of the political tendencies which were present in matriarchal societies. Dzog Chen communities tend to be non-hierarchical, based on cooperation rather than competition, communities of families or loosely formed collections of hermits of both sexes who have no particular "organizations" but who help and support each other without any imposing hierarchies.

Sutric Buddhism forms the base of Tibetan monastic communities, though some Tantrism and sometimes Dzog Chen were also practiced. Tantrism and Dzog Chen predominated amongst those who chose to live apart from the monasteries as yogis in high mountain hermitages or as traveling practitioners with no fixed abode. In these situations women practitioners flourished. I was unable to discover, for example, any stories of women "saints" in the most monastically oriented sects of Tibetan Buddhism, the Gelugpa tradition. When I asked a lama of this sect if men and women had the same capacity for enlightenment, he assured me that they did. Then, when I asked him for stories of great women in his lineage, he drew a complete blank. I asked him how this could be if men and women had essentially the same mind and the same capacity for enlightenment. Then he confessed that there was a slight difference between men and women. He described women as being "slightly less emotionally stable." He said this was his own observation from working with both men and women; however, behind this comment lay hundreds of years of male monks passing judgment on the spiritual capacities of women. Apparently this "slight" difference was supposed to account for a complete absence of any women saints within his monastic sect, in which there are thousands of nuns. The lamas who now are teaching internationally are constantly confronted with questions of sexism and have therefore altered tradition somewhat so that women have become teachers and administrators, but still, even in the West, Buddhist organizations are usually dominated by men.

Sensing the lack of good spiritual instruction in the nunneries and the absence of free time for meditation practices, many Tibetan women seriously pursuing the spiritual path chose to live the life of hermits or wandering yoginis. Machig Lapdron, the female founder of the Chod lineage, who lived in the twelfth century, encouraged the life of the nomadic meditator who lived in caves and cemeteries. Women under these circumstances were very free: they formed friendships with other pilgrims and stayed as long as they liked in places they found conducive to meditation, supporting themselves through begging. We see many examples of this way of living in the stories of the women in this collection.

It is interesting to note that on the other side of the globe in the twelfth century Christian women were making the same choices for the same reasons. Eleanor McLaughlin points out in her essay "The Christian Past, Does It Hold a Future for Women?" that "in medieval Christianity the highest religious and moral values of the society were exemplifed not typically by all clerical bureaucracy, but by the religious and those whom people called 'saints', categories in which women as well as men took an equal and active place."[17]

The point is that often in-depth meditation practice did not take place within the organized monastic structures. More often than not those in monasteries spent their time fundraising, performing rituals for rich patrons, the traditional prayers and "pujas" for protection and blessings of the community. Because Tibet was a country where religion and the state were inextricably linked, the monasteries were often hotbeds of political intrigues and there were even wars between monasteries.

Though some women have become famous teachers of both men and women, most women in Tibet, even if they were highly accomplished, received little acknowledgment from the male hierarchy. Although famous women are few, there were probably many great women practitioners. A-Yu Khadro, for example, was not a particularly well-known teacher, and her biography only appears here because her disciple, Namkhai Norbu Rinpoche, happened to ask her to tell him her story. The average Tibetan has never heard of her, yet she is obviously a great yogini.

There were many great practitioners of both sexes who never achieved particular acclaim, but the reason why women were not often recognized as teachers is probably twofold. As I have stated above, women were not as highly respected spiritually as men in the Sutric Buddhist framework, were not allowed to teach monks, and were supposed to remain under the surveillance of monks. Secondly, it may also be that women manifest enlightenment differently from men; that is, women may be satisfied with "being," and men may have a desire to "do." Therefore, the energy of a male who has reached great spiritual heights may be to build monasteries and retreat centers, open libraries and create schools, whereas a woman might work for others on subtler levels, working with energy and not "doing" anything which would call attention to herself, though this may be a product of patriarchal suppression.

Although many women in Tibet found ways to practice spirituality, they did so in a culture which gave them mixed messages. On the one hand they were subject to religious and cultural negation of women as equal vehicles for spirituality; on the other hand they were supported by the notion of women being the essence of wisdom and the dakini principle. They had to prove themselves in ways that men and monks did not. We Western women are also conditioned by limited examples of truly spiritual women as role models within our patriarchal society. We must seek to recover from the alienation from ourselves and articulate our experiences with very few resources from which we can draw inspiration and in which we can recognize ourselves.

Even within the Tantric tradition, which provides more or less egalitarian values for men and women practitioners, the male point of view is still emphasized, as Alex Wayman points out in *The Buddhist Tantras*, in his discussion of the Kalachakra (Wheel of Time) Tantra:

> When the yogin attains the Great Time his recessive female becomes actualized; when the yogini attains this time her recessive male becomes actualized. This casts a floodlight on the sexual symbolism of mystical visions. Almost all of the Buddhist scriptures were composed by men, as far as is known. Hence these works speak so much about attaining prajna, the void, the state of waking and light. Hence that large body of scriptures entitled Prajna paramita ("the perfection of insight") and the personification of the Prajna-paramita as the "Mother of the Buddhas."[18]

So I would suggest that in order to make the Tibetan Tantric path more available to women, texts emphasizing the development of upaya and the finding and working with male consorts should be developed: perhaps then the principle of the daka (male energy) would become as important as the dakini (female energy) principle.

Women need to become aware of what practices actually work for us, what practices are adapted to our energies and our life situations. We cannot be satisfied with just doing something because it is supposed to lead to enlightenment or blindly obeying the edicts of male teachers and administrators. We need to observe what actually works. Women need upaya (skillful means) as much as men need to balance their energies with prajna (profound knowing) and emptiness (sunyata). Perhaps women could begin writing about and researching upaya. Women tend to have a natural affiliation for the receptive states of meditation, intuitive knowing and compassion, but have a harder time seeing clear ways of working with concrete problems and acting assertively and effectively in worldly situations. So perhaps women should at once take advantage of their natural affinity toward meditation and merging through practices such as those in the Dzog Chen tradition, and at the same time seek to develop their skillful means and to enter into new kinds of sexual relationships which would enhance both these aspects. In this way women within the Tantric Buddhist tradition can have a powerful and balanced spiritual path toward illumination at which point these relative distinctions between men and women break down. I have found that many Buddhists are anxious to leap to this absolute point of view and consider any discussion of possible differences in the spiritual paths of men and women as useless dualistic fixation caused by a lack of understanding of the true nature of the mind. But these people forget that *both* the absolute *and* the relative truth must be considered. It is often those who most adamantly insist that one should go beyond relative considerations about men and women who abuse and undervalue women practitioners the most.

Women also need a spiritual path that speaks to our sense of ourselves biologically. Unless we choose not to have children, a great deal of time and energy is absorbed by pregnancies and childrearing. Children cannot be intellectualized: when a child needs something we must drop everything and relate to that situation concretely – if we don't, sooner or later the situation will become even more demanding and unavoidable. The life of a mother is one of constant interruptions, day and night, when the child is small. I have tried to relate to this situation in a variety of different ways in order to integrate spirituality with diapers, noise and delicate, forming hearts and minds. One possibility is the "time out" approach. This means arranging time for personal retreats, be it for a few weeks or a weekend or even an hour in which I try to pick up the threads of a stable centered state and enter into meditation which goes deeper than the grocery list and telephone calls. This approach also includes time to go to hear teachings without bringing the children along (which I tried to do at first and which actually just disturbs and irritates oneself and everyone else). This approach provides a sense of islands of peace amidst tempests, and I think it is actually necessary.

[18]

One might argue that women should have a spiritual path in which they do not have to remove themselves from their life rhythms in order to practice. I agree with that theoretically, and I would like to see more teachings given which really help in dealing with relationships and childrearing in a positive way. Such things as seeing motherhood as a constant attack on selfishness, an admirable ever-present testing of the Bodhisattva Vow to save all sentient beings before ourselves, provides ground for spiritual development. The arts of psychic and medicinal healing, a sacred sense of the home and preparation of food as a divine act, the one-value approach to diapers and a bouquet of roses, and so on, are all potential methods for spiritual paths for mothers. The possibilities are endless, but I have never heard a male teacher discussing these possibilities. This is natural since these experiences do not generally fall upon men, and I think it is the duty of women who are spiritually awake to make connections between their lives and the teachings. The path of a mother should be given its deserved value as a sacred and powerful spiritual path. It is infuriating to me when I hear, as I frequently do, a man saying that his wife or mother or someone else "does nothing." When I challenge them on this they say "Of course I meant nothing in the outside world, they only cook, clean, shop, create atmosphere in the home, provide emotional support, etc." This is obviously a perfect example of a patriarchal value-system which would give a secretary credit for doing "something" but not a wife. These values have also infiltrated the spiritual path as well, and the tremendous spiritual potential of motherhood as a soteriological path has not been given enough appreciation and support. Someone commented to me when I had finished this book what a great accomplishment it was and what a lot of work it represented. I replied that compared to the work, thought, and energy I have put into even one of my children this book was easy.

Anyway, I am still searching and seeking for practices and ideas that can be concretely applied to daily life situations. I think this is an integral part of spirituality for women. At the moment I use a combination of daily meditation without the children, occasional practice with them when they request it, occasional retreats, and trying to apply the equilibrium, humor, and sense of openness gained by these moments of quiet to the rest of my life. I must confess that I do have a longing to "get on with it" when they grow up, but I realize this is really missing the point so I am trying to integrate spirituality with the rest of my life. It may be that for the deeper states of spiritual development, unless one is already very advanced, extensive solitude or semi-solitude are necessary. We see in the following biographies that all of these women chose this living situation, but I still feel that there is a vast untapped resource of female wisdom within so-called worldly life which could enrich our ideas about spirituality tremendously. Probably these resources have remained untapped because those who have defined the spiritual path for the last few thousand years have been men who associated spirituality with a separateness from nature and all that it represents, in terms of birth, death, children, and so on.

We must still struggle to find spiritual ways that are adapted to us as *women* and which validate and develop us as *women* not as asexual entities who must deny their inherent nature in order to be acceptable on the spiritual path. When we do this we will certainly be of greater benefit to others than if we are trying to ape men, following traditions that were created by men for men.

Even though I believe that on the absolute level the true nature of the mind has no sexual characteristics, on the relative level the means to achieving illumination must be adapted to the individual. The differences between individuals must be appreciated and even celebrated. Women and men are different when we speak from a relative point of view, but how these differences are interpreted and whether these differences are seen positively or negatively is a matter of cultural and religious conditioning.

In order for women to find viable paths to liberation, we need the inspiration of other women who have succeeded in remaining true to their own energies without becoming fixated on their sexual gender and have, with this integrity, reached complete liberation.

Hopefully these biographies of real women, not mythological figures or divinities, can begin to fulfill this need. I have felt from the beginning that there is such a vacuum in this area that these stories were being pulled through me to fill this gap. They have certainly filled a longing within me, and I am joyful that they can be shared with others, not only for the benefit of my generation but so that our children and many generations to come will grow up with these stories to read and will have them to draw inspiration from in their times of need. I have already recounted the stories of Nangsa Obum and others to my daughters and they listened to them wide-eyed, with complete absorption.

The feminine principle in Tibetan Buddhism

The feminine principle in Tibetan Buddhism has many complex aspects. I will not attempt a conclusive study, but I would like to discuss the aspects which appear in these biographies.

Any discussion of the feminine must begin with "The Great Mother or Consort." This aspect of the feminine is mentioned several times in the biography of Machig Lapdron. She may be called "Yum Chenmo," "The Mother of the Buddhas," the "Womb of the Tathagatas," or "Prajna Paramita." This is the primordial feminine which is the basic ground. It is described as feminine because it has the power to give birth.

Trungpa Rinpoche explains the "Great Mother" in this way:

In phenomenal experience, whether pleasure or pain, birth or death, sanity or insanity, good or bad, it is necessary to have a basic ground. This basic ground is known in Buddhist literature as the mother principle. Prajnaparamita (the perfection of wisdom) is called the mother-consort of all the Buddhas. . . . As a principle of cosmic structure, the all-accommodating basic ground is neither male nor female. One might call it hermaphroditic, but due to its quality of fertility or potentiality, it is regarded as feminine.[19]

Starhawk in her book on witchcraft describes a very similar if not identical principle:

[21]

In the beginning of the Goddess is the All, virgin, meaning complete within herself. Although She is called *Goddess*, She could just as well be called *God* – sex has not yet come into being. . . . Yet the female nature of the ground of being is being stressed – because the process of creation that is about to occur is a *birth* process. The world is born, not made, and not commanded into being.[20]

The "Great Mother" is different from the Christian God, because it does not intend to produce a world and set down laws. The whole thing is spontaneous rather than intentional. God separates himself to create the world, but the feminine just gives birth spontaneously.

In Tantric Buddhism the symbolic manifestation of the "Great Mother" is the downward-pointing triangle called Chos.'byung (pronounced "chojung"), meaning "source of dharmas," the cosmic cervix, or the gate of all birth. It is three-dimensional and is white on the outside and red on the inside, but it is not something material. Trungpa Rinpoche explains it thus in his commentary on the Anuttara Tantra of Vajra Varahi in the Kagyu tradition:

The source of dharmas arises out of emptiness and has three characteristics: it is unborn, non-dwelling and unceasing. Essentially it is absolute space with a boundary or frame. This represents the coemergent quality of wisdom and confusion arising from the emptiness of space. The source of dharmas is sometimes referred to as a channel for sunyata or as the cosmic cervix. . . . The shape of the triangle – sharp at the bottom and wide at the top – signifies that every aspect of space can be accommodated at once, microcosm and macrocosm, the most minute situations as well as the most vast.[21]

It is white on the outside because it is unconditioned and non-dwelling, and this is balanced and also activated by the blood-red interior, the transcendental ecstatic lust. Vajrayogini both stands on the triangular source of dharmas and has it in her "secret place," roughly the position of the human womb.

The triangle represents the feminine in many cultures:

[22]

Vulvular V's and the more abstracted triangle represent women as a fertile source. . . . *Fecunda* is *femina*: fecund, or fertile, and female are one. The fertile woman bestows form through her perfected form. The *mons veneris* of the Mother is the triangle of Aphrodite, the "mound of Venus," the mountain connecting man and woman, earth and sky.[22]

The Pythagoreans considered the triangle to be sacred, not only because of its perfect form, but also because it was the archetype of universal fertility.

The Great Mother is described as "the void state of all the dharmas which we call 'Mother of all Creation' "[23] in the biography of Machig Lapdron (see pp. 176–7). In Buddhist philosophy all dharmas (which are fundamental factors or things out of which all experience is built) have no self-existing essence. A person or thing is the summation of its parts and has no self-essence, or soul, and is therefore void of self or ego. This essential emptiness is the primary matrix of existence and is therefore called the "Mother of Creation." It is the basic space that permeates everything and undermines the ego. Voidness is an expression of space. The Great Mother principle is the space that gives birth to the phenomenal world. This process of emptiness or space giving birth to phenomena goes on all the time. It is not a question of "once upon a time," but rather a fundamental process which goes on continually. So this permeating space and boundary, which is fundamental to all form, is the Great Mother, and her symbol is the downward-pointing triangle, the source of dharmas.

The Prajna Paramita, the perfection of profound cognition, is also a part of the feminine principle. It is said to be the "Womb of the Tathagatas" (the Buddhas, those who have gone beyond) or the "Mother of the Buddhas." The Prajna Paramita (see p. 130) is the quality of sharp perception which comes with the relaxation of the ego. Meditation, because it slows down the confused grasping aspect of the mind, allows the natural luminous clarity of the mind, prajna, to come forth. This faculty of profound cognition is the source of, or the womb for Buddhas to grow in and is therefore called "the womb of the Buddhas."

The combination of profound cognition, Prajna, the feminine, and skillful activity, Upaya, the masculine, is represented in male and female figures in sexual embrace in Tibetan Tantric art. This is called the union of yum (the feminine) and yab (the masculine). But when we speak of yab-yum we are no longer at the level of the primordial mother, because the Great Mother has no masculine counterpart, she (it) is basic space and emptiness. When we reach to the level of yab-yum we are talking about descendants of primordial space, energies which are working as polarities. The qualities of these energies are assigned by the culture which gives them labels. As we can see from the opposite attributes given to the masculine and feminine in Hindu and Buddhist Tantras, there is no absolute quality for the masculine or feminine. The Tibetans attribute the dynamic energy to the male, though the lunar energy was also considered masculine and the feminine is the wisdom aspect associated with the sun.

Thus we can see, from the above-mentioned passage in the biography of Machig Lapdron, the way the primordial feminine moves through the dimension of light and finally into female form. This human form might be called yogini or dakini, but Machig had to meet with her roots in the Great Mother before she could experientially move beyond the cultural prejudices that told her that she was weak, and stupid and not spiritually as capable as men. The sense of a noble lineage coming through the Great Mother, Tara, which Machig was shown, can also give a sense of spiritual heritage and inspiration to women. From this point of view we are not evil temptresses or unwelcome renunciants in a religion whose founder admitted women reluctantly, nor are we ignorant householders who might be able to renounce someday; but rather we could connect with the lineage of the divine feminine, the primal matrix, imbued with compassion, actively wrathful and destructive where energy is blocked, ecstatic and playful, understanding the true nature of reality. To understand this heritage more clearly, this alternative genealogy which Machig was shown, we must look more deeply at the dakini, for it is the energy of the dakini which dances through all these aspects of the feminine.

The Dakini Principle

Dakini in Tibetan is "Khadro," which literally means "sky-goer," or one who moves in the sky. The dakini is probably the most important manifestation of the feminine in Tibetan Buddhism, and appears many times in these stories. So we must try to understand her significance and her many forms.

In general the dakini represents the everchanging flow of energy with which the yogic practitioner must work in order to become realized. She may appear as a human being, as a goddess – either peaceful or wrathful – or she may be perceived as the general play of energy in the phenomenal world.

In order to connect to this dynamic energizing feminine principle the practitioner of Tantra (Tantrika) does specific practices. These practices take place at three levels. At the primary level the dakini is invoked and visualized as deity in the form of a dakini. For example, the dakini may be visualized first in front of the practitioner, and then this external figure is united with the Tantrika, and the mantra of the dakini is recited. This is a very general description of the "outer" practice of the dakini.

After one becomes accomplished at the level of the outer practice one begins the "inner" practice. At this stage the dakini is worked with through the activation of the subtle nerves (rtsa), the breath (rlung) and the essence (tig.le).

The third level of practice is called the "secret"; at this point there is a direct contact between the state of the practitioner and the energy of the dakini principle.

In Tantra one of the primary ways of looking at the manifestations of the dakini is as the wisdom energy of the five colors which are the subtle luminous form of the five elements. In Tantrism enlightened manifestation is divided into five aspects called the five families (Rigs.nga). (See biography of Nangsa Obum pp. 92–3.) These five "families" each represent the transformation of a gross passion or neurosis. The transformation of these five negativities into wisdom is the essence of the Tantric path.

In order to understand the five wisdom dakinis we have to

go way back to the beginning, to the basic split. The split is between "I" and "others." This is the beginning of the "ego." The ego sees everything dualistically, there is a space which is "here" and which is "me" and "mine" and another space, "there," which is "them" and "theirs." This barrier between the internal space and the external space creates a constant struggle. The conventional search for happiness is the ego's attempt to redress this split by making it all "mine," but the ironic twist is that the more the ego tries to control the situation, the more the barrier is solidified. In the struggle the ego completely loses track of the basic split that is the source of suffering.

What happens after the dualistic barrier is initially created is that the ego forms a kind of governing headquarters which sends feelers out into the environment to determine what is safe and what will enhance itself and expand its territory, what is threatening and what is merely uninteresting or vaguely annoying. These feelers report back to central headquarters and the reactions to this information become the three fundamental poisons: passion (attraction toward what will increase its territory), aggression (toward what seems threatening) and "ignoring" or ignorance (toward that which seems to be of no use to the ego). From these fundamental poisons develop further elaborations, and we get into conceptual discrimination, further pigeon-holing of perception and more complex forms of the three poisons. We end up with a whole fantasy world centered around the ego. A storyline develops based on these reactions and one thing leads to another. This is what Buddhists call the karmic chain reaction. The whole thing gets so complicated that the ego is kept constantly busy and entertained by the plots and subplots which develop from the basic dualistic split. This clinging to the fantasy that the ego needs to control its territory and protect itself from threats is the basis of all suffering and neurosis. However, since this process has been going on for lifetimes, the thickness of the plots and subplots sometimes becomes overwhelming. Meditation practice slows down the reaction patterns, and gradually things start to settle down and the whole process becomes a bit clearer.

Because the energy of individuals varies, their styles of

relating to the basic split also vary. When the ego's frantic struggle is relaxed, the basic energy of the individual can shine through as wisdom. The way wisdom manifests will vary according to the nature of the individual, and thus we have the five Buddha families. Naturally not everyone fits neatly into a particular category and many people are mixtures of several families.

The five families are: Vajra (diamond), Buddha, Ratna (jewel), Padma (lotus), Karma (action). These are fundamental energy patterns which manifest in all phenomenal experience.

The Vajra family person in the unevolved state surveys and reflects the environment with sharp accuracy; there is a fear of not having the situation covered and, if there are any surprises, the reaction is anger, either hot or cold. The Vajra type is intellectual and conceptual, always trying to systematize everything. When this becomes neurotic, complex systems of how everything works are evolved which have little relationship to the situation at hand. When this angry, controlling intellect is transformed into its original state it becomes "Mirror Like Wisdom." It is associated with the element water, blue or white, the Buddha Akshobya and the dakini Dhatisvari.

The Buddha family person is associated with the element of space or ether. In its neurotic state it is dull and thick: the slang "spaced out" perfectly defines the Buddha family person whose intelligence is lulled to sleep. These people don't bother to wash the dishes or take care of themselves; everything seems to require too much effort. The Buddha family is associated with the "Wisdom of All-Encompassing Space," and when this dullness is purified it becomes open and spacious like the sky and the person is calm, open and warm. The name of the Buddha of this family is Vairocana and the dakini Locanā.

The Ratna family is associated with the element of earth, the south, the color yellow and autumn. In its unevolved state this energy must fill up every corner because it never has enough. There is a tendency to be greedy and domineering, wanting always to be the center of things. The Ratna type needs to accumulate food and possessions. The negative quality of Ratna is pride; they want everyone to think they are very important. When this energy is purified into wisdom it becomes "All Enriching Wisdom." Without the attachment of the ego the expansiveness of Ratna seems to enrich every situation: wonderful things are created and the surroundings are enriched. The Buddha of this family is Ratnasambhava and the dakini Mamaki.

The Padma family person is involved with seduction rather than the acquisition of material things that concerns the Ratna type. The Padma person is interested in relationships and wants to accumulate desirable feelings. They want to draw others in and possess them. The mental pattern involves a dilettantish, scattered kind of activity. Projects are started and then dropped when the superficial glamor wears off. Pleasure is very important, and pain is rejection or abandonment. The wisdom which emerges when this energy is freed from the ego's hold is "Discriminating Awareness Wisdom" and things can be seen with Prajna, profound cognition. Aesthetics become enlightened and great art can be created with this energy which can see the relationships between everything. Padma is associated with the west and spring, the color red, fire, the Buddha Amitabha and the dakini Pandaravasini.

The Karma family person is very active and is always working at something. The Karma family dakini is often portrayed in profile because she is too busy to look at you straight on. This speed comes from the air element and can be very aggressive and impulsive. There is a tendency toward paranoia, a fear of losing track of all the plots that are going on, so they are usually frantically organizing everyone and everything, making sure things are under control. In its wisdom transformation this energy becomes "All-Accomplishing Wisdom," and enlightened activity begins to take place, which benefits many beings. The Karma family is associated with winter, the north, envy, the Buddha Amogasiddi and the dakini Samayatara.

Certain women are said to be emanations of these dakinis, and they have certain signs by which they can be recognized. Because wisdom is an inherent part of the energy, not a separate thing which follows on a linear pattern, the enlightened aspect might escape from the surveillance of the ego at

[28]

any moment and therefore everyone has the possibility of becoming a Buddha or dakini on the spot. We could have little gaps in the claustrophobic game of dualism, and clarity could shine through. Therefore even an ordinary "unenlightened" woman or situation could suddenly manifest as the dakini. The world is not as solid as we think it is, and the more we are open to the gaps, the more wisdom can shine through and the more the play of the dakini energy can be experienced. The primary way to relax the ego's grasp is to practice meditation. All Tantric visualizations and mantras are geared to freeing the energy of wisdom which is being suffocated under the solidified fantasies of dualistic fixation.

By consciously invoking the dakini through Tantric practices we begin to develop a sensitivity to energy itself. When looking at the iconography of the dakini we should bear in mind that through understanding her symbols and identifying with her, we are identifying with our own energy. Tantric divinities are used because we are in a dualistic state. Tantra takes advantage of that, or exaggerates it, by embodying an external figure with all the qualities the practitioner wishes to obtain. After glorifying and worshiping this external deity, the deity dissolves into the practitioner – then at the end of any Tantra there is a total dissolution of the deity into space; and finally after resting in that state the practitioner visualizes herself or himself as the deity again as they go about their normal activities.

There are a vast number of Tantric dakinis, both peaceful and wrathful, in the Tibetan pantheon, each embodying specific qualities which the practitioner may need to activate at certain times according to the instruction of the guru.

The energy which springs from the Great Mother gives birth to the dakini. One of the main dakinis, according to the Annutara Tantra, is Vajra Varahi (see illustration), a form of Vajra Yogini. She springs out of the cosmic cervix, the triangular source of dharmas, burning with unbearable bliss, energy in an unconditional state. She has the three-dimensional triangular source of dharmas just below her navel and she is standing on one. This form acts on the being of the tantrika when he or she visualizes Vajra Varahi, and the effect is the activation of internal energies which dissolve the sense of inner

Vajra Varahi

and outer and plug in to a sense of all-pervading energized space which is primordial wisdom and a kind of burning transcendental lust and bliss.

In order to understand some of the symbolism of one of the most frequently used dakinis, I would like to discuss some of the ornaments of Vajra Yogini in the form of Vajra Varahi (Indestructible Sow). Within Tibetan Buddhism there are many different schools and lineages, and within these there are many interpretations of the symbols. I have chosen to discuss only a few of the symbolic ornaments of the dakini. I have expanded the discussion of these aspects to include the interpretations of similar symbols from other cultures which I found corresponded to the Tibetan interpretation of these symbols.

In the mandala of Vajra Varahi she is a red figure and is surrounded by the four dakinis, the blue Vajra dakini, the yellow Ratna dakini, the red Padma dakini and the green Karma dakini; she herself comes from the Buddha family. All the retinue dakinis look the same as her, except that they have different ornaments on their hooked knives symbolizing their families.

Vajra Varahi is called "Diamond Sow" or "Indestructible Sow" because she has a wild boar's head coming out of the side of her human head. The symbolism of the pig or sow in connection with this goddess is significant. Looking at the history of the sow in other religions may give us some clues as to its representation here. As Nor Hall points out:

Pigs were Demeter's fertility. Gravid sows were buried in mystery pits. They were called the uterine animals of the land, close to motherhood. . . . "Pig" in Greek and Latin was also "cunt" and it was sacred; pigs were not to be eaten during rites. But pork becomes unclean and pigs become "disgusting" when the mother functions of the feminine, and the goddess of the rotting and rutting and springing to life, are no longer revered. . . . In the Mother realm, where the blackness of desire is not feared, where (with the moon-struck poet Levertov) "we rock and grunt and shine", the goddesses are all great white, round maternal sows (Ishtar, Isis, Demeter, etc.).[24]

These ancient goddesses were also portrayed, like the Tantric dakinis, as naked, with exposed, sometimes very vividly painted genitals. The female body in ancient religions was considered sacred, inspiring. The sexual ecstasy that is suggested was also divine. It was not until women themselves were considered profane that the female body was also considered shameful.

The pig could be seen as a symbol of the unpresentable brutish part of ourselves; our animal instinctual nature. The Mesopotamian goddess Ishtar has two faces: "both waterer of green shoots and piglike destroyer. Paying attention to her means admitting paradoxes of intention and action. . . . It means listening to inner voices or going to the oracle of one's dreams when blinded by the too bright constant light of day."[25]

"Diamond Sow" could represent the incorporation of both the animal and the human, the ignorant and the logical, the dark and the light, the unconscious and the conscious parts of ourselves. Both these aspects have their sacred qualities, and both must be there to achieve the power of the goddess.

There are three main objects that usually accompany a representation of the dakini: the hooked knife (Kartik), the trident staff (Khatvanga), and the skull cup of blood (Kapala).

The hooked knife is held in her right hand. It is raised as if to strike. The handle of the knife is a half vajra, four prongs around a central prong, closed at the top. The "vajra" symbolizes the masculine energy which means "thunderbolt" or "diamond" or "indestructible" or "skillful means." Since this is the handle, the dakini must grasp the handle to strike with the knife. Therefore she must grasp the force of this thunderbolt in order to cut. The blade is in the shape of a crescent moon with a hook on the end. This is the shape of the traditional Indian butcher's knife and descends from the Tantric charnel-ground cemeteries in India. There the knife was used to skin and cut up human corpses. Originally dakinis may have been horrific female spirits and low-caste women who lived in the cremation grounds where yogis stayed for their Tantric rituals.

So the knife has two aspects. One is the handle and the other the blade. The cutting edge of the knife symbolizes her incisive insight. The crescent shape suggests the moon. In reading Nor Hall's *The Moon and the Virgin* I was struck by the image of the double-edged axe in the Minoan civilization of Crete and its similarity with the crescent knife. It was the tool carried by the Minoan mother goddess and was once considered "the lightning flash of Zeus's eyes, a thunderbolt fallen to the ground."[26] The association of the crescent moon and the goddess is extensive. In general the crescent moon is associated with the potential of all things to grow and change in rhythmic monthly cycles. The moon changes its face constantly and brings reflection with its silvery light. A crescent moon in the right hand is the waxing crescent symbol of the virgin or the nymph.

The traditional interpretation of the hook in Tibetan Buddhist imagery is that of the hook of compassion. It is the hook which pulls beings out of the cycles of transmigration. The hooked crescent-shaped knife of the dakini with its vajra handle pulls one forth from suffering, chops up the ego-centered self and is guided by the diamond clarity of the vajra.

In her left hand the Vajra Varahi holds a skull cup (Kapala) brimming with blood or white amrita. The Kapala symbolizes the vagina, and the blood (rakta) is the essence of the dakini, the red bodhicitta, the female counterpart of semen, the white bodhicitta, or thought of bodhi, "the thought toward enlightenment." The blood is also thought of as form or phenomenal experience and the skull cup as environment, or basic space.

The witches' cauldron has a similar archetypal significance:

The work of woman is transformation: making something out of nothing, giving form to formless energy. Her instruments in this work are the tripod and cauldron, her elements blood and milk – both liquids held within her are organic, that with which one works. She is both container and contained at this stage. She transforms matter and is herself transformed. She is the procession of form and the forms of the process.[27]

In the Celtic tradition the goddess Ceridwen also has a cauldron:

her cauldron is the womb-cauldron of rebirth and inspiration. In early Celtic myth, the cauldron of the goddess restored slain warriors to life. . . . The Celtic after-world is called the Land of Youth, and the secret that opens its door is found in the cauldron. The secret of immortality lies in seeing death as an integral part of the cycle of life. . . . We are continually renewed and reborn whenever we drink fully and fearlessly from "the cup of wine of life."[28]

There is a passage in the life story of Yeshe Tsogyel, *Sky Dancer*, wherein, after practicing austerities, she has a vision "of a red woman, naked, lacking even the covering of bone ornaments, who thrust her bhaga against my mouth and I drank deeply from her copious flow of blood. My entire being was filled with health and well-being, I felt as strong as a snow-lion, and I realized profound absorption to be inexpressible truth."[29]

The redness of blood is also connected to primordial lust, the passion which binds the universe together, and the white is the masculine, male sexual fluids. In the Tibetan tradition, white connotes the life force, and red the kairmic base consciousness, the feminine menstrual blood. The red-bodied Vajra Varahi, who, in some practices, drips menstrual blood on a mirror, also carries the crescent knife and the skull cup of blood. The red blood suggests the burning interior power of women, primal matrix which can become babies, milk, passion and fierceness, primal lava of life.

The Khatvanga is the third accouterment which is present in an iconographic image of a dakini. It is a staff, with a trident at the top, and underneath the trident, tied to the staff, is a double vajra with three severed heads. The top head is a dry skull, under the skull is a head that has been severed several days, and below that is a freshly severed head. The staff is held in the crook of the elbow of the left arm and extends from her head to her foot. Usually she is dancing, so one foot is raised and the other is standing on a corpse, which represents the negativity which has been overcome.

The three prongs of the trident at the top of the staff symbolize the transformation of the three poisons: passion, anger and ignorance. The three heads symbolize the three "kayas," or bodies. The dry skull stands for the Dharmakaya, a level of being which has no form, but contains the potential for everything. The second "kaya" is the Sambogakaya, symbolized by a head which has been severed for several weeks. The Sambogakaya is the dimension of light, the manifestation of the essence of the purified elements. The deities of the Tibetan pantheon exist in this level, but only very advanced yogins can really see them and enter into their sphere. The Nirmanakaya is represented by a freshly severed head under the other two on the staff. This "kaya" means that the enlightened energy manifests in human form such as Padma Sambhava or the Buddha. The Nirmanakaya is the only kaya which can be perceived by normal human beings. The incarnate Tibetan lamas are called tulku, the Tibetan for Nirmanakaya; the Buddha is also considered a Nirmanakaya manifestation.

The overall significance of the Khatvanga staff is that of the "hidden consort." Here it is the masculine consort of the dakini. If we think of the possible uses of a staff with a trident on top, they are: a support, a spear, and a stake to hold things down. By holding the Khatvanga she shows us that she has incorporated the masculine into herself. This energy is at her service. With this staff she has the power to stand alone because she has integrated the masculine into herself. The same is true in reverse for male figures who hold the Khatvanga as their "secret consort." The Tantric practitioners who visualize themselves as these deities understand that in order to be whole we must embody and appreciate *both* the masculine and feminine in ourselves.

I find the image of the Khatvanga staff held by the dancing dakini a particularly potent symbol. She holds it and yet she does not grasp it. She recognizes it as something she must have near her to use, and yet she also recognizes it as something which is separate.

I was struck by the similarity of the stake of Ereshkigal from the ancient Sumerian myth "The Descent of Inanna" which dates from the third millennium BC. Ereshkigal is the goddess of the underworld who kills Inanna when she descends to witness the death of Ereshkigal's husband and she hangs Inanna on her stake. In analyzing the meaning of the stake, Sylvia Perera states in her book *Descent to the Goddess*:

This sense of the pole suggests an aspect of the impersonal feminine yang energy. It makes firm, nails down into material reality, embodies and grounds spirit in matter and the moment. It is thus supportive, a peg to hang onto through life's flux. Also the stake is like a phallus or dildo of the dark goddess, or the member of Gugalanna her husband, who was killed. Ereshkigal's stake fills the all receptive emptiness of the feminine with feminine yang strength. It fills the eternally empty womb mouth, and gives a woman her own wholeness, so that the woman is not merely dependent on man or child, but can be unto herself as a full and separate individual.[30]

There are two points that must be made in relation to the Katvanga staff. One is that the image of the wrathful dakini holding her "consort" staff is clearly an image which could be an inspiration to women in our culture. We have no such images of the feminine to identify with. Our culture has clearly discouraged women from claiming their feminine potency. Women are not given encouragement to see themselves positively when they are assertive and angry. They are taught to be docile and never to threaten.

The second point is that the staff of the dakini does not preclude a positive and passionate relationship with a real man. Rather the strength she gains by incorporation of the masculine into herself balances the polarized energy within her and makes her more capable of receiving a genuine relationship. Rather than relating to her mate from a stance of poverty, Sleeping Beauty to be awakened by the prince, she is already awake and dancing and does not need to sap the energy of her consort to feel balanced. She can give and receive from the stance of wholeness and richness. In this way she avoids indiscriminate and unwise relationships that may prove to be painful and masochistic.

The assertive feminine also acts as guardian of the earth. The dark goddess energy is seen as an obnoxious upstart when the patriarchy rips apart and poisons the earth. This force of the wrathful dakini is seen in the connection of the women's movement with ecological and disarmament protests.

[36]

In *The One Hundred Thousand Songs of Milarepa*, Milarepa encounters some dakinis who have been offended by being burned by the smoke of a shepherd's foul-smelling fire. They have reacted by creating a pestilence. The dakinis say to him:

According to the reciprocal-relation principle of the Law-of-Causation, when we recover from a disease so will the people. It is the common oath of all worldly Dakinis that if one of us has been made unwell or unhappy, we are all offended and the Devas and spirits support us, throwing the world into confusion.[31]

If we see the dakini as the subtle flow of energy, when someone acts in a way which disturbs the energy of the earth the dakini principle is also disturbed and this will cause disease, famine and warfare.

Beyond formal meditation on the dakini there is the spontaneous manifestation of the dakini in everyday life situations which the Tantrika must learn to work with. In these biographies, and in almost all the stories of great saints in Tibet, the dakini appears at crucial moments. These encounters often have a quality of sharp, incisive challenge to the fixated conceptions of the practitioner. They may occur through a human dakini or through a dream or mirage-like appearance which vanishes after the message is communicated. These encounters often have a grounding, practical insightful quality which is sharp and wrathful. This is the primordial raw energy of the dark goddess. Often a pure ascetic monk must accept this aspect of himself before he can make progress on the Tantric path. For this reason the wrathful dakini is associated with meat and blood.

In the story of Abhayakaragupta,[32] a famous high-caste scholar, a young maiden approached him in the courtyard of his monastery and shoved a piece of bloody meat at him, saying that it had been slaughtered for him. He was taken aback and replied: "I am a pure monk. How can I eat meat that has been so blatantly prepared for me?" At once she disappeared.

Tantric Buddhism forces us to go beyond all our limitations,

[37]

even the limitations imposed by the Buddha, such as not
eating meat that has been killed for oneself. This is because in
Tantrism all habitual patterns, even "golden habits," must be
relinquished so that we may experience reality without
conceptuality. Tantric ritual feasts, "ganachakra," always
include meat and wine for this reason. In any situation we
must not be conditioned by concepts of good and bad. Even in
a seemingly amoral situation a Tantric practitioner can and
must transform negativity directly rather than avoiding it. By
not recognizing this girl who acted as a dakini to test his
understanding, he cut off his progress in the practice. The next
time she appeared to him she was in the form of an old hag.
This time, having consulted with his guru in the meantime, he
recognized her and confessed his failure to acknowledge her
before. This was a turning point in his practice. He went on to
become an accomplished yogi rather than a strict monk.

Through the contact with the dakini, intuitive faculties are
opened and insight occurs; without the activation of these
energies the practice would be flat and intellectual. The dakini
also creates a sense of relatedness and capricious playfulness
which can be terrifying, as Trungpa Rinpoche says:

> The playful maiden is all-present. She loves you. She hates
> you. Without her your life would be continual boredom. But
> she continually plays tricks on you. When you want to get
> rid of her she clings. To get rid of her is to get rid of your
> own body – she is that close. In Tantric literature she is
> referred to as the dakini principle. The dakini is playful. She
> gambles with your life.[33]

The dakinis transmit directly through life experiences,
rather than through complex philosophical arguments. It is
for this reason that the dakini is associated with the Tantric
teachings which work directly with the energy of body,
speech and mind, rather than the more intellectual Sutric
teachings.

The dakini often makes her first appearance when a
practitioner is making the transition from an intellectual
approach to an experiential approach. This is seen in the
biographies of both Saraha and Naropa.

The well-known monk and scholar Saraha left his university to go in search of a Tantric teacher. On the way he saw a young woman making arrows in a marketplace. He was fascinated by her, and when he approached her and asked if she was a professional arrowsmith, she replied: "My dear young man, the Buddha's meaning can be known through symbols and actions, not through words and books."[34] After this he understood the symbolic meaning of the arrow, and then he began living with this low-caste woman, accepting her as his teacher. This outraged the religious community as he had been a pure brahmin. The famous dohas of Saraha, his songs of realization, were his response to the king, the queen and the people, who challenged his religious understanding because he had gone to live with this dakini.

The importance of intimate contact with a dakini should also be mentioned. The Tibetans recognize the importance of sexual yoga in opening up further fields of awareness and insight, and in bestowing the blessing of long life on the Tantrika. Besides the sexual contact, living with a wisdom dakini brings intuitive insights in daily life situations. For example, one day Saraha asked the arrowsmith woman to prepare him a radish curry. While she was cooking it he went into a deep state of meditation (samadhi) which lasted for twelve years. When he came out of meditation he immediately asked for radish curry and she said: "You sit in samadhi for twelve years without getting up, and now you want radish curry, as if it still existed. Besides there are no radishes at this time of the year." When he replied that he would then go to the mountains to meditate she replied: "Simply removing your body from the world is not true renunciation. Real renunciation takes place when your mind abandons frivolous and absorbing thoughts. If you sit in meditation for twelve years and cannot even give up your desire for radish curry, what is the point of going into the mountains?"[35]

A monk should not have any intimate contact with any woman: technically he should not even receive something directly from a woman's hand. The same is true in reverse for a nun. For this reason they cannot benefit from the communication which can come from living with an insightful consort. This is the reason why many great teachers, including some of the women included here, are told by their gurus at a certain point in their practice that they must find a suitable consort. Padma Sambhava sent his own consort, Yeshe Tsogyel, off to Nepal at a certain point, to find a very specific young man to be her consort. Machig Lapdron was also guided by Tara and her gurus and dakinis, to her consort Topabhadra. So the necessity of the consort is not limited to men. The descriptions of dakinis are generally female because most of the Tantrikas we hear of are men. But whether the consort is male (daka), or a female (dakini), a certain concrete presence is needed at times in order to work further with one's energy. Otherwise the channels which can be opened by Tantric sex will remain closed and so yogi or yogini cannot fully develop his or her insight and awareness.

However, it should be noted that this contact with a consort does not come at the beginning of the training when the passions are still out of control and distraction is rampant. Rather, the taking of a consort is suggested as one of the final measures for complete enlightenment. Emotions are very powerful, and unless we can truly use them for further depth of awareness, intimate relationships can become a big obstacle instead of a boon to the practitioner.

One of the best examples of the mercurial changes of the dakini is in the life story of the famous Indian Buddhist teacher Naropa.

Naropa was the greatest scholar at the prestigious Nalanda University. One day as he was reading a book on logic, a shadow fell across the page. When he turned round he saw a hideous old hag. She asked him if he understood the words or the meaning, and when he replied that he understood both, she was furious and told him that he only understood the words, not the meaning. She recommended that he find her brother, who understood the meaning, and then she disappeared into a rainbow. Because of contact with the dakini he decided he must seek true realization outside the monastic university. The dakini appears as an ugly old hag because she is primordial wisdom, ancient beyond conceptuality. She is ugly because Naropa has been suppressing and rejecting this part of himself. This ambassador of primordial wisdom appears in a hideous form because he has been deluding himself, thinking that he really understands when in fact he has been building a deluded castle of intellectuality and prudishness.

Although he did abruptly leave the monastic university and became a poor mendicant in search of a guru, his habitual thought-patterns were much slower to change. His guru, Tilopa, did not appear to him until he had spent years in search of him. Tilopa insisted that he overcome his prejudices and come to know "the mirror of the mind, the mysterious home of the dakini."[36] The guru presented situations that Naropa took literally and conceptually rather than symbolically and intuitively, thus proving his lack of understanding of the dakini and causing him great suffering. For example, when he set out to look for his guru he came across a leper woman who was lying in the middle of his path. Instead of stopping to help her as he should have done if he had been living the teachings of compassion he had been studying, he jumped over her. At that moment she appeared in a rainbow halo in the sky and said:

> The ultimate in which all become the same
> Is free of habit-forming thought and limitations
> How, if still fettered by them,
> Can you hope to find the Guru?[37]

Due to his lack of relationship to the dakini, who exists beyond duality and speaks in a symbolic language, he acted as if there were a "self" to act. He saw everything external as being separate from himself, and fell into the trap of dualism, rather than seeing the mind as a mirror with the capacity to reflect without dualistic notions of good and bad. Her home is the first thought before we solidify what we perceive, when we let perception in without putting all impressions into pigeon-holes.

Being a dynamic principle, the dakini is energy itself; a positive contact with her brings about a sense of freshness and magic. She becomes a guide and a consort who activates intuitive understanding and profound awareness, but this energy can turn suddenly and pull the rug out from under you if you become too attached and fixated. This can be painful. When the energy becomes blocked and we feel the pain caused by our fixation, this is the wrathful dakini. Her anger pushes us to let go of this clinging and enter her mysterious home.

All Tantrikas must be tuned in to the energy of their own bodies and that of the world around them. This means they must have a positive relationship to the dakini, who is energy in all of its forms. The meditation on a form of the dakini such as Vajra Varahi or the five wisdom dakinis is one means of establishing this awareness, but as we see in the stories that follow and in the stories of Naropa, Saraha and Abhaya-karagupta mentioned above, she also appears in dreams, visions and as a human being. She acts as a spiritual midwife, the medial feminine, helping the Tantrika to give birth to the wisdom which she embodies by cutting through conceptualiza-tion and working directly with energy.

The language of the dakini

In our culture, which is dominated by the rational, scientific point of view, we tend to think of language in a very limited way. But mystics and madmen have always maintained that there are other kinds of languages. These are languages which cannot be interpreted or understood by the rational left hemisphere of the brain. The Tibetan lamas speak of a language called "the secret signs and letters of the dakini" (mKha'. 'gro gSang Ba'ibrDa Yig), and another which is a secret code of Tantric terminology called "the twilight language" (sandhyabhasa in Sanskrit). The oral teachings of the Kagyu lineage, or ear-whispered teachings, are called by Milarepa "the dakini's breath."

The language of the dakini consists of letters or symbols which have no set translation. The ability to understand the meaning of this language is the province of only a very few – those who are in contact with the energy field of the dakini. It is a highly symbolic cipher which is so condensed that six or seven volumes of teachings could come out of a few letters. Yeshe Tsogyel, a great dakini, hid many texts by putting them into the dakini cipher; sometimes a whole teaching was condensed into a single symbol and hidden in the earth, a rock, a tree, or water.

In order to discuss the language of the dakini we must first discuss the terma tradition. A terma is a "hidden treasure" which is concealed and then discovered at a later date by a "terton," a person who finds and deciphers the hidden text. The text is usually written in the language of the dakini, and only a terton destined to reveal the terma will be able to translate the text. The content of the terma varies, but it is always something appropriate to the time in which it is discovered and revealed.

The best-known termas are those hidden by Padma Sambhava and Yeshe Tsogyel in the latter part of the eighth century and the early ninth century AD. Usually Yeshe Tsogyel, using her extraordinary memory, took the teachings of Padma Sambhava and hid them in "diamond rocks, in mysterious lakes, and unchanging boxes."[38] These places were called "ternay" (gTer.gnas) and they were protected by spirits called Tetsung (gTer.srung) so that they could not be discovered by inappropriate people. The purpose of the whole process was to give future generations pure and unadulterated teachings coming directly from Guru Padma Sambhava himself, rather than a distorted version, watered down and changed over time. Padma Sambhava is considered by many Tibetans to be a second Buddha. He was in fact responsible for the conversion of the Tibetans because, rather than deny the native beliefs, he worked with magic and mystery and Tantra and Dzog Chen and Bon, creating the basis of what we know as Tibetan Buddhism. Though some Tibetans, particularly those followers of the "reformed" Gelugpa sect, deny the validity of the terma tradition, most Tibetans hold Padma Sambhava, whom they call Guru Rinpoche, and the terma teachings, in highest esteem.

Some of the disciples of Padma Sambhava also hid termas by the method of burying them in the earth. This tradition is called "sater" (sa.gter), or earth treasure. Another kind of terma is that of the "gongter" (dgongs.gter) the "mind treasures." These termas are received "from the birds, trees, all kinds of light, and from heavenly space."[39] In this case the terma does not come from a material source as in the case with earth termas, but is received by means of divine revelation. For example, a terton might be staring into the sky and symbols or letters might begin to reveal themselves from space. If the terton is properly linked to the dakini energy he can write the resulting teachings down in a language comprehensible to ordinary beings. We have instances of this kind of terma in several texts mentioned as "gongter" in the biography of A-Yu Khadro.

Besides termas hidden in various elements, such as "meter" (me.gter) or fire treasure, "lungter" (rlung.gter) or air treasure, and so on, there is also something called "yang ter" ('yang.gter) or "again terma." These are termas which are found by a terton and then, because the time is not right for their revelation, they will be returned to the dakinis and revealed again at a later date. We have an example of this kind of terma in the case of Jomo Memo. Although she received the terma of the Khadro Sangdu (mKhà.'dro gSang.ba Kun.'dus) in the cave of Padma Sambhava in AD 1260, this teaching was not revealed to others, and it was not until it was rediscovered by Khentse Wongpo (mKyen.brtse'i dBang.po), 1820–92, and published in his collection of termas, the famous *Rinchen Terzod* (Rin.chen gTer.mdzod) that it became a revealed terma. He was the primary guru of A-Yu Khadro, and since she had received the transmission of this tantra she was able to transmit it to others.

So from this information we can understand that the "twilight language" is an actual cipher which can only be understood by those blessed by the wisdom dakini. The way the language is translated is not with a dictionary and a grammar book, but through "another way of knowing" which comes from a space which is far from the sunlit rational world dominated by the logos, and at the same time it is not from the dark abyss of the unconscious but rather a twilight world where another function of the mind is possible. This is not merely the intuitive part of the mind, because even very sensitive people cannot understand the language of the dakini. It is a realm governed by the dakinis, and only those who can integrate into the symbolic world of the dakini can understand their half-concealed language.

The language of the dakini may also be used by the practitioner as a method of reaching a state of awareness (rigpa).[40] For example, "The Song of the Vajra" is written in the language of the dakini. Although "The Song of the Vajra" is considered by many to be a mantra, it is different from a mantra in that it is not used to obtain a certain effect, but rather to link the internal energy of the individual who is in a confused state with the universal flow of energy. Because we are in a dualistic state, this separation exists, and therefore the point of this kind of practice is to eliminate the dualistic boundary by entering the dimension of the sound. The sounds of "The Song of the Vajra" have the power to make this possible. It is something like the "music of the spheres" that Western mystics speak of. The sounds vibrate in the body of the individual, and this vibration brings forth waves which massage the vibration of the being, bringing an integration with the spherical sounds of the universe.

It is notable that, in almost every instance in the biography of Machig Lapdron when a dakini appears it is at twilight, and the language of the dakini is also called the "twilight language." Twilight is the time between waking and sleeping, the conscious and the unconscious. It is a time when the switchover takes place, so there could be a gap, a crack in the wall of the ever-protective ego structure where significant communication from something beyond could take place. At dawn we are still beyond the limiting forces of the conscious mind, yet the heavy veil of deep sleep has lifted. We often find the dakini at these transitional points, when we are open to the "twilight" language:

> From eyes shut to eyes opened, mouth closed to mouth open, every night we go through this journey, and yet what happens between the going under and coming up is so little valued. . . . Memory makes initiation, and individuation, the modern parallel – possible. It is essential for psychic growth to throw oneself into the flow of unconscious life, not to forget, not to diminish; not to demean or degrade as "mere fantasy" one's adventures in the other world. . . . This urge to express what was seen and heard beneath the surface of ordinary reality requires a "language of the soul."[41]

The very existence of the terma tradition and the language of the dakini could only evolve within a culture like that of Tibet which provided an environment for profound spiritual development. Tibet's high altitudes, vast open spaces, low population, and lack of mechanical devices provided a silence and spaciousness for the meditator, unequalled anywhere in the world. The culture placed a high value on spiritual practice, dreams and oracles guided heads of state, and the messages from the "twilight world" were heeded and valued.

Descent and re-emergence

The powerful and evocative "descent" myth with parallels in many cultures is found in several of the stories in this collection. The pattern is that of an oppressive or unconscious situation which leads to a crisis and a "death" or descent or initiation in darkness, followed by a resurrection or re-emergence. The experience gained in this darkness sheds light on to the whole being, and through this experience we are irrevocably changed and empowered. This pattern is also found in the myths of Persephone and Psyche, the ancient Sumerian myth of "The Descent of Inanna," in the Greek initiation rites, in Shaman initiatory ceremonies, and in fairytales like "Sleeping Beauty," "Briar Rose," "The Handless Maiden," "The Seven Ravens," the tales of Mother Hulda, and Baba Yaga. It has also been observed by modern psychologists such as Sylvia Perera, Maria Von Franz and Nor Hall. Other women who, without role models or guidance except from each other, have sought to integrate themselves spiritually while living in a patriarchal culture, have also discovered this cycle. If the descent myth is properly understood it can be of tremendous use, because it is a key to the universal initiation process, which we must take part in if we are to develop and understand ourselves. These experiences touch such a deep level that if we can integrate them again, we can undergo a conscious rebirth; rather than being unconsciously shaped by social pressures and customs.

We can appreciate and grow from our black periods, treating them as springboards rather than useless digressions. We can learn the difference between being passively drawn into darkness, and voluntarily choosing an active entry into the veiled world. We can see what and who is necessary to help us digest and incorporate the insights gained during our descents, be they voluntary or forced upon us.

In this collection of stories the biography of Nangsa Obum most clearly illustrates the descent myth. It is a "delog" ('das.log) story, the story of a person who dies and is then resurrected.

I would like to look at some of the events in the life of Nangsa Obum and to see their spiritual psychological meaning in terms of the death and resurrection process.

First, the birth of a heroine or hero in many fairytales comes after a period of sterility followed by the birth of a supernatural child (see p. 67). In our own lives very often we may go through a period of brooding and stopping and starting projects, or just not doing much of anything, before a major transformation or piece of creative work comes forth. In Nangsa Obum's case her parents were doing much meditation on the goddess Tara, without any selfish motives, and this activity produced a miraculous result. This could be understood as the necessity of proceeding in a direction which we feel is good and right even when no material gain is foreseen.

Throughout her childhood Nangsa was a classic example of a "good girl"; her parents were pleased with her "even though she is a girl" (see p. 67). This statement indicates the Tibetan preference for boy babies. When I went to Nepal recently, a woman who was supposed to be a "yogini" told my pregnant friend that if she said 100,000 prayers to Padma Sambhava, she would be sure to have a boy, not, heaven forbid, a girl.

At any rate, Nangsa in her childhood was so "good" she overcame this "disadvantage"; however, she decided she would not marry but would become a yogini instead. She never questioned that this would be her future until she reached puberty. At this point her beauty began to shine forth and in spite of herself she attracted many suitors. Eventually the protective shell of the mother was broken by the Rinang king, who snatched her up "Like an eagle falling upon a small bird," to be the bride of his son.

This motif is common in fairytales: "The original protected state is experienced as one of psychic unity (one we look back upon as the experience of childlike wholeness) is broken into by the emergence of the archetype of the Great Father and his emissaries. Fairytales usually depict this event in the coming of the king's son, the prince who represents the father."[42]

Here Nangsa actually has no choice in the matter; although she expresses her wish not to be married to anyone, even a prince, her parents think it is a great match for her and are afraid to refuse. Since Tibet was a medieval society the local kings had power over the populace and if someone dared to refuse the desires of a king the results could be horrendous. We see this in the life story of Yeshe Tsogyel when she refused to marry a local king: "the official whipped me with a lash of iron thorns, until my back was a bloody pulp, and unable to bear the pain I stood up and accompanied them."[43]

Neither the king of Rinang nor the prince who wanted to marry Tsogyel cared a whit for what was inside these women. They both possessed the mixed blessing of great beauty, which Tibetans see as a result of good karma, and a desire to renounce worldly life. The king hardly even sees Nangsa as human, and in fact asks her if she is human or the daughter of a god, a celestial musician or a serpentine spirit (see p. 70). He sees her as a beautiful piece of merchandise to be possessed for the aggrandisement of his family.

Even in the twentieth century we as women may be threatened with a beating for expressing our spirituality or not wanting to marry someone *or* we may find ourselves getting into and remaining in negative relationships, because patriarchal society teaches a woman that she must be with a man in order to validate herself. If a woman is young and at a point of inner hesitation, it might be a relief if a man defines her life for her. If she falls into this trap and then later tries to assert her individuality, she will meet with tremendous resistance, perhaps even violence. When a woman's own desires begin to conflict with the man's needs, there is an explosion and the anima projection (when a man projects his unconscious feminine side on to a woman) collapses; or she gives in and continues to suppress her own individuality and lives out his projection. If she does this she may try to maintain an inner life of her own, but the conflict between her inner and outer worlds, and her imprisonment in the service of his psychological needs, will inevitably cause her to live in a semi-somnambulant state of depression.

This explosion comes to Nangsa in the form of being beaten to death. But before her "death" the impossibility of her situation already comes to consciousness when she encounters the yogis, who point out the uselessness of her present life, and again when Sakya Gyaltsen manifests as a handsome beggar with a monkey (see pp. 85–7). His choice of beggar and monkey is an interesting symbol. He is a beggar because Nangsa's spirituality is "begging" for attention, and is impoverished. Yet he is handsome, not only to raise the suspicions of the father-in-law, but because her deep longing for her individuality is beautiful. It might seem strange that a guru who is supposed to emanate compassion would aggravate an already painful situation as Sakya Gyaltsen did, but it is often the case that the teacher will submit the disciple to hardships in order to purify his/her karma and speed up progress on the path. In this case he also foresees that she must have this "delog" experience in order eventually to be able to help others.

The monkey symbolizes something which is captured and trained to imitate. It is captured because its appearance is charming, and then through painful training its natural instincts are controlled and it becomes a source of entertainment for free human beings. The beggar uses the monkey, and several other animals such as the parrot, as examples of Nangsa's situation. Finally he tells her that if she does not give him a substantial offering she is no better than the paintings in the temple. This means that unless she is willing to make a substantial commitment to her true self, she will remain a superficial woman, no deeper than a two-dimensional painting.

Although Nangsa appears to be fulfilling her role as loving wife and mother, she is secretly longing to go into retreat and practice meditation. She is isolated from her experience because of the undercurrent of this unfulfilled longing. So her separation from her husband at the time of her "death" is actually an amplification of a separation which has been running under the surface the whole time.

By staying silent and not defending herself from Ani

Nyemo's jealous accusations against her, she unconsciously provokes the confrontation which forces her out of her stagnant, depressing, obedient phase. Her exaggerated gifts to the yogis and the beggar are further unrepressible instinctive actions which bring on her descent and the eventual resolution of the situation. Many women experience this helpless "no way out" feeling after marriage and children. They have given themselves, and they feel that if they are not happy they have failed. Old desires for fulfillment have remained unsatisfied and undermine the situation. The woman in this situation is restless and sad even when she has "everything" that she is told should make her happy. Usually a woman does not see that this discontent is caused because she has lost her own power, but sees it as a personal failure or incapacity. So she continues to try to find ways to find satisfaction within the context she has chosen, but usually she cannot and the demon of depression continually rears its ugly head.

Nangsa was conditioned by her culture and her mother not to trust her ability to follow the life of a yogini. We see this when her mother says:

> "If you really want to practice the dharma, it is very difficult.
> If you think like this why did you have a baby?
> Do not try to do what you are not incapable of doing,
> Practicing the Dharma.
> Do what you know how to do.
> Be a housewife." (See pp. 114–15.)

"You are like a little sheep, who does not want to stay with the other sheep and be fleeced. So do not be sorry if you are sent to the butcher!" (See p. 114.)

Although Ani Nyemo appears as a negative figure who just stirs up trouble, in fact if it had not been for Ani Nyemo, who brought the situation to a head, Nangsa might have just gone on in a silent depression all of her life. Ani Nyemo causes a confrontation between the collective standards represented by the palace life and Nangsa's inner spiritual life. This confrontation eventually leads to Nangsa's release from this duplistic situation.

Ani Nyemo also represents the devalued feminine. She turns against Nangsa because, rather than seeing her as a sister, someone to share with, she sees her as a competitor. A situation dominated by male power often has this effect on women. Rather than identifying with each other, women turn against each other in competition for the males who hold the power. When women are denigrated they become twisted and negative; we do not like ourselves and we see other women negatively, looking for ways to devalue them in the eyes of men so that we can receive the favors of the oppressors.[44]

At this point in the story of Nangsa there are two motifs which are found in Western fairytales. In "The Handless Maiden" an innocent girl, through the plotting of a devil, is misunderstood by her husband and is driven into the forest, where she lives alone. "She is driven into nature where she has to find the connection to the positive animus within, instead of functioning according to the collective rules. She has to go into deep introversion. The forest could equally well be the desert, or an island in the sea, or the top of a mountain."[45]

In Nangsa's case she "descends" into hell (see pp. 91-2), and through her experiences there she comes back to life understanding herself more deeply and she no longer suppresses her spiritual longings. They have been validated by her miraculous coming back to life.

In another fairytale called "The Seven Ravens," a girl has a project of turning her brothers back into humans from ravens, and in order to do this she must not talk or laugh for six years and must make shirts made of star flowers for each of them. During this time she is married to a king and she leads a double life, continuing her silence and work on the shirts as well as her wifely duties. Her mother-in-law stirs up trouble by taking her children away and then accusing her of murdering them. Von Franz analyzes this story like this:

> Although she is productive and has fulfilled her normal feminine life, yet there is something going on behind the screen, a second process, which leads to misunderstandings. Sometimes the step-mother, or the mother-in-law, can alienate the king from his wife. Then she is slowly driven into complete isolation and her heroic deed consists in

keeping silent; but the pressure in the situation does not force her to disclose her secret, in spite of the threat to her life. She stands the misunderstanding of those around her and her highest endeavour is applied to keeping the religious secret . . . Keeping the discussion within, and not allowing disruptive forces to bring it into the open and destroy it, is one of the ultimate vital battles in the process of individuation.[46]

Nangsa protects her spiritual process with silence. Often, deep inner processes must be kept secret; otherwise they will be frozen or distorted by those whose values remain in the materialistic world, like Nangsa's husband and in-laws.

The "death" of Nangsa itself has great archetypal significance, for similar motifs are reported in shamanistic traditions, ancient Greece, and here in Tibetan initiation ceremonies, in the story of Jomo Memo, and even in the long retreats of some of the other women in this book.

The pattern is basically one of initiation. Initiation is an active choice to enter into darkness. It is a conscious closing off of the sunlit world and entry into the deeper parts of one's being. In Tibetan initiations one is given a red band of cloth which is symbolically placed over the eyes during the initiation. One enters a different dimension by passing through darkness.

In ancient Greece at the site of the oracle cave of Zeus – Trophonios – the oracle seekers had to lower themselves into a cave through a small hole similar to a birth canal, and after three days they were helped out by "therapeutes" or helpers.[47]

The shaman initiatory rites were very similiar to the "delog" descent. In Central Asia the Yakut shamans recount how "the evil spirits carry the future shaman's soul to the underworld and there shut it up in a house for three years (only one year for lesser shamans). Here the shaman undergoes his initiation. The spirits cut off his head, which they set aside (for the candidate must watch his own dismemberment) and cut him into small pieces, which are then distributed to the spirits of the various diseases. Only by undergoing such an ordeal will the future shaman gain the power to cure. His bones are then covered with new flesh and in some cases he is also given new blood."[48]

It is quite possible that the "delog" stories and the "Chod" ritual in Tibet descend from this kind of shamanistic ceremony. However, the difference is that the "delog" is catapulted into the underworld involuntarily. In the Tibetan "delog" stories in most cases a grave illness precedes the journey to the underworld. "Before the journey the 'das.log' has terrible visions and hallucinations, he imagines himself in the middle of frightening storms and whirlwinds, he hears a fearful noise, and he believes himself attacked by mighty hailstorms, which shatter his bones and lacerate his head, he feels like a shipwrecked man at the bottom of the sea or as if thrown to the heights of the sky, he believes himself dead, for the real world disappears from his view and he sees the world of the hereafter."[49]

The "delog," like the shaman, returns from the underworld empowered by the experience and an authority on life after death. This information is used to convince the living that the results of their actions in this world will reap results in the hereafter.

The journey into the underworld experienced in depression can also have this function. A depression can lead to the depths of oneself and dark deadness, which if used properly, and if the sick person pulls through it, can be like the introversion of the hermit who voluntarily enters the bedrock of himself and emerges with a knowledge which can help others. This experience can become a jumping-off point which allows growth and rebirth to take place. The important thing is that, when the person re-emerges, he or she is able to remember and make use of the descent experience, for otherwise it serves no purpose.

A-Yu Khadro, Jomo Memo, Drenchen and Machig Ongmo all underwent years of voluntary isolation in order to reach the deeper states of consciousness. A-Yu Khadro literally dwelled in darkness for many years, developing the inner lights through her Dzog Chen practice, which required complete darkness. These were all voluntary descent experiences.

Western women emerging from crisis situations also often choose to live alone, intuitively knowing that the confrontation with oneself that this brings will lead to a deeper understanding. These women (in our society, which sees them as pitiable and unfortunate) can take strength from the stories of these Tibetan yoginis.

These Western women also seek the support of other women or psychotherapists to help them to emerge from their descents, just as the yoginis sought the guidance of their teachers and spiritual friends, and the Greeks needed the help of the "therapeutes" to make sense of the memories they brought back from the oracle cave.

Speaking of the descent myth in terms of her experiences in controlled therapeutic regressions, Jungian analyst M.L. Von Franz describes the descent process in relation to the story of "The Handless Maiden":

> In the Middle Ages there were many hermits, and in Switzerland there were the so-called Wood Brothers and Sisters. People who did not want to live a monastic life but who wanted to live alone in the forest had both a closeness to nature and also a great experience of spiritual inner life. Such Wood Brothers and Sisters could be personalities on a high level who had a spiritual fate and had to renounce active life for a time and isolate themselves to find their own inner relation to God. It is not very different from what the shaman does in the Polar tribes, or what medicine men do all over the world, in order to seek an immediate personal religious experience in isolation.[50]

Because re-emerging people have often undergone a re-evaluation of themselves, and the knowledge gained makes them "different," they can be seen as threatening to those who knew them before. Nangsa's husband and relatives found her threatening in her decisiveness. Jomo Memo was so changed after her experiences in the cave of Padma Sambhava that she was called a demoness ("memo") and had to leave her native land. She found in Guru Chowang someone who could understand the knowledge she had gained and guide her in her further development.

Up to the point of her "death" Nangsa had been "good," fulfilling the expectations of the collective standards that surrounded her. After her descent she realized that complying with these standards was not genuine goodness and did not lead to a positive result. Goodness is not necessarily truth, and through her experience she gained the courage and confidence in herself to follow her heart.

Her final break with submission came when she returned to her parents for a visit after her "delog" experience. It is interesting that the final confrontation came when she was weaving. Weaving has traditionally been the work of women. Women weave the fabric of familial life, they weave genes and blood and nourishment to make children. Nangsa was sitting in a loom harness singing a song about how she had been woven into a pattern which was not of her choice. This song irritated her mother to such an extent that she became furious. But Nangsa could not be intimidated as she had been before and insisted that she would find a way to leave in order to unite her internal longings with her external situation. When her mother threw her out and kept her son, Nangsa gathered together her courage and finally departed to find her guru. She had to face the loss of her son and the frightening journey into the unknown. She realized the sadness of this loss but saw that this emptiness also created the possibility of finally leaving a situation which had been wrong for her for a long time. "Having and knowing that bedrock of self-validation and belief is very important, because it enables us to take risks and function in the world with courage without being paralyzed by fear of disapproval or disapproval itself."[51]

Nangsa shows heroic qualities throughout her life, but her courage at this point is really amazing. She not only risks the severe wrath of her husband and father-in-law, but she has also been abandoned by her mother and her son has been taken away. However, her courageous step is validated in the end when the power of her teacher and herself triumphs over the material strength of her husband's army. The end result of her choice to follow her heart's longing is the elevation of all those involved. Had she not made this choice, not only she, but everyone else, would have been degraded in the process.

If we avoid the descent because of fear of what we will discover about ourselves in the "underworld," we block ourselves off from a powerful transformative process. This process has been recognized by modern psychologists and ancient mystery religions alike.

The sacred biography

The sacred biography is called "rNam.thar" in Tibetan, which literally means "complete liberation." The "rNam.thar" are specifically geared to provide records for those on a spiritual quest, in much the same way that someone about to climb a high mountain would seek out the chronicles of those who had made the climb before. The sacred biographer is primarily concerned with providing information which will be helpful and inspirational for someone following in the footsteps of the spiritual adept or "saint." Establishing a mythical ideal and the communication of the sacred teachings takes precedence over providing a narrative portrait or "likeness" of the subject as a personality. The personality is stressed only in so far as it relates to the spiritual process of the individual.[52]

In looking at these stories we must remember that, although the sacred biography may seem fantastic and unreal to those outside its religious tradition, to those within the tradition it is considered historical. As Mircea Eliade points out, "the religious experience of the Christian is based on an imitation of the Christ as an exemplary pattern."[53]

There are basically two kinds of sacred biographies. One is that of a religious founder, in which case we are describing a person who creates the religious ideal and the story describes the miraculous acts of this individual. This kind of story is represented here in the biography of Machig Lapdron, who is miraculous and destined from before her conception to be a great religious leader and founder of her own lineage.

The second category of sacred biography is that of those individuals who attain an ideal already recognized within their religious community. This kind of story describes the "path" stage, emphasizing the process rather than the result. Since the function of the sacred biography is to provide guidance and inspiration to the aspirant during the process leading toward enlightenment, naturally information concerning the passage toward illumination is more appropriate than elaborate details of the activities of the saint once she has attained the religious ideal.

The sacred biography can also be understood by contrasting it to another kind of life story: the life story of those who represent the average individual within a society. It is this kind of life history which is sought after by the anthropologist, who seeks to know, not the religious ideal of the society, but the life of an average individual within a given society.[54]

In these biographies, which serve as role models for the Tibetans seeking "liberation," what is valued is not the material rise to fame and fortune that we so often find in Occidental biographies, but the spiritual development of the person. The sacred biography, "rNam.thar," or the liberation story is the only kind of biography that existed in Tibet which indicates Tibetan cultural values. The decision-making process of the individuals, in this collection of biographies, demonstrates the value system of the Tibetan culture. Decisions were guided by dreams, visions and intuitions. A-Yu Khadro, for example, found the place where she spent the latter half of her life in retreat, through a vision she had at dawn, between sleeping and waking. Throughout her life story her life choices are guided by her visions and dreams.

Another notable aspect of this collection of biographies is that, although they are all sacred biographies, each one is a different type of hagiography. For this reason I have written a short prologue before each story indicating something about its historical context and a description of the kind of biography it represents.

Notes

1 Carol Christ, *Diving Deep and Surfacing: Women Writers on a Spiritual Quest*, p. 1.
2 Ibid., p. 13.
3 I.B. Horner, *Women under Primitive Buddhism*, pp. 101–2.
4 C. Christ and J. Plaskow (eds.), *Womanspirit Rising: A Feminist Reader in Religion*, pp. 228–9.
5 Ibid., p. 51.
6 Starhawk, *The Spiral Dance*, pp. 27–8.
7 C. Christ and J. Plaskow (eds.), *Womanspirit Rising*, p. 5.
8 Diane Paul, *Women in Buddhism*, p. 308.
9 Nancy A. Falk, "The Case of the Vanishing Nuns," in Falk and Gross (eds.), *Unspoken Worlds: Women's Religious Lives in Non-Western Cultures*, p. 215.

10 Ibid.

11 Therigata's, *Psalms of the Early Buddhists*, trans. C.A. Rhys Davids, London, 1964, p. 250.

12 C.C. Chang (trans.), *The One Hundred Thousand Songs of Milarepa*, vol. I, p. 142.

13 Agehamanda Bharati, *The Tantric Tradition*, p. 202.

14 Ibid., p. 213.

15 Sylvia B. Perera, *Descent to the Goddess: A Way of Initiation for Women*, p. 20.

16 See Eva Dargyay's *The Rise of Esoteric Buddhism in Tibet*, pp. 16–27, for a hagiography of Garab Dorje.

17 Eleanor McLaughlin, "The Christian Past, Does It Hold a Future for Women?" in C. Christ and J. Plaskow (eds.), *Womanspirit Rising*, p. 103.

18 Alex Wayman, *The Buddhist Tantras*, p. 83.

19 Chögyam Trungpa, *Maitreya IV*, pp. 23–4.

20 Starhawk, *The Spiral Dance*, p. 24.

21 Chögyam Trungpa, in "The Diamond Path and The Silk Route," catalogue, ed. D. Klimburg-Slater, Los Angeles, University of Southern California Arts Council, p. 236.

22 Nor Hall, *The Moon and the Virgin*, p. 44.

23 See biography of Machig Lapdron, p. 177 below.

24 Nor Hall, *The Moon and the Virgin*, pp. 81–2.

25 Ibid., p. 14.

26 Ibid., p. 9.

27 Ibid., p. 169.

28 Starhawk, *The Spiral Dance*, pp. 83–4.

29 Keith Dowman, *Sky Dancer*, p. 71.

30 Sylvia Perera, *Descent to the Goddess*, pp. 39–40.

31 C.C. Chang (trans.), *The One Hundred Thousand Songs of Milarepa*, p. 336.

32 See R. Ray, "Accomplished Women in Tantric Buddhism," in Falk and Gross (eds.), *Unspoken Worlds*, p. 237.

33 Chögyam Trungpa, *Maitreya IV*, p. 25.

34 Herbert V. Guenther (trans.), *The Royal Song of Saraha*, p. 5.

35 R. Ray, "Accomplished Women in Tantric Buddhism," in Falk and Gross (eds.), *Unspoken Worlds*, p. 236.

36 Herbert Guenther (trans.), *The Life and Teachings of Naropa*, pp. 41, 47, 51, 53, 62, 67, 69, 72, 75, 77, 79, 80, 83.

37 Ibid., p. 30.

38 Eva Dargyay, *The Rise of Esoteric Buddhism in Tibet*, p. 88.

39 Ibid., p. 90; cf. n. 6, Part II.

40 "Rigpa" is the awareness of the primordial state of "awake," that

awareness which is present when one experiences the clarity, "non-thought" and emptiness of self (sunyata). It is sometimes described as the "naked" state, because the mind is stripped of discursive thought and subconscious gossip in this "presence." The practitioner learns to recognize and cultivate this state through various practices such as "The Song of the Vajra."

41 Nor Hall, *The Moon and the Virgin*, pp. 27–8.
42 Ibid., p. 135.
43 Keith Dowman, *Sky Dancer*, p. 16.
44 E. Neumann, *Amor and Psyche*, pp. 12–25, 29–30, 70–7, 132–4.
45 M.L. Von Franz, *The Feminine in Fairytales*, p. 84.
46 Ibid., p. 136.
47 Nor Hall, *The Moon and the Virgin*, pp. 25–7.
48 M. Eliade, *Shamanism*, pp. 36–7.
49 G. Tucci, *The Religions of Tibet*, pp. 198–9.
50 M.L. Von Franz, *The Feminine in Fairytales*, p. 86.
51 Chris Sarfaty, "Towards Autonomous Affiliation: Issues of Dependence and Autonomy for Women in Love Relationship Crisis."
52 F. Reynolds and D. Capps (eds.), *The Biographical Process: Studies in the History and Psychology of Religion*, Introduction.
53 M. Eliade, *Myths, Dreams and Mysteries*, p. 30.
54 See the biography of a Tibetan noblewoman, R.D. Taring, *Daughter of Tibet*, for a biography of this genre.

1
NANGSA OBUM

PROLOGUE

This text is a translation of a native Tibetan folk drama, performed by wandering troupes of actors in the courtyard of a monastery or the village square. The villagers gather round making an active vocal audience, cheering the heroine and hissing the villains. The drama might go on for several days, with pauses for tea and meals. Parts are sung in a kind of wavering chant-like voice interspersed with the voice of a narrator reciting parts of the story which are not spoken by the actors. The whole thing is accompanied by drums and cymbals for sound-effects.

Dramatic operas of this genre are called "Ach'e Lhamo," named after the goddesses who intercede at desperate moments. This drama is dedicated to, and part of, the cult of Tara. Nangsa is a devotee of Tara, and it is to Tara that she prays in moments of duress. Tara is the popular female form of the Buddha: nothing is below her station, she will help in even the most mundane matters. The Tibetans say that even those who have not had the Tara initiation can call on her and she will respond. She is the champion of the downtrodden, and functions somewhat like the Madonna in Roman Catholicism. Where the Buddha seems too removed and sublime, the maternal compassion of Tara can be invoked.

According to the myth of Tara's origins, she is an incarnation of the princess "Moon of Wisdom," who in ancient times, through her supreme thought toward enlightenment (Bodhicitta), made the vow to help sentient beings caught in the web of suffering. At this point, she was advised by monks to take on the form of a man. To this she replied: "Since there is no such thing as a 'man' or a 'woman', and no such thing as a 'self' or a 'person', or 'awareness', this bondage to male and female is hollow . . . Oh how worldly fools delude themselves!"[1] Following this she made a decision which gave birth to Tara as an enlightened energy in the female form. She vowed: "Those who wish to obtain supreme enlightenment in a man's body are many, but those who wish to serve the aims of beings in a woman's body are few indeed; therefore may I until this world is emptied out, serve the aim of beings with nothing but the body of a woman."[2]

Since that time, through many thousand billion years, she has saved countless beings from suffering in worldly existence. So she became a deity by the perfection of her own meditation practice and by the vow to help others, taken aeons ago.

The story of Nangsa Obum takes place in the eleventh century in Central Tibet. This period was one of tremendous religious activity and fervor in Tibet. Many of the most important teachers lived at that time, and some of the most important lineages, such as the Kagyu lineage, began during this period. Machig Lapdron, Milarepa and Phadampa Sangye were all Nangsa Obum's contemporaries. Many new texts and teachings were being brought from India. This period is known as the restoration or renaissance of Buddhism in Tibetan chronology. The original influx of Buddhism, approximately from AD 650 to 836, was supported by the monarchy, the Buddhist kings of the Yarlung Valley, in Central Tibet. During this time Buddhism changed from being a foreign religion supported by the monarchy, to being the dominant religion of Tibet. The last of these kings was Langdharma, an anti-Buddhist, who was murdered in 842. Following his death there was a period of civil war and chaos, and it was not until approximately 978 that Buddhism was restored. This period was marked by the new translations of Smirti, in Eastern Tibet, and Rinchen Zangpo (958–1055) in Western Tibet, under the protection of a line of Buddhist kings. These translations are known as "The new Tantras." Milarepa's teacher, the famous Marpa the Translator (1012–98) travelled to India several times and returned with new teachings and a tradition of poetry, based on the didactic Indian model, but including personal insights and imagery from the practitioners' experience. We find examples of these "songs" in *The Hundred Thousand Songs of Milarepa* and in the story of Nangsa Obum.

The biography of Nangsa Obum is of the genre of Tibetan tales concerning the "delog," "one who dies and then returns to life." The "delog" would report on the fate of the dead. Having seen the suffering of those in hell, who had arrived there because of evil deeds such as killing, cheating and stealing, they would report back to the living. Their tales would awaken fear, and the desire to change before arriving at this unfortunate end. The general effect of these stories was to raise the moral standards of the populace. I have omitted the didactic prologue in this translation.

Notes

1 Steven Beyer, *The Cult of Tara*, p. 65.
2 Ibid.

THE BIOGRAPHY
OF
NANGSA OBUM

Birth and childhood

Nangsa Obum was born in Tibet, in the province of Tsang in the area of Upper Nyang in the county of Gyaltse, to an ordinary family called Jangpe Kur Nangpa. In that place was a man called Kunzang Dechen, and a woman called Nyangtsa Seldron. Together they did extensive practice without interruption, and without thought of personal gain, of the sadhana[1] of Tara of the Khadira[2] forest.

As a result of doing this practice about 100,000 times this woman had a great many auspicious dreams. She recounted one of these dreams to her husband, saying:

"I dreamt that in the heavenly realm[3] of Tara,
On the throne of conch shells,[4] sits the female Buddha,
Protectress of the past, present, and future.
From the seed syllable TAM[5] in Tara's heart,
Emanated a light which entered through the top of my
    head,
And entered my central channel,[6] and dissolved into my
    heart centre.
A lotus tree sprang up in my body,
Dakinis were making offerings to the tree,
Butterflies were fluttering about sucking nectar from the
    lotuses.

[66]

This kind of dream must be a good sign.
Please tell me the meaning."

Kunzang Dechen was very happy and responded:

"My life-long friend, listen to me!
Dreams can be illusions,
But this is prophecy!
The light shining from the TAM in the heart of the Arya
    Tara,
The clear light dissolving into your heart,
Means the blessings of the female Buddha of the Three
    Times has entered your heart.
That lotus flowers were blooming in your body,
Means that you are the queen of the dakinis,
That it was surrounded by butterflies sucking nectar,
Means that both pure and impure beings
Will be benefited by your body, speech and mind.
When you were young and pretty you had no son.
Now you have white hair and will have a daughter.
She will be better than any boy!
Say prayers and make offerings everywhere!
This is a very good dream, be happy!"

So they made offerings to the Jewels,[7] to beggars, and to the
monastic community so that they would say prayers for them.
In the Year of the Horse, in the Monkey Month, on the tenth
day, the day of the dakini, a Thursday, Nyangtsa Seldron gave
birth to a daughter.

When the baby drank her first milk she spat it into the sky
and said:

"Homage to Arya Tara, consort of the Three Times!
I have been born in order to help all sentient beings.
It is by your kindness that happiness and fortune may come
    to this earth.
By the brilliant luminosity of your activity
One hundred thousand beings will enter the Dharma!"

She was named Nangsa Obum by those who heard her say these words. Every month she grew as much as a normal baby grows in a year. She was beautiful and kind, like a daughter of the gods. Her parents were very happy, and praised her body, speech and mind often, saying:

"Good daughter of the father!
Good daughter of the mother!
Like an ornament, you beautify.
Listen, Nangsa Obum, all the beauty of the universe is
    unified in you.
As soon as one sees you, one feels happy,
Your body is beautiful like the daughter of a divinity.
Your incomparable voice is like the song of Brahma,[8]
It cannot be compared to the sweetest sounding birds.
As soon as one hears your voice one feels happy,
Praise your sweet voice.
You who have devotion to the gurus and all the Great Ones,
You have great compassion for all beings,
As soon as you have a thought it brings happiness to others.
Praise the mind of the daughter Nangsa.
It is marvelous to have a daughter like you,
For two old people like us.
Having you is like a donkey having a mule,
Or an old bull having a female yak."

Then Nangsa responded:

"Homage to the mother of the Buddhas of the Three Times!
Listen to me, father and mother!
Without a doubt you are my parents,
But I also have my outer, inner, and secret parents.
The external father is Kunzang Dechen.
The external mother is Nyangtsa Seldron.
The inner father is Avalokitesvara.[9]
The inner mother is the white and blue Tara.
The secret father is Mahayana Mahasuhka, "The Great Bliss
    of the Great Vehicle,"
The secret mother is Prajna,[10] clear and pure.

[68]

Homage to the outer, inner, and secret parents in
their union of bliss and emptiness."

Night and day she repeated mantras of Avalokitesvara and the
white and blue Tara. She was very compassionate and wise.
All the Tantras and Sutras were integrated into her being. She
went to bed late and woke up early, helping her parents on
their farm.

Marriage

The family became quite rich, and by the time she was fifteen
she had suitors from all over Tibet hoping to marry her.

But for Nangsa the teachings of the Buddha were the most
important thing. She always thought about practicing meditation and had no thoughts of marriage. Her parents had no
other children, but Nangsa was better than 100,000 children.
She could do both meditation and worldly work. They
accepted none of the suitors and kept her at home. She was
with them a long time, and then a very harsh nobleman
decided to find a wife for his son Dragpa Samdrub.

One day there was a festival in the local town where a lama
was to give an initiation, and everyone was going. Nangsa also
decided to attend with her parents because she wanted to take
part in this initiation.

She was so well dressed and beautiful that everyone who
saw her had some kind of wish about her. They were
astonished that there could be such a beautiful woman. Her
face was like a shining moon. Her hair was silky like new
shoots of rice. Her hair had been dressed by her parents and
ornamented. She had on earrings and necklaces of the highest
quality. Nothing was missing in her costume. She brought
many offerings for the lama giving the initiation, and these
were carried behind her by a servant as she rode ahead on a
horse. They also brought a large picnic to eat during the day.

When they arrived at the monastery to take part in the
festival, they first made their offerings, requested initiation,
prostrated themselves and circumambulated. Then they went
over to where many women were watching the dancing.

The king of Rinang, Dragchen, with a large entourage, was watching the festivities from a high balcony in the lama's quarters. Although he was supposedly watching the dancing, at the sight of all the women he was powerless and couldn't keep his eyes off them. When he spotted Nangsa he whispered something into the ear of his servant, Sonam Palkye, who went into the crowd and pounced on Nangsa like an eagle attacking a rabbit, or like a falcon falling upon a small bird. He led her back to the king of Rinang, Dragchen, who took hold of the hem of her skirt with one hand and offered her a bowl of chang[11] with the other, saying:

"You have a beautiful body,
You are lovely to listen to,
You have a lovely smell,
You probably have a sweet-tasting mouth,
You are soft to touch and have all the five desirable
   qualities,[12]
Whose daughter are you?
Are you a goddess?
Or the daughter of a Naga?[13]
Or a nonhuman celestial musician?
Come on, tell me, don't be secretive!
Girl, who is your father and what is your mother's name?
What province are you from and what is the name of your
   house?
I am from Upper Nyang in Rinang.
I am the head of the province,
My name resounds like thunder over my kingdom.
I have a son, my heir, Dragpa Samdrub,
Who is outwardly like an iron mountain,
But inside he is a jewel.
He is approaching eighteen and you should marry him."

Nangsa thought: "Oh no, my appearance has worked against me. I want to practice the Dharma but now it looks like I'll have to marry this prince."
Then she sang this song:

"Victorious Great Mother, Arya Tara,

Look at this impious uncompassionate girl,
Listen, King Dragchen!
I am from Upper Nyang, the area of Gyaltse,
My house is called Jangpe Kur,
My father's name is Kunzang Dechen,
My mother's name is Nyangtsa Seldron,
My name is Nangsa Obum,
I am the daughter of common people.
The poisonous Tagma tree has a beautiful flower
But since it comes from a poisonous tree
It isn't fit to put on one's altar.
Likewise there is a kind of inferior turquoise
Which is not fit to put next to the superior variety!
Although small birds are good at flying
They aren't capable of flying as high as eagles!
Although the girl Nangsa might look pretty
In what way is she suitable to be the bride of an important
    person?
Please let me go!
Obum wants to study the Dharma!"

Then the attendant gave the king some turquoise threaded on
a red silk thread and an arrow with five-coloured silks.[14] The
attendant said to the king:

"Although one says one does not want to,
Inside that's all one thinks about,
This is a sign of a man wanting to be someone's husband.
Although a woman might swear she has no desire to do such
    a thing,
Deep down she really does,
This is a sign of a woman wanting to be someone's wife.
This woman won't say that she wants this,
In front of all these people,
So you should put the turquoise around her neck
And give her this arrow adorned with silk, and finalize
    things."

So the king thought this must be right, and he said:

"Beautiful Nangsa, you are like a goddess to look at.
I am Dragchen and my voice resounds like thunder.
I am the most powerful man in these parts,
So if you don't listen to what I say you are actually quite
    stupid.
We won't send you to practice the Dharma.
Although you say you want to stay at home,
We won't leave you there.
Although the sun is high in the sky
Its rays still strike the lotus that grows in the earth.
Although there is a difference between high and low,
Through the proper karmic connection
The two can benefit each other.
Although the arrow is long and slender and
The bow is relatively short,
The two work together harmoniously.
Although an ocean is great and the fish are small,
They benefit each other through their harmonious
    connection.
Although my son is very powerful and
You are just a common woman,
It doesn't matter;
Because of your harmonious karmic connection you should
    marry."

Holding the five-colored silks and the turquoise aloft he
placed them on her head and said he would take her for his
son's wife, and proclaimed that Dragpa Samdrub had chosen
his bride, saying:

"Now no powerful people are allowed to take her away.
The weak people can't steal her.
Those in between have no right to her.
Likewise no one can say she's flown away into the sky, or
    been buried in the earth,
This is the prince of Rinang's new wife.
Everyone should understand I am now in charge of Nangsa.
There should be no confusion about it."

So saying, having placed the turquoise and silk on Nangsa's

head, he said to her and her servant: "Now you should take these and hide them when you get to your parents' house.

So Dragchen and his entourage returned home, and Nangsa returned to her parents' house. Dragchen began to prepare for the marriage – making the chang, organizing jewelry and the bride's price. Then with all this they set out for Nangsa's house.

When they arrived the attendant, Sonam Palkye, went and knocked on the door. Nangsa's mother, seeing the king and a whole party approaching, said to her husband: "Listen to me, Kunzang Dechen. Dragchen and all his entourage are approaching our house on horseback. It would be good if we invited them in." He replied: "Listen to me, Nyangtsa Seldron, listen to Kunzang Dechen! The king at our door is as bad a sign as an owl sitting on our roof. He is an important person. Ask him what his business is, then, if he won't go away, I suppose we'll have to invite him in."

So Nyangtsa Seldon went to the door, offered them chang, and asked them why they had come. Dragchen explained what had happened at the Dharma festival. Nangsa's mother was very happy and rushed up to tell her husband, who was also happy about this event.

He said: "This is the only reason they've come here. Now our daughter has certainly found a good place to go. There is nowhere better in Rinang, so if Dragchen asks I will certainly promise him Nangsa. Invite them in to see me!"

So the officials all came upstairs. Nangsa's parents offered them the best they had, and the king presented the chang, some jewels and the bride's price. He said:

"Girl Nangsa and you parents, listen here!
From today onward the king of Rinang, Dragchen, has taken
    Nangsa for the wife of his son Dragpa Samdrub.
You can't say your daughter has flown up into the sky or
    been buried in the earth.
No powerful people are allowed to take her away,
Weak people can't steal her,
And those in between have no right to her.
Nor can you parents refuse to send her with us.
Nor can you Nangsa say that you will not go with us.

Now you are the queen of the king of Rinang.
In three days' time five hundred horsemen will come to
    collect you!

"Also listen to this! When you come to my palace, you will
shine like the moon among stars. You are the most beautiful of
all the women in the crowds of the market place. Do you
remember the turquoise and silks that I gave to you? Bring
them here now. I asked you to hide these things because if
your parents saw the crown jewels they might have been
angry, not knowing where you got them. However, now is the
time to show them."

Nangsa brought them, and Dragchen presented them again,
formally, in front of her parents. Then the king and his
entourage departed for home.

Nangsa, having no desire to get married and no desire to go
with these people, only wanted to practice the Dharma. So she
decided to talk to her parents. She said to them: "Mother and
father, listen to me! You have kindly given me this body.
Seeing all meetings end in separation, I have no desire to get
married to this man, Dragpa Samdrub. The three jewels are
beyond this relative existence. I would like to break the
commitment to this husband and practice the Dharma. Even a
rich man's wealth is not secure – he may lose it. I won't remain
as the property of the king of Rinang.

"There are seven jewels[15] that are beyond impermanence. I,
this woman, want these jewels only. I want to practice the
Dharma. Even the well-made houses eventually decay; I won't
stay in the house of the Rinang king. I would like to stay in a
cave in solitude, a place that doesn't fall down like a man-made
house."

Her parents responded: "You are a human who looks like a
goddess, you are so beautiful, but listen to us! The son of the
king of Rinang has a fiery heart; if you don't marry him he will
be furious. He is the most powerful man in the world: please
don't say you won't marry him. If you insist on going to
practice the Dharma and leave now, he will kill us. If you go to
practice the Dharma and he kills us, this won't lead to
enlightenment. So please marry him and don't go to practice
the Dharma."

Her parents spoke with such desperation that Nangsa promised not to go away and not to insist on practicing the Dharma.

Then Dragpa Samdrub's representatives came to fetch Nangsa. Her parents had divided up their things, giving her her own share of all their possessions. Before she left they advised her thus:

"You are the daughter better than a thousand sons!
Please listen to us!
For when you go to Rinang we are giving you these things:
The statue of Tara made of turquoise,
As well as Buddha images and expensive stupas.
We are giving you a lot of jewels: coral, turquoise, gold and
    silver of immeasurable cost.
We are giving you silk and brocade clothes.
We are giving you rice, barley and other food,
All this we will give you to take to Rinang.
We are sending Dzompa Kyi to serve you.
When you are with the Rinang family
Wake up at cockcrow!
When you are with the Rinang family
Be like a dog at the door who is the last to sleep!
When you are with the Rinang family
You must respect your husband and father-in-law,
Not thinking of yourself.
Work for everybody else and be ashamed of your mistakes!
Dragpa Samdrub is your husband because of your past
    karma.
You will live with him all of your life –
Serve him well![16]
Be kind and fair to everyone at the Rinang family's house.
We pray to see you often!"

Having heard all this, Nangsa left with the official party. They went on horseback, all ornamented; on the way, there was dancing, music and singing. When they arrived there were many days of celebration.

After the wedding she lived with Dragpa Samdrub for the

next seven years. Then a son was born who was as beautiful as a little god and they named him Lhau Darpo. A big party was given to celebrate his birth. Everyone was saying Queen Nangsa did not have the five bad qualities[17] of a woman, but she did have the eight good qualities[18] of a woman. She was industrious in serving her father-in-law, husband, and son. She was very kind to both her male and female servants and helped everyone. She worked hard in the fields, was good at sewing, and made delicious food. Everyone in the kingdom of Rinang, both high and low, respected Queen Nangsa very much, not only because she had had a good son, but because they approved of everything she did.

Death

Nangsa was so beautiful and Dragpa Samdrub loved her so much that he never left her, even for an hour. Since she was so good, Dragchen and Dragpa Samdrub considered giving her the keys to the house, which would mean giving her the power over all the goods in the palace. This power had previously belonged to Dragchen's sister, Ani Nyemo, and she did not want to give this privilege to Nangsa. Nangsa respected Ani Nyemo, but everyone else disliked her and spoke badly of her behind her back because she was of bad character. Ani Nyemo always said terrible things about Nangsa to the king, her husband and Lhau Darpo, and to the servants. She wouldn't give Nangsa the keys and even gave her poor food and no new clothes. She kept the good things for herself. This made Nangsa very sad, and she wished from her heart, more than ever, to renounce samsara and practice the true Dharma; but even this she could not tell her husband.

One day she was thinking about this while nursing her son in her room, and she started to cry and sang this song to her son:

"I take refuge in the Lama and the Three Jewels,
Guru, Deva, Dakini,[19] please grant your blessings!
Protectors, please prevent obstacles from arising!
This woman wishes to become accomplished in Dharma!

[76]

My son, children are like a rope that pulls a woman into
  Samsara.
Lhau Darpo, you make it impossible to leave,
And I cannot take you with me as this would create obstacles
  in my practice.
I wanted to practice the Dharma but I got married instead.
I tried to help my husband, but I made Ani Nyemo jealous.
I cannot return to my parents, because I am married.
Woe is me," she cried sadly.
"My beautiful form, you, my son, and the rest of my relatives
  are big obstacles for my Dharma practice.
But Ani Nyemo is like my guru because she had made me
  turn to the Dharma.
When you can get along by yourself,
If I am still alive,
Nangsa will go to the Dharma.
Obum will not stay here.
She will stay in a simple retreat place."

Then she took her son into the garden. Her husband was
there washing his hair. After he had finished he came and put
his head on her lap and fell asleep. It was autumn, and most
flowers had become withered and were falling to the ground;
the few fresh blossoms had many bees around them. Nangsa
saw them and thought:

"Although I love my parents,
I am separated from them.
Although I want to help my husband,
I cannot because of Ani Nyemo.
Although I want to practice the Dharma,
I cannot because of this worldly life."

Then she started to cry. A tear fell into the ear of Dragpa
Samdrub. He awoke and found her crying quietly. He said:

"Queen Nangsa you are so beautiful
I never have enough of looking at you.
Queen Nangsa, please listen to me!
We are rich enough to buy you any jewels you may desire.

[77]

We know the difference between Dharmic and Samsaric[20]
    action.
We have on our laps a beautiful boy.
You are the Queen of Rinang.
There is no reason to lament.
Why are you crying, please tell me the truth?
Whatever is wrong I will make it right!"

Nangsa thought: "Before, I never told my father-in-law and
husband about the jealousy of Ani Nyemo, because it would
make problems between the families. Now my husband is
asking me why I am crying. Previously I could not tell him that
I wanted to go to practice the Dharma, but maybe now I can.
Also if I tell him maybe Ani Nyemo will realize that I am not
trying to take the keys from her." Thinking this, she began this
song:

"Only father, I bow at the feet of the Guru!
I bow to the Mother of the Buddhas, the Dakinis!
Karma gave me you, Dragpa Samdrub, as my husband,
So please listen to what I am singing!
When I was with my parents in my native place
My beautiful face and my beautiful body
Became an obstacle to my Dharma practice,
Preventing me from practicing and leading me to this house
Which is not mine.
When I became the queen of Rinang
I had respect for the family and servants;
I was especially respectful to Ani Nyemo.
I have no hesitation in saying that I have always been most
    respectful to her.
But even so she has been very unkind to me.
If I give her chang she gives me water.
According to her I am dumb.
If I answer others I am blathering.
If I go out, I am a whore.
If I stay in, I am like an image in the temple, never moving.
When I see the kind face of my husband, Dragpa Samdrub,
I think I would like to help him for all my life.
When I look at Lhau Darpo

I think I'll work in Samsara.
When I look at our servants
I think I shall remain the wife of the king of Rinang.
When I hear Ani Nyemo speaking spitefully about me
I think of answering her back,
But then I think about impermanence.
I think I will practice the Dharma.
I do not have what is necessary for the next life.
I do not have what is necessary for this life because
I do not have my parents.
I sing this song for them
I would be so happy to see them."

Then Dragpa Samdrub said: "Nangsa, you are thinking of your parents because you haven't seen them for so long. So we will take you to see them soon. I do not know if it is true that Ani Nyemo is jealous or not, but if it is I will talk to her. Anyway, now is the time to cut the grass and make the hay. We should start in three days, so we will have to hire extra help. Go to collect the scythes from Ani Nyemo."

When the haymaking started, Ani Nyemo came with Nangsa to oversee the workers. Nangsa was standing there watching when two yogis approached. They were from Tingri, a guru and his disciple. When they saw Nangsa they sang this song:

"I bow to the father Guru!
Please take all sentient beings out of Samsara!
Give us some food in exchange for some Dharma teaching.
This body of yours is like that rainbow in the distance:
It has many beautiful colors but no permanent substance.
Now is the time to practice the Dharma.

Your beautiful body is as lovely as a cockatoo,
But even though you have a nice voice
What you say has no meaning.
Now is the time to practice the Dharma.

Even though your beauty is as famous as a dragon
It has no significance.
Now is the time to practice the Dharma.

Even though you are as beautiful as a painting
This beauty has no real value.
Now is the time to practice the Dharma.

When the great enemy impermanence comes to claim you,
You will not be able to escape,
Death will not give you a moment's respite.

Death cares nothing for your beauty.
Even if you have the power of a king
You cannot stop death.
Even if you are a very fast runner
You cannot run away from death.

Now you have a precious human body[21]
And this may be your only chance to practice the Dharma.
You should not pass away without practicing the Dharma."

Nangsa thought: "They are singing this for me." She was
filled with emotion and felt like making offerings to the yogis,
but Ani Nyemo was there and she was afraid she wouldn't let
her. So she told the yogis: "Go over there and you will find Ani
Nyemo, that woman with the brown ugly face."

They went to Ani Nyemo and asked if they could have some
food. Ani Nyemo was very angry. She dropped what she was
doing, stood up and said: "You poor beggars, don't come to
me! In the summer you beg butter and food, in the winter you
ask for chang and get drunk. If you stay in the mountains you
don't meditate. If you stay in town you don't work. If you had
the capacity you would become real bandits; but instead you
are petty thieves, lying and stealing. You pretend to teach the
Dharma, when in fact you lead people astray. To the likes of
you I will give nothing! If you want something, go to that girl
who is like a peacock, and who has the voice of a nightingale,
and whose mind is strong as a mountain. Ask her, the wife of
the Rinang king; I am just her servant, I have no authority to
give!"

So the lamas went back to Nangsa and told her what Ani
Nyemo had said. She couldn't believe what Ani Nyemo had

said, and was so saddened by it that she gave them seven
sacks of flour. She asked them: "Where do you come from and
where are you going? Please make offerings to gurus and
Buddhas that I may be able to practice the Dharma when I get
older." Then one of the yogis sang her this song:

"Obeisance to the Guru!
Please release sentient beings from the ocean of suffering!
Please listen to us, Nangsa!
Thank you for your offering.
I come from La To,
From Lachi, snow mountain.
I am a disciple of Milarepa,[22]
My name is Rechung Dordrag.[23]
Now we are going to central Tibet, to the Yarlung valley.
There must be connection between you
Who stay in the town,
And we who stay in the mountains,
In order to reach Buddha's level of development.
The root of our connection is dedication.
You have given us food,
We have given you some explanations of the Dharma.
That is the karmic cause for future Dharma practice.
So we will pray to the Buddhas
That you will be able to practice the Dharma."

When she heard this her devotion increased, and she gave
them a few more sacks of grain. The gurus blessed her and
continued on their way.

Having seen what Nangsa was doing, Ani Nyemo got very
angry. She tied her skirt up around her waist, got a long stick
and approached Nangsa. Looking at her very pointedly she
said:

"You look beautiful from the outside,
But you are a demon inside,
You demoness, who look like a peacock,
Listen to me!
There is a guru in Tingri called Phadampa Sangye.[24]
In Lachi there is another famous guru called Milarepa.

[81]

If you give to everyone who passes through
There is no reason to call yourself the mother of your son.
This field is famous for its barley,
If you want to give everything to the yogis,
Why don't you go with them?"

Nangsa replied:

"Obeisance to the Three Jewels!
Please help this girl who is without Dharma practice!
Please listen to me Ani Nyemo!
I was not sure about giving food to the yogis,
So I sent them to you.
You said you were just a servant,
And sent them back to me.
Even if they are not good yogis
They are poor, so I gave to them.
If when they leave they say: 'I went to Rinang, and they
    gave me nothing,' that is not good. In the Dharma
tradition if you are rich, it is good to offer to the poor.
Like bees that just collect and store honey,
It is useless to have a lot and not use it.
Please do not call the disciples of Milarepa beggars.
Please do not call me a demoness for giving to Milarepa's
    disciples.
You should take delight in my goodness."

This made Ani Nyemo furious and she said:

"You ghostly demoness,
You are not giving because of devotion;
You just make offerings because these yogis have nice voices
    and are good-looking.
You think your husband will just make again
What you throw away.
Whatever I say,
You answer me back twice.
Maybe you think you are the queen here,
But I am the real member of the Rinang family.
I am in charge here.

[82]

Don't you know that by now?"

Then Ani Nyemo went on:

"Until now I have used only words with you,
Now it seems I must show you with my hands!"

First she grabbed her and pushed her onto her back, then
she jerked her forward onto her face. Then she pulled seven
hairs out of Nangsa's head and put them into her chuba.[25]
Then Ani Nyemo suddenly realized she was beating her
nephew's adored wife.

So she went to Dragpa Samdrub and pretended that she had
been so upset that she had pulled out her own hair in dismay,
when in fact the hair she showed him was Nangsa's hair. Then
she sang to him:

"Please listen to Ani Nyemo, Dragpa Samdrub!
Our Queen Nangsa never works,
But does things she should not do in the fields.
This morning two handsome yogis came by;
She was so attracted to them she gave them
Almost everything in the field.
She was shameless and was practically seducing them on the
    spot.
When I told her take it easy,
She beat me until all my bones ached.
Look at what kind of wife you have!
You are going to have to choose between your wife and your
    aunt:
Think carefully about your choice!"

Dragpa Samdrub thought: "Ani Nyemo would not lie, since
she is in charge. Nangsa is young and beautiful and the mother
of a boy, so everyone treats her well. She has grown spoiled.
Children and women must be constantly controlled."

He went to find Nangsa and found her in a corner, crying.
Feeling very sad he sang her this song:

"You demoness, listen to me,

The king of Rinang, Dragpa Samdrub!
Look at what you have done!
You did what you should not have done with those cheats.
And you beat my aunt!
If you leave a dog on top of a house,
It starts to bark at the stars.
If you treat a donkey like a horse,
It starts to kick the horse.
Like a boatman who is careless and lazy in shallow water,
You are careless and lazy because I am easy with you.
Like a person who already knows a dog,
Does not pick up a stick when approaching him,
Like this you treat me carelessly!
Look at how demonic you are, Nangsa!"

Nangsa thought: "I have not done anything and Ani Nyemo has gone to tell Dragpa Samdrub. On the other hand, if there is no anger one cannot practice compassion. If I tell the truth my husband will not be angry with me, but I will separate relatives. If I tell the servants the truth, they will dislike Ani Nyemo even more. So I shall not answer."

When Nangsa made no response he assumed that Ani Nyemo had been telling the truth. He thought Nangsa was crying because she was feeling guilty. So he grabbed her by the hair and pulled her to and fro, kicking her. Then he beat her with the blunt side of his big knife until she was bleeding from her hands and legs and had three broken ribs.

She was screaming so much that her servants heard her and came running. They prostrated themselves before Dragpa Samdrub and said: "Please listen, great king! Even if Nangsa has displeased you, you can communicate with words. She is the person with whom you will share your whole life and the mother of your son. How can you beat her so much? Nangsa's face is like this full moon, but now it is covered with marks like the moon streaked with clouds. Her body is like a flexible young bamboo tree, yet you have managed to break three ribs. Please do not beat her! Queen Nangsa, please do not cry!"

Then they took Queen Nangsa and Dragpa Samdrub to their rooms.

Not far away was a monastery called Kyepo Yarlung, and there lived a good guru called Sakya Gyaltsen.[26] He was the guru who advised Milarepa to go to Lodrag Marpa Lotsa.[27] He was especially known for his knowledge of the precious Dharma of Dzogpa|Kyenpo,[28] although he was accomplished in all the lineages. This guru, due to his omniscience, realized that Nangsa was a special dakini, and was experiencing suffering due to past karma, but this suffering was purifying her further. He saw that she would die and then come back into the same body[29] to help sentient beings. In order to speed up this process he manifested a phantom body,[30] looking like a very handsome beggar with a monkey. This phantom beggar went under Nangsa's window and sang this song:[31]

"You whose beauty is superior to a goddess's,
Who are inside that window,
Please listen to me!
Please listen to my voice and look at my monkey!
In the jungle of Eastern Kongpo
There is a kind of monkey,
Even if they can play they still cling to their mother,
And get food from her!
This monkey had no karmic link with his mother,
So I got him!
He does not like having the rope on his neck;
When I train him he has to suffer.
Though the training brings him so much suffering,
If he felt no pain he would not learn much!

In the forest in the extreme South of Tibet,
Many birds and their babies live.
Those that are able to, fly high,
Those that are not able, rest in the branches of the trees.
The garrulous parrot has come into the king's hand.
On his foot is an iron chain
Which causes him suffering and difficulties.
In order to learn how to imitate the sound of a human voice,
He undergoes all kinds of suffering.
And the clever talk of a parrot is only imitation.

[85]

In the West, in Nepal, the land of rice,
Live golden mother bees and their offspring.
The fortunate ones take the essence from the flowers,
The unfortunate just buzz around where there is the smell of
    rice chang.
Those who are small and still less fortunate are caught by
    children and tortured.
Bees having left their hives experience all kinds of suffering.
It is because of their association with sweetness that bees
    must experience all this suffering.

In the North, in the grasslands of Mongolia,
Each ewe has a lamb and they nourish themselves on grass.
Although they are not fat,
They are healthy and accompany pilgrims on the road.
Then they fall into the hands of a butcher,
And undergo the suffering of a butcher's hand on their
    bodies.
Because of their meat they undergo hardship.
This is the story of the sheep's delicious mutton.

In Upper Nyang every woman has a child.
Fortunate ones move in solitude, staying in hermitages.
Others stay at home with their parents.
Beautiful women go to noblemen as their brides.
They undergo sufferings at the hands of the likes of
    Ani Nyemo.
They experience suffering because of her jealousy.
This is what happens to beautiful women.

If you do not keep impermanence and the thought of death
    in your heart,
Even though you are pretty, you are just like an Indian
    peacock.
If you do not practice the Dharma,
Having attained the human body,
Your sweet voice is no better than the sound of the singing
    blackbird in the willow trees.
If you give me nothing,
You are no more productive than the paintings of

ornamented deities in the temple –
With all your ornaments and jewelry."

At the end of the song the monkey stopped his dance.
Nangsa had heard the beggar's voice and her son had been
watching the monkey. Nangsa thought: "I must give something to this man. If I give him anything like barley or jewels, it
might make someone angry; it would be best to give him
something that is really mine. I want to consult with him about
where to go to study the Dharma and who the good teachers
are. I should not be attached to my child or I will be like the
animals in the yogi's song. I must promise to go away and
practice."

So she called him into her room and sang him this song:

"Please listen to me,
You beggar with monkey!
My father and mother are old,
Like evening shadows.
Now that they are old
I cannot help them.
Thinking thus, renunciation arises in this woman.
Nangsa will not stay here,
She will practice Tantra.[32]
Obum will stay in retreat!

When I look at my husband,
I think of the fluttering flag on the roof.
Even though he is my husband he is not stable.
He believes what other people say before hearing my side.
Thinking thus, renunciation arises in this woman.
Nangsa will not stay here,
She will practice Tantra,
Obum will stay in retreat!

When I look at my son,
He seems like a rainbow;
Even though he is cute,
He will not lead me to enlightenment.
Thinking thus, renunciation arises in this woman.

Nangsa will not stay here,
She will practice Tantra,
Obum will stay in retreat!

When I look at Ani Nyemo,
I realize she is like a serpent,
So jealous that even meditation makes her angry.
Thinking thus, renunciation arises in this woman.
Nangsa will not stay here,
She will practice Tantra,
Obum will stay in retreat!

When I look at my servants I feel sad:
Nobody listens to them,
As if they were small children.
Thinking thus, renunciation arises in this woman.
Nangsa will not stay here,
She will practice Tantra,
Obum will stay in retreat!

If I want to practice holy Tantra,
Which monastery should I go to?
Which lama, with great blessings, do you recommend?
You travel around all the time so you must know.
Here is some coral and turquoise,
Tell me the truth!"

The beggar stood in front of her bowing respectfully. He
said:

"You human who look like a goddess, listen to me!
Beautiful Nangsa, listen to me!
I have been everywhere in Tibet.
There is nowhere I have not been.
Everything I say is the truth.
I have never told a lie.
Tibet is a very religious country,
There are many teachers.
But one of the most famous is Milarepa in Lachi.
But that is too far from here,

You are alone and cannot go to him.
In the North, which is a nice place to live,
On the mountain that looks like a lion jumping,
Behind the mountain that looks like an elephant lying down,
There is a nice monastery called Ser Yarlung and a lama
  called Sakya Gyaltsen.
That lama is a great Dzog Chen master.
He is learned and powerful.
If the queen wants to practice Dharma
Please go there."

When Nangsa Obum heard the name Sakya Gyaltsen, the hair on her arms stood on end and tears came into her eyes. She gave the beggar three high-quality turquoises and five big corals, that she was wearing on her own body.

The Rinang king, Dragchen, her father-in-law, was on his way to check how the work was progressing, and as he was on the stairs near Nangsa's room, he heard the exchange with the beggar, a young man with a nice voice. He thought he heard Nangsa, but the male voice was not that of his son, so he peeked through a crack in the door. He saw his grandson Lhau Darpo playing on the floor with a monkey and Nangsa giving her jewels to the young man.

He thought: "Yesterday Nangsa was giving barley to yogis and beat up Ani Nyemo when she told her not to give everything to beggars. So my son beat her a little. Now she has forgotten that and today she has brought this beggar into our house. How can she be our queen? If I leave her at it she will ruin the child as well!"

Dragchen flung open the door. The beggar and the monkey disappeared out of the window. He grabbed Nangsa by the hair and said: "Yesterday you gave barley to some yogis. We told you not to give, so why are you inviting this beggar in and giving him your jewels? Surely Dragpa Samdrub and Ani Nyemo are right. You are a whore. You are a demoness. You do what you should not do."

Nangsa did not have time to answer before her father-in-law started to beat her, even though her wounds had not healed from the previous beating.

Then he took away Lhau Darpo and gave him to a wet

nurse. Nangsa was so sad that she died of a broken heart. Lhau Darpo was so sad that he cried all night, feeling that his mother had died of a broken heart. So the wet nurse thought she must take Lhau Darpo to see his mother without anyone knowing. When she got to Nangsa's room and opened the door she thought Nangsa was sleeping. But when she touched her body she found it completely cold. She could not believe Nangsa was dead, and kept on pressing and shaking her. Finally in horror she ran to Dragchen and Dragpa Samdrub. They ran to Nangsa's room and saw her, but they thought that she was pretending to be dead because they had been mean to her. Dragchen grabbed her right hand and Dragpa Samdrub her left hand and they pulled her up, saying:

"Listen to Dragchen and Dragpa Samdrub, Nangsa Obum!
Look at the moon that seems to disappear as in an eclipse.
It may be that a cloud has covered the moon,
But it cannot be an eclipse if the day is not right.
Please wake up, Nangsa, precious friend,
Please, mother of kings, arise!

Look at the flower in the garden.
It looks old when it hails,
But it can't be dead until autumn.
Please do not sleep, girl!
Please wake up, Nangsa!

In this beautiful house, in this beautiful room,
Queen Nangsa is acting dead.
It is possible that you have pain in your body;
But it is not possible for you to be dead."

They pulled her up, but she did not respond: she was cold and really dead. So they had a big funeral and gave away a lot of things to create good karma.[33] Then they asked for a divination[34] as to how to proceed, and the response was that Nangsa's lifespan was not up and she would come back to life. She should be put on an eastern hill, and then after seven days they would not have to worry about the body. They put her in a casket and wrapped her in white cloth. Then they took her to

1 The author in Manali, north India, 1970, when she was an ordained Tibetan Buddhist nun (see pp. xxi–xxvi)

2 A Tibetan nun with prayer wheel near the great Baudha Stupa in Kathmandu. She supports herself by begging and lives independent of a monastic situation, as did A-Yu Khadro, Drenchen Rema, Machig Lapdron, Machig Ongjo and Jomo Memo (see pp. 14–16)

3 Namkhai Norbu Rinpoche, master of Dzog Chen teachings (see p. 236, and n. 1, p. 258)

4 Namkhai Norbu Rinpoche practicing the Chod. The human thighbone trumpet is used at a certain point in the ritual to call discontented spirits to feast on the amrita of the transformed body of the practitioner, which has been chopped up to feed others. The practice is based on the cutting of egotism (see pp. 144–9) and the Prajna Paramita Sutra. The ritual and its instruments have their roots in pre-Buddhist Tibetan shamanism

5 Urgyen Chodron "Amala," consort or Sang Yum (Secret Female Consort or Mother) of Abo Rinpoche, in Manali, India (see p. xxxiv)

6 A Tibetan laywoman making her morning rounds reciting mantras near the Baudha Stupa (Choten) in Kathmandu. Behind her is Urgyen Rinpoche's monastery

7 Yudron, who was a nun when she was young, under the famous woman teacher Shug Sep Jetsun Rinpoche, Ani Lochen, and her eldest son, Jigme, who is on a five-year retreat in Kathmandu Valley. She brings him food and supplies when he needs them (see p. xxxiv)

8 A Tibetan monk reading a religious text next to the Baudha Stupa in Kathmandu. This kind of activity is said to accumulate merit creating positive results for the practitioner or those who pay the reader. Machig Lapdron was a professional reader in her youth. She read the Prajna Paramita Sutra for those who requested this service from her guru. She was famous for the speed at which she could read (see pp. 158–9)

9 A mandala of Vajra Varahi and the figure of Machig Lapdron, founder of the Mahamudra Chod lineage. Phayang monastery, Leh, Ladakh (see pp. 22, 31–6)

10 Vajra Yogini statue, Kathmandu Valley (see p. 249)

11 Tibetan nomads on pilgrimage in Ladakh. They are spinning prayer wheels which contain tightly wrapped rolls of paper on which hundreds and thousands of mantras have been written. The malas, or mantra beads, which they hold in their left hands are made from bodhi seeds and are used to count the mantras which are recited

12 Gorzang retreat center, Ladakh. Here yogis and yoginis in the Drukpa Kagyu lineage of Shakya Shiri do long retreats

13 Traditional lama dance depicting the life of Padma Sambhava, Hemis, Ladakh

14 (below) Performance of a religious drama in the courtyard of a monastery in Hemis, Ladakh. The folk opera of Nangsa Obum's life story is performed in similar circumstances (see p. 63)

15 The steep front stairs which approach Swayambhu Stupa from the east. This is the formal way of approaching the stupa and entering its mandala (see p. xxvii)

16 This huge vajra
(indestructible diamond scepter)
which symbolizes the masculine
and skillful activity, lies at the top
of the staircase to the
Swayambhu Stupa, just in front of
the Buddha Akshobya, and the
Buddha Vairocana

17 Swayambhu Stupa from the
northwest with the hills
surrounding Kathmandu Valley in
the background

18 Cave in Kulu Valley, northwest India, inhabited by Tibetan yogini nuns. Drenchen Rema, Machig Ongjo and A-Yu Khadro probably lived in similar caves in Tibet

19 Two young Tibetan nuns living in a group hermitage in Kulu Valley sound the long Tibetan horns during a feast offering. A group of men and women living around this mountainside gather to practice like this several times a month, when they are not in closed retreat

20 A group of nuns living in caves (see opposite) gather to make food for a Tantric feast offering

21 Gyalwa, a Tibetan monk, standing outside the three-year retreat center at Namo Buddha, Kathmandu. On his right is a freshly made meditation box similar to the one he will live in for his three-year retreat. This box will be placed inside a small cell in the hermitage, with just enough room for full-length prostrations

22 A Tibetan couple outside their cave in the hills above Rewalsar (see opposite page, below). He is wearing one of the traditional dresses of a yogic practitioner, the red and white shawl and skirt (shandup). A-Yu Khadro lived in a similar way when she was traveling with Togden Semnyi (see pp. 247–51)

23 The above couple inside their cave, where they dedicate themselves to the practice of meditation and are supported by the gifts of patrons and by begging

24 One of many caves inhabited by yogis and yoginis above the lake at Tso Pema (Rewalsar) near Mandi, India

25 The lake at Rewalsar, also called Tso Pema (Lotus Lake), which was allegedly formed when the king of Mandi tried to burn Padma Sambhava and the princess of Mandi, Mandarava, alive because he discovered they were living together. They had in fact been practicing advanced stages of Buddhist Tantra together and they integrated with the element of fire, created the lake and were unharmed by the fire

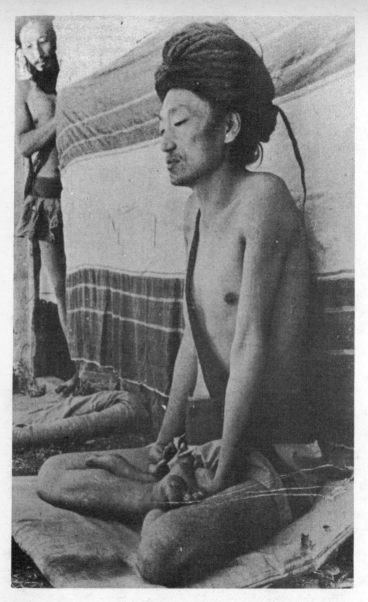

26 Togdens (yogis) from Tashi Jong, north India, 1970. These yogis practice the Six Yogas of Naropa and wear only thin white cotton clothes, symbolizing that they have accomplished the yoga of inner heat (tummo) like Milarepa

an eastern mountain shaped like an elephant's trunk. They left her there with guards, for seven days.

Her mind left her body like a hair being pulled out of butter. She was in the Bardo[35] and she met Ah Lang Go, the Lord of Death, who was sending the people who had done many good deeds on a white path to the three higher realms, while the people who had done bad deeds were taken to the three lower realms, including the eighteen hells. In hell were people who had done cruel things cooking in a big black pot. Others were suffering in cold, like that of high mountains. This was the cold hell realm. She was so afraid she could not feel. She put her hands together in prayer and said:

"Please, Arya Tara,
Please grant your blessings, Mother of Dakinis.
You are the Lord of Death who knows karma!
I have not done anything bad, and I have even helped many
    people with my compassion.
I know that if one is born one must die,
So I am not attached to my body.
I have known that all possessions are impermanent,
So I have given many away.
I know that at the time of death,
One is separated even from the closest of kin,
So even to them I have not been attached.
I have not even got angry with my enemies.
Please be compassionate to me!"

The Lord of Death was accompanied by two gods, one white and one black. They counted her good and bad actions with white and black stones. There were very few black but many white ones. Then she looked into the mirror of karma and saw that she was a special kind of dakini. The Lord of Death said to her: "Listen carefully to me, woman Nangsa Obum! Listen to the King of Death, the powerful one! The Dharma King sees black and white, virtue and sin! When I see the white virtuous actions these people are taken on the white path to freedom. Then my name is noble Avalokitesvara. I am the embodiment of compassion, the King of the Three Times! When I take people to the hell realms my name is Shinje, the Lord of Death.

When I inflict pain on others with bad karma I am very
terrifying. In my kingdom if anyone does anything wrong he
must be punished. If you have black karma even a great guru
cannot help you. Once you are in hell it is very difficult to
leave. When you are in hell how can you get enlightened? But
you are no ordinary woman, you do not have a lot of negative
karma. You are the phantom body of a dakini. Even if your
body looks like that of a goddess, your mind is not conditioned
by that, it can overcome everything. If you have a mind that
always thinks of Dharma you will become enlightened. But the
best thing is to have both outer and inner practice of Dharma.[36]
You must go back now and enter your old body again and help
others, being a delog."[37]

Nangsa was very happy. She received his blessing and, taking
the white path, entered her body and was alive again.

When she awoke on the eastern hill she was wrapped in a
nice white cloth, sitting in the meditation posture with seven
aspects.[38] There was a rain of flowers and she was doing Vajra
Yogini practice. She was surrounded by rainbow light. Then
she put her hands in a prayer position and said:

"I bow to the Guru, the Deva and the Dakini!
Please take me out of the ocean of suffering.
In the East is the Vajra family Dakini.[39]
You have a white body like a conch shell,
Carrying in your right hand a damaru,[40] tro lo lo!
In your left a little silver bell, si li li!
You work compassionately with thousands of white
    assistants.
Please help me to avoid obstacles.

In the South is the Ratna family Dakini!
You have a golden body and a semi-wrathful appearance,
Carrying in your right hand a golden damaru, tro lo lo!
In your left is a little silver bell, si li li!
You produce enriching action with thousands of golden
    assistants!
Please help me!

In the West is the Padma family Dakini!
You are the color of coral, your face is a little more wrathful,
Carrying in your right hand a golden damaru, tro lo lo!
And in your left, a little silver bell, si li li!
Surrounded by thousands of red assistants,
You have the power to subdue the three realms!

In the North is the Karma family Dakini!
You are green like the color of turquoise.
In your right hand is a golden damaru, tro lo lo!
In your left is a little silver bell, si li li!
Surrounded by thousands of wrathful green assistants,
You cut off the obstructing energies of the ten spheres.

In the center is the Buddha family Dakini![41]
You are blue like lapis lazuli,
In your right hand you hold a golden damaru, tro lo lo!
In your left is a little silver bell, si li li!
Surrounded by thousands of blue assistants,
You are able to accomplish all actions peaceful and wrathful.
Please grant me the supernormal powers!"

When the people who were guarding her body heard her
voice they thought it was a "rolang."[42] The cowards ran away
and the brave were about to stone her when she said: "Stop! I,
Nangsa, am not 'rolang.' I have been to hell and back and now
am alive again." Everyone was astounded and made obeisance
to her. After receiving her blessings they ran to tell the Rinang
family.

Lhau Darpo had been very sad because of his mother's
death. He had not been sleeping or eating. When the body
guardians arrived he was up on the roof with his nurse. He
said: "Where is my mother's body? Please show me where it is.
Even if I cannot see her in this life, I pray that I will meet her in
the Buddha fields."

His wet nurse was also very fond of Nangsa and was crying.
Lhau Darpo shaded his eyes with his little hand and looked
toward the East, and sang this song:

"My grandfather killed my mother when I was with her.

Now this little boy is like a small bird left on the ground.
If my mother could hear my sad song how happy I
   would be.

Look on yonder hill: there are no vultures looking for the
   body, not even any crows,
There is only dense rainbow-colored light.
Please take me there to my mother's body."

At that moment the people who had been guarding Nangsa
announced that she had come back to life. They had seen her
wrapped in white cloth surrounded by rainbow light and a rain
of flowers had fallen. Dragpa Samdrub and Dragchen went to
her with great remorse to ask her to return to Rinang, saying:

"We bow to the Gurus,
We pray to the Dakinis.
Listen here, Nangsa, listen to the Dragchen father and son!
Your body seemed like young bamboo,
We didn't know it was the body of a dakini.
Your voice is empty like that of a dakini,
We are sorry we didn't do what we promised before.

Your mind is like a silver mirror,
Like bliss and emptiness.
Forgetting this, we did many stupid things.
We apologize!

We sentient beings are ignorant.
Whatever we did to your body, speech and mind,
We did in ignorance.
Please forgive us,
Take us wherever you want to go!"

Then Dragchen said:

"Even if you do not like me,
Think of my son and come back;
He is the man you are destined to be with,
Please come back!

Do not think about Ani Nyemo,
Think of your son,
He is a part of your body.
Do not think of Sonam Palkye,
Remember Dzom Kye, your servant since childhood.
Even if you do not think of the others, remember your
    precious parents,
They are here, so please come back!"

Even though he pleaded with her in this way she just thought of
her dislike of Samsara and said:

  "I bow to the five poisons transformed into the five
    wisdoms!
I bow to the five Dakinis of the five directions!
Please listen, Dragchen and Dragpa Samdrub,
The Rinang nobles, father and son,
Please listen to this girl with painful karma and without
    Dharma!
My mother's daughter, Nangsa Obum!
Before I died I stayed in luxurious houses.
When I exemplified impermanence, and my body was on the
    eastern hill,
I felt very sad looking at it.
Thinking of the meaninglessness of Samsaric life.
I do not feel happy in your house!

When my mother's daughter, Nangsa Obum, was alive, I
    rode a spirited horse,
But now I do not feel like riding.

When my mother's daughter, Nangsa Obum, was alive, I
    lived with many servants,
But when I died I had to go alone;
So all that is meaningless![43]

When my mother's daughter, Nangsa Obum, was alive, I
    wore a lot of jewels.
But when I died I could not take any of it with me,

Pretty jewelry leads to quarrels.

When my mother's daughter, Nangsa Obum, was alive,
She used to eat very well,
But when she died she had to leave her body,
So now I do not care about my body!

When my mother's daughter, Nangsa Obum, was alive, you
    listened to others,
But when I died you confessed and asked for forgiveness.
Quarrels arise from worldly friends.
King Dragchen, I have no attachment to you.

When my mother's daughter, Nangsa Obum, was alive,
You beat me horribly,
But when I died you decided to do virtuous actions for my
    benefit.
Disputes arise from worldly friends:
Dragpa Samdrub, I have no attachment to you!

When my mother's daughter, Nangsa Obum, was alive,
I worked hard for my son.
But when I died he could not help me,
He was like a rope pulling me into Samsara.
Problems arise from worldly children.
I have no attachment to you, Lhau Darpo!

Now I will go to practice the Dharma.
If I leave you there are plenty of other young girls.
You can marry any of these beautiful girls,
And stay in the hell of Samsara!"

They all thought about what she had said and realized it was
true. They were transfixed with their hands together, unable to
go home. Then her son, Lhau Darpo, climbed into his mother's
lap and started to cry, saying:

"Mother Nangsa, your body was dead and you came back to
    life,
This is a shock to me.

If it is real, it is amazing.
If it is a dream it is very sad,
If you are rolang please kill me,
If you are dead and have come back to life please take me
   with you!
A little boy like me without his mother is like
A monk without his guru.
Please take me with you!

A little boy like me without his mother
Is like a kingdom without a king;
A kingdom has no meaning without a king.
Please do not go away without me!

I am a little boy who has been separated from his mother,
I am like a young man with no courage.
Even if he talks very much,
He cannot protect his parents,
Or injure his enemies.
Think about this and do not leave me!

I am a little boy who has been separated from his mother,
Like a girl with no hair,
Even if she has many ornaments,
She will not get a husband.
Think of that and do not leave me!

I am a little boy who has been separated from his mother,
Like a horse that can run fast but cannot be controlled,
It cannot be sold.
Think of that and do not leave me!

I am a little boy who has been separated from his mother,
Like a mule with a weak back,
Even if it is fed well,
It is useless.
Think of that and do not leave me!

I am a little boy who has been separated from his mother,
Like a businessman with no money,

Even if he works hard he does not get anywhere!
Think of that and do not leave me!

I am a little boy who has been separated from his mother,
Like a Mani wheel[44] with no blessings,
No one will bother with it.
Think of that and do not leave me!

I am a little boy who has been separated from his mother,
Like a bird without wings,
Even if it tries to fly it will fall down again and again,
Think of that and do not leave me!

I am a little boy who has been separated from his mother,
Like a place where there is no grass and no water,
People may come,
But they will not stay!
Think of that and do not leave me!

I am a little boy who has been separated from his mother.
I will be a leper, no one will want to be near me,
Without you I am like that!
So please think of that and do not leave me!
Please come back home!"

Nangsa, seeing her son in this state, felt sorry for him and
started to cry; but then she realised that if she went back to the
palace she would have further obstacles. So she put her hand
on his head and said:

"Only Father, the Guru, obeisance!
The heart of the Dakinis, I bow to you!
Please listen to my song, Lhau Darpo,
I am not rolang,
I am a delog.
I was dead but I came back to life,
So you can be happy.
There is nothing and no one who does not die,
But there are few who die and come back to life.
It is difficult to be a delog.

[98]

Death may come at any time.

I am like a snow mountain,
And you are a snow lion,
Do not be attached to me!
I am just like an ordinary snow mountain,
Unlike my husband who is a big one,
So I can be melted by the sun . . .
It is very dangerous.

You are a golden eagle,
Do not be attached to me,
I am just a small rocky hill,
I might get blown up by lightning.

You, a beautiful deer,
Do not be attached to me, I am like a grassy hill,
There are other, better meadows,
I am dangerously small when autumn comes.

You are a little golden fish,
Do not be attached to me,
I am like a small lake that may dry up in the sun,
There are big oceans that are safer.

You are a beautiful bird,
Do not be attached to me,
I am like a little garden that may dry up.
There are bigger gardens.

You, a beautiful golden bee,
Do not be attached to me,
I am just an ordinary flower.
There are big lotuses nearby.
I could be destroyed by hail.

My little son, do not be attached to me,
The delog Nangsa Obum.
The Rinang family is more secure,
I may die,

Listen to my words and keep them in your mind, Lhau
   Darpo!"

Then he pleaded with his mother again, saying:

"You who are caring for me very compassionately,
My only mother, listen to me, Lhau Darpo!

If my mother and father had not made
The seed of my being,
How could I become a rope pulling them into Samsara?

If I am a snow lion,
If I do not stay with you, the snow mountain,
Even if lightning does not kill me,
My blue mane won't grow,
So until I get my blue mane please stay!
After I get my blue mane we will both go to practice the
   Dharma.
Until that time the sun will not melt you,
You can stay in the shadows.

If I, who am like an eagle,
Staying on a high rocky mountain,
Am not connected to the mountain,
Even if I am not killed,
I will not grow my big wings.
So please wait until I am big enough to fly,
Then we will fly high in the sky and practice the Dharma.
Until then we will not be exploded by lightning,
Because we will get a powerful guru to protect us.

If a little deer like me,
Is not in a forest,
Even if it is not killed by hunters,
It won't get its beautiful horns.
So please do not go until I get my beautiful horns.
Then we will go together to practice the Dharma.
Until then hail will not destroy you,
Because we can tell the clouds to go elsewhere.

[100]

If a little fish like me,
Is not in you, the mother, water,
Even if the fisherman's hook does not catch me,
I will never be able to swim fast.
Until I get this strong body,
Please, mother lake, stay here!
When I am strong enough, you and I will practice the
    Dharma together.
Until then the sun won't dry you up,
Because we can pray to the nagas, who live under the water.

If a little songbird like me
Is not attached to a garden,
Even if an eagle does not kill me,
I will never get my beautiful voice.
So until I get my beautiful voice,
Please stay here,
Then we will go to practice the Dharma.
Until then you will not be dried up in the autumn,
Because we can tell time not to let this happen.

If a little bee like me,
Is not connected to you, the mother flower,
Even if birds do not kill me,
I will never get my silver wings.
Until I can make my own honey,
Please, wild flower, do not go away!
Until then you will not be destroyed by hail,
Because we will keep a magic vase to stop the hail.

If I, little Lhau Darpo,
Am not with you, the kind mother,
I will not grow up.
Until I can get along by myself,
Please do not leave me!
When I am big enough we can go together and practice the
    Dharma.
You will not die before then, because we will do a special
    initiation and pray to Amitabha, the deity of long life.

If Ani Nyemo talked about you to my father,
Causing him to beat you,
Remember compassion is the most important thing in
    Dharma, and do not be angry.
Your friendly little boy is crying, and if you do not have
    compassion, and do not listen to me,
That is not Dharma, mother!

If you have compassion, even if you live in an ordinary
    house,
You are practicing the Dharma.
If you do not have compassion,
There is no difference between you,
And the wild animals who live in caves."[45]

When Lhau Darpo finished singing this song, everyone,
including Dragpa Samdrub, and the rest of the family began to
plead with her to come back with them.

Everyone in the kingdom was pleading with her to come
back. Even Ani Nyemo was feeling sorry and asked for
forgiveness, begging Nangsa to come back. She said: "Even
under the threat of death I will never do what I did before." So
saying she went in front of Nangsa and vowed that she would
cause no more trouble.

Nangsa thought: "The whole kingdom is requesting my
return. Lhau Darpo seems so small and wise. He is already
speaking the Dharma at his age. Ani Nyemo has made this
vow in front of everyone. This must be the blessings of the
Three Jewels."

So she agreed to go back, and they put beautiful clothes on
her as well as a lot of jewelry, and left for home. There was a
rain of flowers and three claps of thunder. Her body was the
Nirmanakaya[46] emanation of the Buddha. Her voice was the
empty sound of the Sambogakaya. Her mind was the bliss and
emptiness of the Dharmakaya.

She thought: "I will go to the Rinang family and teach the
Dharma. I will especially turn the mind of Ani Nyemo." Then
she taught the preciousness of the human body, impermanence, karma, the suffering of Samsara, the benefits of the

Dharma, and many other teachings.

But even after receiving these teachings, her father-in-law, her husband and Ani Nyemo had so many negative karmic traces that they did not change. They were only afraid that she would leave and disgrace them so they treated her like a queen.

Nangsa was so sad because she was unable to turn their minds toward the teachings of the Buddha, and because she had been unable to go away to practice herself, that she was not eating or sleeping.

Dragchen, Dragpa Samdrub, and Ani Nyemo sang her this song:

"Listen to us, you with the beautiful body,
Who take the minds of all the boys,
Queen Nangsa, listen to us!

We apologized to you,
And were very sorry about what we did to you,
And will never do anything like it again,
Even on penalty of death.
But now we have done nothing to you,
So why are you so sad?
You do not sleep at night,
Or eat during the day.
There is no reason to be so sad,
Are you ill?"

Nangsa answered:

"I bow to the Three Jewels,
Bless me, Deva and Dakinis.
Destroy obstacles, Dharma protectors.
Please grant my wish to follow the Dharma!
Listen to Nangsa Obum, you three!
Listen to the delog Nangsa!
I am not sad for worldly reasons,
I do not have any of the sicknesses from imbalance of the
    four elements,[47]
I have no other wishes either.

[103]

I am sad only because you are not letting me go to practice
  the Dharma.
Even though this room looks like a heavenly realm,
And the food tastes like amrita,
Even if you relatives were gods, I would still feel sad.
Even if Lhau Darpo were a godly prince,
I would not be attached to him.
If you three do not want to practice the Dharma
At least please let me go,
If not to practice the Dharma,
At least let me see my parents."

Dragchen thought: "Before, we listened to Ani Nyemo and
beat Nangsa until she died. Now we haven't done or said
anything, but she is still sad and not relaxed in her mind. If I
say anything I'll cause trouble like before. If I do not let her go
she will keep on doing what she should not do, and not doing
what she should do. She will continue talking about leaving
and going off to practice the Dharma all the time."

Then he thought: "Nangsa has not been home since she
came here. Though we promised her she could go we always
postponed it; we have abused her and it is true she misses her
parents. I will send her home and send the little boy with her.
Then she won't run away and perhaps her parents can get her
to do some work."

Return home

The king sent Nangsa and Lhau Darpo home with lots of gifts.
On the way Dzom Kye carried Lhau Darpo, and Nangsa
walked. Then they reached a river which was running so high
that they could not cross it by bridge and were going to have to
take a ferry. She sang a song to the ferryman, who was on the
other side of the river:

"I am longing for my mother, so please come here!
I am thinking of Nyangtsa Seldron,
So please bring the boat here!
I remember my father,

[104]

Please bring the big boat with the horsehead!
I am thinking of Kunzang Dechen,
So please bring the boat!"

The ferryman answered:

"There are thousands of people crossing here everyday;
We have so much work there is no time for you!
If you are thinking so much of your parents,
Jump in and swim across."

Nangsa answered:

"Please do not speak like that;
Bring the big boat with the horsehead ornament.
If you feed a horse well and it does not carry you,
Why keep it in the stable?

If you throw seeds on the ground,
But nothing grows,
You have to buy food,
And there is no reason to plant.
If you practice the Dharma,
But you think of the Buddha as an enemy,
There is no reason to stay in retreat.
If there is a boat in the water,
But it does not carry people,
There is no reason to have a boat."

The ferryman replied:

"Even if you talk very sweetly,
You cannot talk to water.
In the mountains the bandits are the most powerful,
On the river the ferryman is in charge.
If you have magic powers why don't you fly?
If you do not have magic powers,[48]
Then you must give me the fare!
If you have magic powers make a bridge,
If not, give me the money!

[105]

If I do not get the money there is no reason to have this boat.
When a man who thinks of shooting an arrow, buys a bow,
If it does not shoot there is no reason to buy it!
I thought I would make a profit,
That is why I am in this business.
There is no reason to wear a lot of ornaments,
If no one in the market place looks at you.
I became a ferryman to earn a lot of money;
If I don't make money,
It is just a lot of hard work,
And bad times for me."

Nangsa thought: "It is true that in the mountains the bandits
are the most powerful. Here the power is in his hands, so I
must pay." But before she did so she sang him this song:

"You are right, and surely I will pay you.
I remember my parents,
But above all I remember impermanence.
Once I have visited them,
I want to go to practice the Dharma.
I will pay you so hurry up and come here!
The turquoise is for my guru,
The smaller corals I will give to you.
After meeting my parents,
I must go away and practice the Dharma,
So please hurry over here with the boat!
The gold ring with the beautiful jewel,
I must save for my guru,
But my other ring I will give to you.
So please hurry over here with the boat.
I must practice the Dharma without delay!
I have another turquoise and coral saved for my guru.
But I have some amber that I will give to you.
I want to meet my parents once,
Then I will go to practice the Dharma,
So please hurry!"

She then started to take off her ornaments and gave them to
the ferryman. He noticed her beauty and her pretty voice and

was very surprised. He asked: "Who are you, beautiful girl?"

Nangsa replied: "I am Queen Nangsa Obum, the wife of the Rinang king." He had heard the story of the Delog Obum, so he gave her back everything and prostrated himself before her. Everyone else in the boat was very happy to meet her and hear her voice. So they requested her to sing a song . . .

> "If the corals and amber around my neck were Dharma
>   protectors,
> How nice it would be!
> If the shell bracelet on my right hand were
> A conch shell calling the monks from the monastery,
> How nice that would be!
> If the diamond bracelet on my left hand,
> Were a mala for mantras,[49]
> How lovely that would be!
> If all the rings on my fingers were wisdom and means,[50]
> How nice that would be!
> If the golden spoon hanging by my side,
> Were a bell and cymbals,
> How lovely it would be!
> If the silver mirror hanging at my side,
> Were the mandala[51] of the Buddhafields,
> How nice it would be!
> If my shawl were a nun's shawl,
> How nice that would be!
> If my blue skirt were the maroon skirt of a nun,
> How nice it would be!
> If my apron[52] meant
> I was going to study the Dharma,
> How joyful I would be!
> If you were all monks and nuns listening to me,
> How nice that would be!
> But as it is
> I feel so sad!
> I will leave to practice the Dharma as soon as possible!"

Because Nangsa had such a nice voice and the meaning of her words was clear and simple, people bowed to her and they each individually promised to stop creating bad karma and to do good deeds. Nangsa was very happy that her song had made people turn toward the Dharma.

After the boat ride they proceeded to her parents' house. They were overjoyed when they spotted her in the distance. Her father brought her a white scarf[53] and her mother a little chang, and they went the length of an arrowshot to meet her. Then Kunzang Dechen sang her this song:

"My daughter Nangsa, the dakini, Lhau Darpo and Dzom
   Kye,
Listen to this old man:
Before the snow mountain melted,
The snow lion returned.
Thank you for returning, you have grown a handsome blue
   mane.

Before the rocky mountain,
Fell from a stroke of lightning,
The little eagle came back,
Thank you for coming back,
Have you grown your wings?

Before the forest dried up,
The little faun came back,
Thank you, it has been a long time,
Did you get your antlers?

Before the little lake dried up,
The little fish came back,
Can you swim well?

Before the garden dried up,
The songbird came back from the jungle,
Thank you for returning,
Have you developed a beautiful voice?

Before the garden flowers were destroyed by hail,
The little bee came back,
Thank you for returning,

Did you get your silver wings?

Before your old parents died,
You came back, Nangsa,
We have not seen you for a long time,
Are you well?"

Nangsa answered:

"You are the giver of mind and body,
Listen to the delog Nangsa Obum!
Everyone that is born, must die,
But those who die and come back to life are few.

The little snow lion had a lot of problems in the snow,
But it could not kill her.
She is most joyous to see Mount Kailash.[54]

The eagle had a lot of arrows shot at her,
But she survived,
And is happy to see the rocky mountain.

The little deer had a lot of hunters pursuing her,
But she has sharp horns,
She is happy to see her native forest again.

The little gold fish had a lot of hooks tempting her,
But she was prudent
So she is happily back in her old pond again!

Nangsa was killed accidentally,
But then came back to life again,
She is very happy to see you, her parents, again."

Then Nangsa told the story of everything that had happened
in Rinang, how she had been killed and visited hell, and then
how she returned to her body and became delog.
    She told them everything in detail and her parents cried and
smiled and held her hand and said they had heard of people
coming back from the dead, but never thought it would

happen to their daughter. They treated her and her party very kindly and prepared a lot of things to send back to the Rinang family.

Then one day Nangsa passed the weaving room and saw on the loom a cloth that she had left uncompleted when she left for Rinang. So she decided to finish it before leaving to help her parents. But her mother said: "You should not work, it would be shameful. We have plenty of servants."

Nangsa replied: "Why should I be ashamed of working? What is shameful is that I have a precious human body and I am not practicing the Dharma. This is a real cause for shame. You think of me as the queen of Rinang, but I think of myself as the lowest person. I cannot help my own parents and I cannot practice the Dharma. Even ordinary work that is started should be finished. This time I am not going to ask anyone for help, I am going to do this myself."

She began to work on the weaving, and many old friends came to visit her, having heard of her experience. They offered her chang. They found her working, and once, as she was talking to them, she decided to sing them a song, to turn them toward the Dharma, using images from her work:

"I bow to the Guru, Deva and Dakini,
Please help this girl who has no Dharma practice!
Listen to me, my friends, you young girls!
Listen to the delog Nangsa,
I will sing you a song using the loom as an example,
To teach you a little Dharma.

If the square hole for me to sit in was a meditation hut of
branches,
How happy I would be!
If the mat I sit on were a meditation cushion,
How happy I would be!
If the delog Nangsa were a meditator,
How happy I would be!

If my assistants were those who bring the food to someone
in retreat,
How happy I would be!

[110]

If the four pegs holding the loom were
Holding up four gyalsten,[55]
How happy I would be!
If the batten were the Guru's instructions,
How happy I would be!

If the sling that supports me while I work,
Were the sign of renouncing Samsara,
How happy I would be!

If the warp and the woof
Were bliss and emptiness,[56]
How happy I would be!

If the weaving thread,
Were the thread of meditation,[57]
How happy I would be!

If the ropes supporting the loom,
Were discipline and virtue,
How happy I would be!

If the long white string,
Were leading the way to the Buddha fields,
How happy I would be!

If the vertical tension string,
Were a line to pull us out of Samsara,
How happy I would be!

If the down-pulling string
Were pressing closed the door of Samsara,
How happy I would be!

If the opening stick that separates the threads,
Separated and clarified good and bad,
How happy I would be!

If the tension adjuster,
Were the Bodhicitta,[58] offering and serving others,
How happy I would be!

If the long detangling stick,
Could untangle the two veils,[59]
How happy I would be!

If the rolling stick which rolls the finished cloth,
Were the accumulations of merit and wisdom,
How happy I would be!

If the border adjuster,
Were bringing one-taste,[60]
How happy I would be!

If the sound of the loom
Were the sound of Dharma teaching,
How happy I would be!

If the piece that goes back and forth bringing the string,
Were the Dharma that brings happiness and removes
    suffering,
How happy I would be!

If the 84,000 strings[61]
Were the various teachings suitable for various people,
How happy I would be!

If my mind were as wide and long as the cloth I am making,
How happy I would be!"

After hearing this song some of the girls changed from doing
negative actions to doing good and positive actions. This song
was quite easy to understand, though there were a few
complicated words. Some thought that Nangsa just wanted to
go to Dharma because her life was so easy, she had a beautiful
child, a rich husband, cleverness and so on. So they said to
her: "You should not renounce everything when your life is so
good, Nangsa."

Nangsa replied:

"Please listen to me again, friends!
The precious human body is difficult to attain.
If you do not practice Dharma there is a great danger
Of falling into the lower realms.
Life is as brief as lightning between clouds.
Even if you friends do not want to practice the Dharma,
I am going.
Our life is like a drop of water on the grass,
Which can evaporate from little heat.
Even if you friends do not want to practice the Dharma,
I am going.
Life is like a rainbow in the grass,
Even though it looks nice,
It has no real worth.
Even if you friends do not want to practice the Dharma,
I am going.
Our life is as long as that of a butcher's sheep,
We are doomed to death.
Even if you friends do not want to practice the Dharma,
I am going.
Life is like the setting sun,
It looks strong and beautiful,
But before you know it, it is gone.
Even if you friends do not want to practice the Dharma,
I am going.
Life is like an eagle flying,
Now it is here but soon it will disappear.
Even if you friends do not want to practice the Dharma,
I am going.
Life is like a waterfall cascading from a high mountain,
Even though it makes a big sound,
It lasts only a moment then you pass it and it is gone.
Even if you friends do not want to practice the Dharma,
I am going.
Life is like a beggar's food,
Even if they have a lot in the morning,
By evening it is gone.
Even if you friends do not want to practice the Dharma,

I am going.
Life is like people walking in the streets,
For a moment we see them and then in a moment they are
    gone.
Even if you friends do not want to practice the Dharma,
I am going.
Our life is like a light,
The wind blows it and it doesn't rest anywhere.
Even if you friends do not want to practice the Dharma,
I am going.
Life is like a beautiful face,
It is with us when we are young,
But when we get old it will become ugly.
Even if you friends do not want to practice the Dharma,
I am going.
If I can find a good guru to teach me about impermanence,
Even if you friends do not want to practice the Dharma,
I am going."

Nangsa's mother overheard this song and said:

"You who are as dear to me as my own heart,
Listen to us, Nangsa Obum!

Would you like to run off and leave us to practice the
    Dharma?
Would you want to leave your husband to practice the
    Dharma?
Would you like to leave your son and run off to practice the
    Dharma?
Would you like to leave your subjects and go off to practice
    the Dharma?
Would you like to leave the palace and go to practice the
    Dharma?

If you really want to practice the Dharma, it is very difficult.
If you think like this, why did you have a baby?
Do not try to do what you are not capable of doing,
Practicing the Dharma.
Do what you know how to do,

Be a housewife."

Nangsa responded:

"Helpful mother, Nyangtsa Seldron, listen to me!
Listen to the voice of your daughter, Nangsa Obum!
The sun shines in the four corners of the universe:
When the sun stops shining I will stop desiring to practice
   the Dharma, and stay at home.
If the sun keeps going,
I will go also, to the Dharma.
If the moon stops waxing and waning,
I will stay at home.
But if it does continue to wax and wane, I will go to the
   Dharma.
If the lotus flower stops blooming in the summer,
And dying in the winter,
I will stay at home and not practice the Dharma.
But if it continues I will not stay at home,
I will go to practice the Dharma.
If the river stops and reverses its course,
I will stay at home and not practice the Dharma,
But if it does not, I will not stay at home,
I will go to practice the Dharma.
If fire stops burning up and burns down,
I will stay at home and not practice the Dharma,
But if it does not, I will not stay at home,
I will go to practice the Dharma.
When the prayer flags on top of the mountain, stop blowing
   in the wind,
I will stay at home and not practice the Dharma.
But if it does not, I will not stay at home,
I will go to practice the Dharma.
After birth there is always death.
If this is not true,
I will stay at home and I will not practice the Dharma.
But if this is true, I will not stay at home,
I will go to practice the Dharma.
And since it is true that death follows birth,
I want to go to practice the Dharma.

You are an old woman now,
If you became young again I will not go to practice the
  Dharma,
But if not, I will not stay at home,
I will go to practice the Dharma."

Then her mother thought: "She is used to being a queen and she won't listen to me, so I'll have to get a little angry at her." So she said to Nangsa Obum:

"Listen to me, daughter Nangsa Obum. We treated you so well when you were here and now you won't listen to us. Now you are like a karmic enemy. If I speak nicely to you, it is like putting manure on land that does not respond. So do not feel sorry for yourself when hail beats you. You are like a little sheep, who does not want to stay with the other sheep and be fleeced. So do not be sorry if you are sent to the butcher!

"You are like someone who is sick and when medicines are brought you will not take them. Do not have regrets if you die and go to another life.

"You who are like a violin which makes a sour sound even when it is tuned. Do not be upset when the violin maker comes to overhaul you!

"You who, with your beautiful body and voice, do not want to make the Rinang king happy and do not listen to your parents, do not feel sad when you are neither a nun nor a laywoman. Do not think you are my daughter or I am your mother if you behave so badly."

She took a handful of ashes and threw them into Nangsa's face, and was going to beat her with a stick, but Nangsa's friends stopped her. She then threw her out of the house and went inside and would not let Nangsa back in.

Leaving home to practice the Dharma

Nangsa rented a house from a friend and thought: "Everybody has one birth and one death, but I must have very bad karma because I will have two deaths. I do not know when I shall have my second death, so I think I will go now and practice the Dharma. Especially since the Lord of Death told me to go back and help sentient beings before I go back to him. I have tried to help my mother but she did not want to hear it and got angry. But I did not respond angrily so I did not make any bad karma. Now even my son, begotten by actions in our past lifetimes, has been taken from me. This apparent tragedy may in fact be a great boon in disguise. Now I am free to practice the Dharma. If I stay here longer, my relatives will soon come to fetch me. So I should hurry up and go. I would like to go to see Milarepa, but it is too far from here and it is dangerous to go alone. So I will do as the beggar with the monkey suggested and go to see Sakya Gyaltsen."

So she left that night when everyone was asleep. When she reached the Tse Chen bridge, "The Great Summit" bridge, she saw the moon rising in the East and thought this was an auspicious sign, so she sang this song:

"When Nangsa arrived at the Tse Chen bridge,
The full moon rose simultaneously.
This means the kind guru will teach me,
And I will help many sentient beings
Like the moon, whose light shines without partiality."

She flicked the water with her finger three times[62] and then continued on her way. When she arrived at the base of Yarlung, the sun rose. When she arrived at the monastery the monks were blowing the wakeup conch shell. Sakya Gyaltsen, thanks to omniscient vision, was aware of her approach and who she was, but pretended not to know. He sent a monk to detain her. The monk said to Nangsa:

"You beautiful girl, listen to the monk Tsultrim Rinchen!
Where did you come from today?
Where are you going this evening?
Who are your father and mother and relatives?
Who is your husband? How rich are you?
How many children do you have?
What is your name and why did you come here?
Do not try to deceive me, tell the truth!"

Nangsa replied:

[117]

"Guru's servant Tsultrim Rinchen,
Listen to this ignorant girl!
I am from the top of Nyang To,
I do not know where I will go today,
My food is what I am carrying,
My father's name is Kunzang Dechen,
My mother's name is Nyangtsa Seldron,
My own name is Nangsa Obum.
My husband's name is Dragpa Samdrub,
I have a son called Lhau Darpo,
I am poor in nothing except the Dharma.
I have a lot of ornaments and friends,
But I was unhappy with worldly life and I have come to
    study the Dharma!
Please let me see the guru."

Tsultrim Rinchen responded:

"You of beautiful body and voice,
Listen to me, Nangsa Obum.
You and the snow lion are both so beautiful,
You will have a hard time practicing.
You are beautiful, like the eagle,
So I do not think you can practice the Dharma,
You had better go back home.
You are like the jungle deer,
So strong you have no need of Dharma,
So you had better go back.
You are like a big fish in the ocean,
So strong you do not need Dharma.
You and the peacock are both so beautiful,
You do not need the Dharma,
You had better go back.
You and the songbird both have such beautiful voices,
You should not need the Dharma,
You had better go back to where you came from.
You and this flower are the same.
You do not need the Dharma,
You had better go back to your home."

[118]

Nangsa said:

"Listen to me, Tsultrim Rinchen!
The snow lion and I are both beautiful,
But it is because of karma that he has a big blue mane,
This does not have to harm his Dharma practice.
Please do not talk to me like this, let me enter!

I am like the eagle,
But he gets his wings due to karma,
This does not have to affect his Dharma practice.
Please do not talk to me like this, let me enter!

The deer and I are strong,
But he gets his big horns due to karma,
This does not have to affect his Dharma practice,
Please do not talk to me like this, let me enter!

The fish and I are both strong,
But we are like this because of karma,
This does not have to affect our Dharma practice.
Please do not talk to me like this, let me enter!

The songbird and I are both nice to hear,
But this is due to karma,
It does not have to affect our Dharma practice,
So please do not talk to me like this, let me enter!

The flower in the garden and I are pretty,
But this is due to karma,
It does not have to affect my Dharma practice,
So please do not talk to me like this, let me enter!"

Then Tsultrim Rinchen, seeing her great beauty and hearing her voice, realized she wanted the Dharma very badly, so he went in and reported to the guru. The guru did not let her in immediately, but went upstairs and closed the door. Nangsa stood below and sang this song:

[119]

"You who understand primordial purity, dear guru,
I came here due to great devotion to you,
I am disgusted with Samsara.
Please give me an audience!
In this quiet place in Yarlung,
You are the only important thing to me,
So please do not throw me away like a dead bird!
Catch me like a little fish, with the hook of compassion!"[63]

The guru answered:

"If you are an incarnation of Tara, you can be accepted.
But ordinary girls cannot practice Dharma,
A beautiful young woman like you will find it hard to
    practice,
So you had better go home.
If you cut off your hair[64] your parents will be angry with me.
I did not invite you here, you had better go back!"

Nangsa replied: "Beautiful Yarlung that looks like Tsari,[65] I
came here to learn Dharma from you. If I cannot do that, going
into a cave for retreat would be as meaningless as a wolf going
into his lair. I came here because I do not want to wander
meaninglessly; even if I do not have food I will still practice the
Dharma. If you refuse to teach me I will kill myself with this
knife." So saying, she unsheathed her knife. Tsultrim Rinchen
grabbed her hand and called to the guru to open the door
otherwise Nangsa would kill herself.
    The guru said:

"I thought a goat got mixed up with the sheep.
I wanted to know what was brown sugar and what was
    brown sealing wax.[66]
I have tested you to be sure about your commitment.
I did not tell you to kill yourself.
I will teach you the visualization stage and the post-
    visualization stage.[67]
Do not worry!"

With this he ended the song and let Nangsa enter his room. She offered him all of her ornaments and clothes and prostrated herself before him. He saw that she was a good vessel for the milk of the Dharma. Knowing that at the end of her life she would be able to help many people, he gave her the body, speech and mind initiation of Vajra Yogini, the Mandala of Tsendura.[68] He gave her many teachings in Sutric and Tantric Buddhism.[69] Then he gave her a little hut and she proceeded to meditate. After a short time many good signs came to her. Then he gave her instructions on how to avoid obstacles. Both the guru and Nangsa were very happy.

Attack of the king and prince

During this time Nangsa's parents and Lhau Darpo went to call on Nangsa at her friends' house. But they had no news of Nangsa and no idea where she had gone.

Her parents thought perhaps she had gone back to the Rinang palace so they went to see if she was there. When they arrived they were told that she was not there. They told the Rinang family the story of what had happened. King Dragchen came to know she was in Yarlung studying with Sakya Gyaltsen. Dragpa Samdrub, her husband, ordered all the boys over eighteen and all the men under sixty to gather together and make an army to attack Sakya Gyaltsen and get Nangsa Obum back.

The disciples of Sakya Gyaltsen heard what was afoot and were angry at Nangsa. They were saying: "Because this demoness came here, we all must die!"

As the huge army approached there were cries and screams and the smell of gunpowder. The number of horsemen was so great, you could not see the ground. Some monks and nuns were trampled and some were injured. Tsultrim Rinchen was trying to carry Sakya Gyaltsen, who was too old to walk, but they could not get away because the monastery was surrounded. Then Sakya Gyaltsen was captured by Dragchen's soldiers. They tied him up and took him to the king. Nangsa was in her meditation hut; her mind was open like the sky, and she understood that her guru had been captured. So she went out with her meditation belt[70] and a white cloth wrapped around her. She grabbed the horse of the king with one hand and that of Dragpa Samdrub with the other, and sang this song:

"Listen to me, you two, father and son!
When the snow lion goes to the mountains,
Please do not create obstacles!
When the eagle is flying in the sky,
Do not shoot arrows at it!
When the little deer is eating,
Do not let the hunters harm it!
When the little golden fish is swimming,
Do not tempt it with sharp hooks!
When the little songbird is singing,
Do not let the big eagle harm it!
When like the sun I travel in the sky,
Please Rahu[71] do not come and eat me!
Please do not try to harm Sakya Gyaltsen,
Nangsa Obum wants to practice the Dharma,
Please do not stop me!
These other disciples are trying to practice Dharma,
Please do not disturb them either!"

The father and son saw Nangsa without ornaments looking like a yogini. They also saw that Sakya Gyaltsen had been captured and was being brought before them. They were furious and made cursing gestures at him, saying:

"Listen, Sakya Gyaltsen, and the rest of you!
Listen to the Rinang father and son!
You are an old dog that has seduced our snow lion!
Why did you attack our snow lion with the blue mane?
You are a horrid cock,
Why did you try to rape this white grouse?
Why did you pull out her feathers and wings?
You are an old donkey living in a dirty stable.
Why did you rape our beautiful wild horse?
Why did you cut off her mane?
You nasty old bull why did you have sex with our beautiful
   white female yak?

[122]

And shave off her mane?
You dirty old cat,
Why did you rape our pure tigress and cut off her fur?
You, the obscene Sakya Gyaltsen, have done something very
  bad!
You have made love to our Queen Nangsa.
Furthermore why did you take her hair ornaments?
In the sky there are many stars and planets,
But none of them can compete with the sun.
If you try to compete with the sun,
It will rise and wipe out your light!
It is too late for apologies,
In Central Tibet there are a lot of kings,
But who compares to the Rinang king?
When the Rinang king destroys the monastery
And takes the guru, it is too late for apologies!"

Then Dragchen took his bow and Dragpa Samdrub took his
sword and was about to chop up the guru; but the guru
reached out and grabbed the mountain on one side and moved
it to the other side. All the monks that had been injured were
healed instantaneously. All those who had been killed were
brought back to life. No matter what the army tried to do to the
guru, they could not hurt him. He flew up into the sky in the
lotus position and sang a song:

"You men with human bodies and animal minds,
You men with black karma, you listen to me!
You, father and son!
On earth there is someone better than the Rinang king,
That is why Nangsa Obum is here.
If you do not put the lotus in the garden, on a shrine,
There is no reason to have it.
I am disturbed that you threw this lotus on the ground,
To rot in a dirty place.
A big strong horse is useless,
Unless you take him into a field.
Unless you let him run
There is no reason to give him food and water.
I feel sad to see a horse getting old in the stable.

An arrow with good eagle feathers is useless
If it does not hit the target.
There is no reason to have a beautiful bow
If the arrow gets old in its case.
If the beautiful goddess,
Does not want to be the Queen of the Lord of Wealth,[72]
Even if she is caught with the lasso of richness,
It is useless.
It would be sad for Nangsa to grow old living with a hunter!
Her good qualities will be wasted if you do not let her
    practice the Dharma.
Her precious human body will be useless,
She will grow old in the kingdom of the king with bad
    karma.
This would be sad.
I knew where to shoot the arrow and I pulled the bowstring,
I am beautiful so I wear ornaments,
I am rich so I can give loans,
I know the doctor so I have the medicine,
I know many practices, so I showed you my magical powers,
I will not show them at the wrong time.
But you, who have the ten qualities of demons,
Have to be convinced, so I have shown you my powers!
Now you, Nangsa, must show your powers,
So they will become devoted to you!"

Immediately Nangsa showed her powers by making her
shawl into wings. She flew up into the air and sang this song
from the air:

"You, father and son and the rest of you, listen to me!
Listen to Nangsa Obum!
You have tried to make a snow lion into a dog,
But this is impossible!
Now I am on the snow mountain showing my mane!
You tried to tame a wild yak and turn it into a cow,
But this is impossible,
That is why I did not stay with you.
Now I am showing off my horns!
You tried to saddle the wild mule who lives in the forest,

That is why I ran away.
Now I am showing you my power.
You tried to make a wild bird into a hen,
But you cannot do that,
That is why I am in the forest showing off my plumage.
You tried to make a rainbow into a piece of cloth,
This is impossible,
Though it is visible it is not a concrete substance.
Now I show you this power.
You tried to make a delicate cloud into a cloth,
You could not so that is why I am staying here.
Now the cloud is showing you its capacity to make rain.
You tried to make a wild monkey into a servant,
But this is impossible.
Now I am showing you how I can climb!
You tried to make the delog Nangsa Obum into a wife,
But even though you put tsendura into my hair parting,[73]
You cannot hold me.
Here I am, flying above you,
I have flown to Tsari,
I have some bamboo from Tsari to prove it!
Like a yak that has worked hard plowing,
Now I show you the furrows.
If I want to fly like an eagle,
I fly like this!
If I want to dive like a hawk,
I do it this way!
People who can fly like birds are rare,
Only Milarepa and us.
Rinang soldiers, do not make terrible karma by hurting us.
You had better apologize to Sakya Gyaltsen."

The soldiers were amazed to see them flying about; they
dropped their weapons and collapsed prostrate on the ground,
singing this song:

"Great Lama Sakya Gyaltsen!
Beautiful Nangsa Obum!
We are demons, we Rinang soldiers;
Please listen to this song of pardon!

You, the guru, are the real Cakra Sambhava![74]
You, Nangsa, are the real Vajra Yogini!
But we did not know that, because of our ignorance
We thought you were a nasty guru.
We destroyed the monastery,
Some monks and nuns were killed,
Making our karma worse.
We especially displeased the lama yab yum.[75]
So we beg your forgiveness!
We beg you to be our guru!
We are rich in bad karma and as poor in good karma as
    beggars!
All of our lives have been spent in accumulating bad karma,
But please do not throw us into the lower realms again!
We promise to never do such things again.
Even if our very lives are threatened!
Please give us some teaching that is easy to understand and
    practice!"

Sakya Gyaltsen and Nangsa prayed from their hearts that the
bad karma of the noblemen and the army would be purified:

"For those who have done wrong,
Repentance is like the sun rising in the darkness,
This is fantastic!
Even those with the worst karma can rectify it,
If they purify with the four methods.[76]
If you want to change your actions after this, please listen to
    me!
The guru is like a field that has everything.
The precious human body is like a rare flower,
Difficult to find!
Practicing the Dharma is like finding the wish-fulfilling gem.
Death is like lightning,
Life is about as stable as a lamp in the wind.
It is easy to fall, like a falling star.
Being born and dying is like the rising and setting of the sun
    and moon!
When you die the mind comes out of your body,
Like a piece of hair from butter.

Your possessions are like the bees' stock of honey: it can be
    taken!
Friends and family are like those you meet in the market
    place.
Relatives are like companions crossing a bridge.
Karma is your shadow,
The eighteen hells are the Lord of Death's prison.
The realm of hungry ghosts is like the valley of the poor.
Animals have a hard time staying alive.
Like stars in the daylight,
The minds of animals are like the dreams of a deaf-mute.
The asuras are as angry as snakes.
The beautiful bodies of the gods
Are like borrowed jewels.
Even the human realm is like a city of the ghosts that feed on
    smell,
They are never satisfied.
All the six realms are full of suffering,
Nirvana is like being happy,
And not sharing it with anyone.
The Hinayana is like a young girl.
The Mahayana is as strong as a powerful man.
The Sutras are the seeds of all the yanas.
The Vajrayana is like the fruit.
So if you want to be liberated,
First you need a good Dharma friend,
You must be devoted and imitate this person.
The human body is difficult to obtain;
Even if you do obtain it,
It is subject to impermanence.
Now you should practice the Dharma.
Think about Samsara and its suffering,
Your own experiences and their meaninglessness.
Do not get attached.
Think how good it will be to be in the field of Dharma.
Wear the three ways of learning,[77]
Then leave the Hinayana path and enter the Vajrayana,
Like the Buddha's sons who have reached Nirvana,
Practice the Six Paramitas[78] and the Four Essentials of
    Partnership![79]

Then you must have a strong mind,
To carry all sentient beings to the Buddhafields.
That is why you must get started.
Remember all the people you have beaten,
And how bad your karma really is.
There is also the path of the yogi,
A superior path that can bring you to liberation in one
  lifetime.
You should attain the four initiations,[80]
And prepare yourselves for the Vajrayana.
Practicing the visualization and post-visualization stages.
When you know all of this well,
You will be unified with Vajradhara."[81]

All of those present promised to do as she had said. The
father and son, who had less bad karma, saw the guru as
Cakra Sambhava and Nangsa as Vajra Yogini. Nangsa's son,
who was fifteen by this time, was given the kingdom of
Rinang. Dragchen and Dragpa Samdrub left worldly life to
practice the Dharma. Sakya Gyaltsen promised that if they kept
their promise to follow the Dharma, they would not die before
they had reached the fruition of the practice.

Nangsa stayed in the mountains and not only flew, but left
her thighprint and footprint in many places as though stone
were butter. Dragpa Samdrub returned to Rinang to crown his
son and then returned with Ani Nyemo and stayed with
Nangsa and Sakya Gyaltsen. Lhau Darpo ruled virtuously
following the Dharma. Everyone in the kingdom followed the
Dharma carefully. Dragchen and Dragpa Samdrub, Nangsa
and Sakya Gyaltsen and all his disciples, had plenty to eat and
enough supplies to remain in retreat. They gathered merit for
future happiness and used all material things with compassion.

NOTES

1 Sadhana: a Tantric practice involving visualization of a deity and mantra repetition.

2 Tibetan Seng.lDeng: the acacia tree which predominates in the thick forests of Northeast India and Bengal.

3 Heavenly realm; Buddha Realms, "fields," "spheres," or "heavens" are other dimensions of existence where beings exist in much subtler forms than our bodies. Normal humans find it hard to believe that anything exists beyond what they can experience, but the more advanced beings can reach these dimensions and tell of them. The Christian heaven is probably a derivative of Christ's experiences in these dimensions.

4 Conch shells: an archetypal symbol of the feminine. The sound which emerges from the spiral symbolizes primordial pure space. The conch spiral also symbolizes the eternal mandala, without beginning or end.

5 Every deity has its essence or seed in a certain vibration or sound. From this sound comes the deity, it is therefore called the "bija" or seed syllable.

6 Central channel: a subtle energy channel running from the top of the head to four finger-widths below the navel, or straight to the perinium. The Central channel, Uma (dBu.ma), is transparent white with a reddish tinge. It is luminous and perfectly straight, and hollow like a reed.

7 Jewels: this refers to the three jewels (dKon.mChog gSum): (i) the Buddha, (ii) the Dharma (the Buddha's teachings), and (iii) the Sangha (the community of nuns and monks, or other fellow practitioners of the Dharma). The Dharma is sometimes confused

with dharma(s) which are elementary factors, moment points, separate, but connected to the process of perception.

8 The Lord of the Universe in Hinduism, similiar to the concept "God."

9 Avalokitesvara: the divine form of compassion, called Chenrezi in Tibetan, is the most popular deity in the Tibetan pantheon, whose mantra is "Om Mani Padme Hum Hri." One of his most common forms is a young white figure with four arms; two in front of his heart hold a jewel and one holds a crystal rosary and the other a flower.

10 Prajna Paramita (Tibetan Shes.rab Par.phyin). This is the "perfec-tion of profound cognition" which leads to liberation. According to the Kagyu and Nyingma sources I consulted, in the Vajrayana tradition it is really not quite accurate to translate Shes.rab as wisdom, because it is not a state like Ye.shes, which may be translated as wisdom, but rather a faculty, a tool, to reach Ye.shes. This tool, often described as a sword or a torch, rediscovers, or cuts away illusion to reveal, or illuminate, the primordial state which is always perfect but obscured by impurities and inaccurate view, like the sun hidden behind clouds. So prajna is a tool to discover wisdom, not wisdom itself. (Cf. Trungpa, *Meditation in Action*; sGampopa, *The Jewel Ornament of Liberation*; also Introduc-tion, above, pp. 21–3).

11 Tibetan beer made of fermented barley or rice or millet.

12 The five desirable qualities: desirable to see, touch, taste, smell and hear.

13 Nagas (Tibetan Klu): serpentine creatures of the underworld with powerful abilities to affect human beings through such things as skin disease, and they are also said to hold wisdom in their dark watery kingdoms. Nagarjuna was said to receive the Madyamika teachings (dBu.ma) from the Nagas. Both Indians and Tibetans lay great store by the powers of the Nagas. There is a whole series of stories of Nagas called the kLu.'bum ("One Hundred Thousand Nagas") which divides them into three groups: white, black and multicolored. The Nagas are closely connected to fertility because of their connection with water.

14 Arrow with five-colored silks (Tibetan: mDa'.Dar Tshon.sna lNga): this symbolic arrow has its roots way back in the Pre-Buddhist pastoral folk religion of Tibet. The arrow was adopted by the Buddhists and is used in the longlife initiation and other rituals. The five silk scarves which are tied to it are symbolic of the five elements which are activated by the arrow.

15 The Seven Jewels: (i) faith, (ii) discipline, (iii) generosity, (iv) hearing and understanding the Dharma, (v) feeling ashamed of

one's unwholesome actions, (vi) using the faculty of Prajna to know what to take up and what to reject, (vii) the development of the Prajna which comes from listening to, contemplating and practicing the Dharma.

16 This admonishment indicates the way a woman should ideally behave according to Tibetan cultural standards.

17 The five bad qualities of a woman: (i) thinking about other men after marriage, (ii) lack of generosity, (iii) wanting to do what cannot be done, (iv) wanting to do what should not be done, (v) killing her husband.

18 The eight good qualities of a woman: (i) friendliness, (ii) always having male children, (iii) doing what should be done, (iv) ability to do any kind of work, (v) not being jealous of other women, (vi) speaking meaningfully, (vii) having faith in the Dharma, free from wrong views, (viii) even if her husband is not there she does as he likes.

19 The deva is the patron deity, who is chosen by the guru according to the temperament of the disciple. The guru, deva and dakini (Sanskrit), (Tibetan: Lama, Yidam, Khadro) are added to the fundamental Buddhist refuge, the Buddha, Dharma and Sangha (the Three Jewels) in Tantric Buddhism. So in Tibet there were actually six Refuges. The most important was considered to be the guru, because without a teacher the other five could not be useful.

20 Dharmic action is action which is in accord with the teachings of the Buddha (the Dharma); and Samsaric action is action based on ignorance and leads to transmigration in the endless cycle of suffering.

21 A precious human body: only the human body has the capacity to reach enlightenment even though all beings have Buddha nature. What is required is a precious human body which is not simply a human body but a human body with certain qualifications which are the working basis for the attainment of Buddhahood.

22 Milarepa is Tibet's most famous "saint". After undergoing many trials and tribulations in his youth, he lived in caves, many of which were in Central and Southern Tibet. His life story has been translated by Evans-Wentz, *Tibet's Great Yogi Milarepa*, and C.C. Chang translated a book of his encounters with his students and his poetry in the book *The One Hundred Thousand Songs of Milarepa*.

23 Rechung was one of Milarepa's closest disciples. Both he and Gampopa were heart sons of Milarepa. From Gampopa comes the branch of the Kagyu lineage that became the Karma Kagyu, and from Rechung descended a line which was less monastic. Both have remained unbroken lineages which still continue into the present.

24 Pha.dam.pa Sangs.rgyas: an Indian teacher (d. 1117) from the south of India, who visited Tibet more than five times. He was the founder of the sDug.bsngal Zhi.byed school. When he first came to Tibet he was not accepted as a Buddhist, but was considered a Saivite holy man, but eventually he was revered by the Tibetans. He is also the inspiration behind the Chod school (gCod) which he taught to Machig, and her teacher Kyoton Sonam Lama (sKyo.ston bSod.nams bLa.ma), though it was Machig who founded the Chod school. Both Zhi.byed and Chod were based on the teachings of the Prajna Paramita (see n. 10, above). The Zhi.byed was eventually absorbed into other schools, whereas the Chod practiced by and popularized by Machig Lapdron was to maintain itself as an independent current though it was adopted and modified by other lineages to some extent. Both teachings emphasize the practice of non-clinging as a means to liberation (cf. prologue to biography of Machig Lapdron on Chod, and Tucci, *The Religions of Tibet*.) Machig Lapdron's encounter with Phadampa Sangye took place during his third trip from India to Tibet.

25 Chuba: a full-length Tibetan dress which folds over in the front and ties at the waist. The upper part is used as a pouch-like pocket.

26 It could be that Sakya Gyaltsen was Machig Lapdron's brother (see biography of Machig Lapdron, below, p. 168).

27 Marpa was the guru of Milarepa, known as Marpa the Translator, because he brought many teachings back from India and translated them into Tibetan. These teachings form the basis of the Kagyu (oral lineage). See Nalanda (trans.), *The Life of Marpa the Translator*.

28 rDzogspaChen.po'i sKor: teachings based on a nongradual approach based on working with the energy of the body, speech and mind. The principle of Dzog Chen is that there is a fundamental primordial state of absolute unconditioned being (Ngo.bo.nyid Kyi.sku) which is the ground; this state of being manifests itself as unadulterated intelligence (Rig.pa). The introduction to Rigpa, the development of awareness of the state of Rigpa, and the release from the clouds of nonawareness and confusion (Ma.rig.pa) constitutes the path. The fruit or result of the Dzog Chen path is remaining continually in the state of Rigpa. Although instantaneous understanding (gCig char) can occur, it only does so when a disciple is already spiritually mature, therefore Dzog Chen also has a series of purification practices and meditation practices working to prepare the individual for a continual state of Rigpa. The three main series of Dzog Chen teachings are: Sems.sde, kLong.sde, and Man.ngag.sde. Dzog

Chen practices are also associated with Terma (see Introduction, pp. 42–4 above). (For further information on Dzog Chen see Introduction, pp. 13–14 above.)

29 See Introduction, "Descent and Re-emergence," pp. 46–56 above.

30 One of the "siddhis" or magical powers of one who has reached the level of the sGyu.lus (illusory body) is to be able to project as many bodies in as many places as necessary in any form, in order to help others. These bodies are called phantom bodies but they appear as if they were real. See Tucci, *The Religions of Tibet*, pp. 108–9.

31 See Introduction, pp. 49–50 above.

32 Tantra: the text actually says "Dharma with Deities," which means the Buddhist teachings plus the Tantric teachings which use visualization of deities etc. See Introduction, pp. 10 and 29 above.

33 The accumulation of merit is a fundamental concept and is considered essential for results in meditation. It is based on the idea that one's actions (karma) create an imprint in the stream of one's being and if these actions have been positive (kindness, generosity, patience, etc.) then merit (Sod.nams) accumulates in this stream. These accumulations are brought from lifetime to lifetime and when enough merit has accumulated the spiritual path becomes possible. If one has not accumulated sufficient merit one will either not be attracted to spirituality, or will find oneself distracted and progress will be difficult. Tibetan teachers often begin a lecture by saying that people are there because of their accumulation of merit. (See sGampopa, *The Jewel Ornament of Liberation*.)

34 Divination (Tibetan: Mo). Tibetans make many of their decisions on the basis of divination. They employ many different methods: using their malas (rosaries), a mirror, dice, complex knots, skipping stones, etc. Sometimes it is interpreted by using a book similar to the *I Ching*, and sometimes through numerological analysis.

35 The Bardo is the name generally used for the time between death and rebirth, though "bardo" actually just means "between." There is an elaborate terma on the "bardo" between death and rebirth, giving instructions on reaching liberation during this time, called the Bardo Thodal, or *The Tibetan Book of the Dead*. (See translations by Evans-Wentz and a more recent translation by Freemantle and Trungpa.) In Tibetan teachings there is a similar idea of the weighing of one's good and bad deeds to that of Christianity. However, in the Tibetan teachings the decision determines only one's next rebirth rather than a judgment for eternity. After the

judgment one is sent to one of the six realms. There are three higher realms (gods, humans and jealous gods (asuras)) and three lower realms (animals, hell and hungry ghosts). The longest lifetimes are those in the realm of the gods and in the hell realm. There are eighteen hell realms which include various kinds of tortures divided between the freezing hells and the boiling hells. Though these realms may be interpreted as psychological states experienced by humans (see *Cutting Through Spiritual Materialism*, Trungpa) the average Tibetan interprets them very literally (see sGampopa, *The Jewel Ornament of Liberation*).

36 Although up until this point Nangsa has practiced the Dharma inwardly, this encounter gives her the strength to integrate her inner values with her external situation.

37 Someone who had died and been resurrected after experiencing the after-death world (Bardo).

38 Posture with seven aspects, the classic meditation posture: the legs in the lotus posture, spine straight as a spear, hands palms up, one hand over the other (right above for men, left for women) with thumbs joined, held beneath the navel with the shoulders back and even, chin slightly tucked in, eyes open but relaxed, gazing straight ahead from the tip of the nose, tongue and lips relaxed, tongue may curl back to touch the palate.

39 For description of all the Buddha families see Introduction, pp. 27–8 above.

40 Damaru: a small ritual drum similar to the Chod damaru, but smaller. (See prologue to Machig Lapdron, p. 148 below.)

41 The Buddha family dakini is sometimes blue and the Vajra family dakini is sometimes white depending on the Tantra.

42 Rolang (ro.langs): if a corpse is revived after death it is either "delog" or "rolang." The "delog" is a person who is resurrected after a visit to the netherworld. A "rolang" is the possession of a corpse by a malevolent spirit. The "rolang" are much feared by the Tibetans and they love to tell stories about terrifying encounters with "rolang," whereas the "delog" are looked upon as great religious teachers.

43 One of the things which Tibetan lamas always emphasize in their teachings is that we do not know when we will die and should therefore act in a way which is beneficial to ourselves and others now. One cannot live one's life as though it were a rehearsal for the real performance. We should be aware that we could die at any moment and not procrastinate in practicing the Dharma and applying in our lives what we have understood intellectually.

44 Mani wheel: a prayer wheel, most commonly filled with the

mantra OM MANI PADME HUM. A cylinder filled with a roll of mantras, which is spun round by a weight, to gain merit.

45 Just removing oneself from the world is not spiritually beneficial, unless one does it with motivation to help others. Otherwise it could become a source of pride or repression. Even if one were to stay a hundred years in retreat, without compassion, it would be the same as animals who live all their lives in caves, there would be no spiritual benefit.

46 See Introduction, p. 35 above (Kayas).

47 According to Tibetan medicine, one of the reasons for illness is an imbalance of the elements of earth, air, water and fire. For further explanation see *On Birth and Life: A Treatise on Tibetan Medicine*, by Namkhai Norbu, pp. 18 and 36.

48 Magic powers are "the ordinary siddhis": these are the powers that come as signs of progress in meditation practice. Although they are extraordinary from the point of view of the world, they are called ordinary to make it clear that these powers are not the real point of doing the practice. The ordinary siddhis are by-products of the practice; the real point is to go beyond attachment and return to the primordially pure state of wisdom. The ordinary siddhis include the power to pass through walls, to transform stones into gold, to walk on water without sinking, to enter fire without getting burned, to melt snow with one's body heat in extreme cold, to travel to a far distant cosmos in a few seconds, to fly in the sky and walk through rocks and mountains, extraordinary abilities to read minds and know the future, and the development of all the senses far beyond their ordinary capacities. One can also radiate beams of light from the body and stand in sunlight without casting a shadow, make one's body vanish and other so-called miracles.

49 The Tibetans use a string of 108 beads, like a rosary, in order to count the mantras they have done. The mala (Sanskrit), Tring.wa ('Phreng.ba) (Tibetan), may be made of bodhi seed, coral, wood, crystal, etc., and for practices involving wrathful deities, human skull malas can be used.

50 When a Tantric practitioner reaches a certain point, it is customary to wear on the left hand a ring with a bell on it symbolizing the feminine "Prajna," and on the right hand a ring with a Vajra, symbolizing the masculine "Skillful Means." This is a symbol of the integration of the external and internal energies of the masculine and feminine.

51 Literally a mandala is something with a center and a fringe, and three-dimensional energy pattern with a center and concentric circles or squares. It is used very often in Tantric practice with a

deity at the center surrounded by retinues, a palace and gates with protectors outside. The function is the transformation of the meditator into the energies of the deities by means of intensive visualization of this mandala and repetition of the corresponding mantra (mystic formula). There are various levels of understanding the mandala beyond these formal representations, including seeing all the phenomenal world as a mandala.

52 The wearing of an apron symbolizes that a woman is married. Tibetan women wear colorful striped aprons all the time, not just for cooking.

53 Because Tibet was at such a high altitude, rather than giving garlands of flowers, they gave long, thin white scarves called "kata" which were ceremoniously presented at appropriate occasions. They symbolize the offering of pure mind.

54 Mount Kailash (Tibetan: Tise Snow Mountain) is situated in the Trans-Himalayan Range and is regarded as the most sacred of all pilgrimage places by Hindus and Buddhists alike. "Whether Kailash is spoken of as 'throne of the gods' and the 'Abode of Siva and Paravati', or as the 'Mandala of Dhyani-Buddhas and Bodhisattvas', or as 'Meru', the spiritual and phenomenal center of the world, the fact which is expressed in the symbolic languages of different traditions, is the experience of a higher reality, which is conveyed through a strange combination of natural and spiritual phenomena, which even to those who are unaffected by religious beliefs, cannot escape. Like a gigantic temple rising in regular tiers of horizontal ledges and in perfect symmetry, Kailash marks the centre of the 'Roof of the World', the heart of the biggest temple, the seat of cosmic powers, the axis which connects the earth with the universe, the super-antenna for the inflow and outflow of the spiritual energies of our planet." (Lama Anagarika Govinda "Pilgrims and Monasteries in the Himalyas," *Crystal Mirror*, IV, pp. 245–6.)

55 A temple banner which resembles a small parasol called a rGyal.mtshan, it symbolizes the protective aspect of the Buddha, Dharma and Sangha.

56 Through the control of the prana and the mind, bliss emerges; it is mixed with realization of Sunyata (emptiness) and this union produces luminosity.

57 The spinning of a thread is used as an example of how to work with the mind in meditation. If the wool is held too loose, it becomes lumpy and thick, but if it is held too tight, it breaks, so it must be held with full attention neither too loose nor too tight.

58 Bodhicitta (Tibetan: Byang.chub Sems.bskyed): this is the motivation to achieve enlightenment for the benefit of all sentient beings.

This is the thought or attitude of a Bodhisattva. It is a concept very much emphasized by Tibetan lamas and distinguishes the Mahayana (Great Vehicle) from the Hinayana (Lesser Vehicle). When a practitioner progresses beyond selfish motivation toward practice of Buddhism the Bodhisattva vow is taken, and should be renewed every day.

59 The two veils are the two principal obstructions keeping one in Samsara. When the two veils are removed the innate wisdom of the individual shines through and it is the removal of these veils which constitutes the path. They are: incorrect view of how things are (i.e. seeing everything through the veil of dualism and "ego") and, secondly, the instability of emotions, which are basically passion, aversion and bewilderment, though these three multiply into hundreds of emotional states.

60 This actually means that if one experiences things as they really are without entering into judgment of good and bad, happy or sad, etc., they will be given "equal value" and therefore will be experienced without anxiety. It does not mean that everything tastes the same, but rather that all tastes and experiences are experienced without an overlay of judgment.

61 It is said that the Buddha taught 84,000 different methods to suit the individual needs of his students. This includes being able to communicate with animals, spirits and gods, etc.

62 This is the traditional way of offering liquids. Here she was probably making offerings to the Three Jewels, the Buddha, the Dharma and the Sangha.

63 Here is the image of the hook I described in the Introduction, p. 33 above.

64 Cutting off the hair is done when one renounces the world. Even if monastic vows are not taken, often people going into retreat shave their heads to avoid the time it takes to take care of one's hair and symbolizing the renunciation of vanity. Even when one takes refuge the lama cuts off a strand of hair symbolizing renunciation and creating a bond with the disciple. Hair cutting also symbolizes a new spiritual orientation.

65 Tsari: the name of a valley between Assam and Tibet. It is a much-frequented pilgrimage place where a special pilgrimage culminates every twelve years.

66 In Tibet they use a crumbly kind of light brown wax for sealing packages, etc., which looks a bit like brown sugar.

67 Kye Rim (bsKyed.Rim; Sanskrit Utpatti Krama) and Dzog Rim (rDzogs.Rim; Sanskrit Sampanna Krama) are the two aspects of a Tantric practice. The first, Kye Rim is "the Arising Stage," the process of evoking the deity from nothingness, sounding the seed

syllable of the deity and visualizing the deity in any number of ways, such as as oneself, in front of oneself, in the palm of the hand, in the vase, etc. Then wisdom is invoked from all quarters of the universe and the deity is filled with this wisdom; this is the joining of the Jnanasattva (wisdom being) with the Samayasattva (being evolved by a vow), then the mantra is repeated and at the end the deity is absorbed back into the seed syllable and into space. At this point the Dzog Rim phase, the "Stage of Perfection," begins. This is a "formless" practice which follows the "form" of the Kye Rim and is a result of it. It is a state of openness, a gap of a particular kind created by the changes in the identity of the body, speech and mind undergone during the arising stage. At this point one is not "doing" anything but is experiencing the afterglow of the Kye Rim. This experience of potentiated emptiness, or luminous emptiness, is then brought into one's daily life and the Tantric practice is complete. As the Tantras become more advanced the Dzog Rim phase predominates over the Kye Rim phase.

68 In the Vajra Yogini practice a mirror covered with the red powder called "tsendura" sindur is used as a mandala. The mantra is inscribed through the powder around the edge of the round mirror, and in the center a crossed triangle, like the star of David, is inscribed.

69 Tantras and Sutras: Tantras contain the practices involving the uses of visualization, mantra recitation, yoga and divinities. There were two main divisions of Tantras: those which belong to the rNying.ma school, and those which were introduced after the second diffusion which could be validated through Sanskrit originals, the "new Tantras," (rGyud.sar.ma). The Sutras form the philosophical and ethical framework for the Tantra. The two main Sutric schools in Tibet were the Madyamika, propagated by Nagarjuna, emphasizing "the Middle Way" – relativism, and emptiness – and the Yogacara "mind only" school, propagated by Asanga. The Sutras include the exoteric forms of Buddhism while the Tantras contain the esoteric.

70 A cinch of heavy fabric is used to support the back during long hours of meditation, in order to keep the back straight and the legs in a certain position, creating a good flow of energy in the body.

71 Rahu: the god of the night who eats the sun.

72 The king of wealth is called "Norzang."

73 When a woman is married the red tsendura powder is put in her hair parting.

74 Cakra Sambhava ('Khor.lo bDem.mChog) is a dark-blue wrathful male figure, standing, embraced by the female form of Vajra

Varahi (rDo.rje Phag.mo). Cakra Sambhava has.traditionally been associated with the Mother Tantras and the sixty-four aspects have to do with the sixty-four spokes of the navel chakra.

75 The guru and consort: this seems to imply that Nangsa practiced sexual yoga with Sakya Gyaltsen.

76 The four methods or powers which make a confession effective: (i) a feeling of deep and genuine regret and contriteness for what one has done and confessing it in front of a Buddha or the Sangha; (ii) the power of acting in a positive way as an antidote to negative tendencies, such as recitation of Sutras, Mantras, setting up a Buddha statue, good deeds, etc.; (iii) desisting from evil actions in a disciplined way, like diverting the course of a terrible river, changing for the good and avoiding past patterns of negativity; (iv) the method of relying on the Buddha, the Dharma and the Sangha and always cultivating the thought of enlightenment for the benefit of sentient beings (Bodhicitta). See sGampopa, *The Jewel Ornament of Liberation*.

77 Three ways of learning: Tsultrim (Tshul.khrims) discipline or morality, Sherab (Shes.rab) profound cognition, Tingnezin (Tinge.nge.'dzin meditation.

78 Six Paramitas: generosity, discipline, patience, industriousness, meditation and prajna.

79 bsDu.ba Shi: the Four Essentials of Partnership: (i) mKho.ba sByin.pa: generosity, (ii) sNyen.par Smra.ba: polite language, (iii) 'Jig.rThen Don mTun.pa: having a common worldly interest or project, (iv) gDul.ba'i Don la sPyod.pa: taking care of disciples.

80 Four Initiations or Empowerments: The Tibetan word Wong (dBang) means to empower or potentiate, while the Sanskrit equivalent, Abhisekha, literally means to anoint. In this tradition in order to practice a Tantra it is necessary to have the "wong" and the "lung" of the Tantra. This means personal contact and transmission through body, voice and mind from the guru, or in some cases a direct transmission from the deity to the practitioner (as in Machig's case, p. 163 below). The empowerment transmits a seed experience which will be ripened by doing the practice. The "lung" is the hearing of the words, the reading of the texts. The Tri (Khrid) is the explanation of how to do the practice. Without the "Wong," "Lung" and "Tri" there could be no results from the practice; simply reading a Tantra will not suffice. There is a great emphasis on lineage (rGyud) in Tibetan Esoteric Buddhism, and the teachings must pass from one person to another, like links in a chain, of mother's milk to a baby. Artificial milk is not possible; without fresh, personal contact, the teaching dies.

The true nature of the empowerment is something which occurs at a nonverbal level between the guru and disciple. During a formal ceremony the disciple is shown and touched by various symbolic objects, such as a crystal, a knife or a bell, and if the disciple is ready and tuned, in a moment the transmission takes place, a kind of flash of experiential insight which is beyond intellect and words. The more advanced the empowerment /or initiation, the fewer externals and rituals accompany the empowerment. On the most direct level a transmission takes place from mind to mind, and may occur during an everyday situation. But in whatever way it happens this transmission must take place in order that the empowerment may be effective.

The four empowerments: (i) The vase empowerment is for purification of the body. Water is poured on the head imitating the Eastern method of bathing. The initiation is for cleansing and transforming the body into a suitable vessel to receive knowledge. (ii) The secret mystery initiation helps to activate illuminated communication and to reach a level of a superior field of energy. It is the identity of oneself with the state of being of the Buddha. (iii) The third initiation has to do with breaking loose the blocked forms in the thinking process and entering a level of unfixated being. At this level sometimes sexual practices are introduced to aid the circulation of the prana and further open awareness. (iv) The fourth initiation goes beyond definition. It is the simultaneous realization of all the above.

81 Vajradhara: the iconographic depiction of primordial wisdom. He is dark-blue like the autumn sky and youthful and beautiful wearing all the Sambogakaya ornaments and silky luminous rainbow-like clothes.

2
MACHIG
LAPDRON

Machig Lapdron

PROLOGUE

Machig Lapdron is one of the most renowned and beloved of Tibetan women mystics. She is said to be an incarnation of Yeshe Tsogyel, the eighth-century consort of Guru Padma Sambhava who brought Tantric Buddhism to Tibet. There are many biographies of Machig, but this is the longest and most complete one that I have seen.

In the "Life of Yeshe Tsogyel,"[1] Padma Sambhava predicted that Yeshe Tsogyel would be reborn as Machig Lapdron; her consort, Atsara Sale, would become Topabhadra, Machig's husband; her assistant and Padma Sambhava's secondary consort, Tashi Khyidren, would be reborn as Machig's only daughter, and so on. All of the important figures in Tsogyel's life were to be reborn in the life of Machig Lapdron, including Padma Sambhava himself, who would become Phadampa Sangye.

Naturally there is no way to prove these connections scientifically, and for a Westerner it may seem strange that family trees are cited through reincarnation lineages rather than blood lines, but many Tibetan hagiographies (sacred biographies) commence with a history of the incarnations going back hundreds of years. Even the biography of Machig begins rather disconcertingly with the biography of a man. It turns out that this man is in fact the preceding incarnation of Machig. The extraordinary switchover into the body of a girl in Tibet from a yogi in India, through the intercession of dakinis, is an exceptionally supernatural occurrence. It is not that he dies, but rather that his consciousness is transferred to

[143]

Tibet. At the end of the story we return to his body, which has remained unchanged for fifty or more years, in a cave in Southern India. In order to understand this kind of story we must surrender our Western frame of reference, which limits our ideas of what is possible and what is impossible, and understand that, at higher levels of spiritual development, the material world can be manipulated by the consciousness, and many things become possible. In this story we find people flying through the air, cremated bodies producing sculptured forms, and various other psychic phenomena. Having witnessed some of these phenomena myself, I ask the readers to put aside their ideas of the limits of the mind and body, and open themselves to further possibilities.

In Tibet and India yogis developed the mind and body while we were concentrating on scientific discoveries. We achieved our own miracles with the development of television, telephones, airplanes and so on, which two hundred years ago would have seemed equally fantastic and miraculous. Meanwhile the Tibetans were working in the laboratory of the mind, developing themselves in the silent recesses of mountain retreats and caves. Considering the time and concentration that went into their research and training, the "miraculous" phenomena which have resulted are not so very strange.

Machig Lapdron was an integral part of the great renaissance of Buddhism which occurred in the eleventh century in Tibet. During this time there was a great deal of exchange between Tibet and the scholarly and yogic schools of India, which later ceased as Buddhism died out in India, shortly after Machig's time. There were many religious pilgrims traveling around Tibet and to India and Nepal. This prompted cultural and spiritual developments, and it must have been a very exciting time to have lived in Tibet.

In order to give an idea of what the Mahamudra Chod is, I will start with a short explanation of this practice, which is the primary teaching that Machig Lapdron is famous for.

The philosophical basis for the Chod is the Prajna Paramita Sutra. Machig was thoroughly immersed in this teaching from childhood, because she became a professional reader at an early age, and the most popular text to be read was this Sutra.

Professional readers were people who could read very quickly. They were sent out to the homes of lay devotees to read through a text a certain number of times. The logic behind this was twofold: first, the hearing of a text would be beneficial to the householders immersed in worldly preoccupations, and secondly, the recitation of such a text would cause the accumulation of merit. Because the Buddhists believe that every act has a certain result, a positive act causes the accumulation of positive results, and therefore a kind of stockpiling of good karma could be accumulated by having sacred texts read aloud. What was considered important was the number of times something was read, rather than the understanding of the meaning; therefore the faster the reader was, the better. In this way the patron could accumulate more merit in less time and have to spend less on maintenance and gifts for the reader. Machig, from a very young age, was an extraordinarily fast reader, and so she was highly valued as a professional reader. She probably repaid her teacher by being his reader.

It was not until she made contact with Lama Sonam Drapa, who questioned her understanding and told her to reread her texts, that she gained real insight into the teaching. This, combined with her contact with Phadampa Sangye, master of the School of Pacifying Suffering (sDug.bsngal Zhi.byed), led her to a real understanding of the teachings – intuitive as well as intellectual.

The Prajna Paramita is a very profound philosophical doctrine and I will just outline the main ideas in it, in order to clarify the Chod. First we start off with the confused egocentric state of mind. This state of mind causes us to suffer, and so, to alleviate the suffering, we start to practice meditation. What happens in meditation is that the speedy mind begins to slow down and things begin to settle, like the mud sinking to the bottom of a glass of water when it is left alone. When this settling has occurred a kind of clear understanding of the way things work in the mind takes place. This understanding is Prajna, profound cognition. Then, according to Buddhist doctrine, through the use of this Prajna, we begin to see that, in fact, although we think that we have a separate and unique essence, or self, which we call the "ego," when we look closely, we are a composite of form, sense-perceptions, consciousness, etc., and are merely a sum of these parts. This realization is the understanding of Sunyata, usually translated as emptiness, or voidness. It means there is no self-essence, that we are "void of a self." If we are void of a self, there is no reason to be egocentric, since the whole notion of a separate ego is false. Therefore we can afford to be compassionate, and need not continually defend ourselves or force our desires onto others.

In order to reinforce and develop the understanding of egolessness and in order to develop compassion for all sentient beings, Machig developed the Chod practice. In this practice, after various preliminaries, the practitioner performs the offering of the body – this is the essence of the Chod practice. "gCod" literally means "to cut," referring to cutting attachment to the body and ego. First the practitioner visualizes the consciousness leaving the body, through the top of the head, and transforming itself into a wrathful dakini. This wrathful dakini then takes her crescent-shaped hooked knife and cuts off the top of the head of the body of the practitioner. This skull cup is then placed on a tripod of three skulls, over a flame. The rest of the body is chopped up and placed into the skull, which is vastly expanded. Then the whole cadaver is transformed from blood and entrails into nectar, which is then fed to every conceivable kind of being, satisfying every kind of desire these beings might have. After all beings have taken their fill and been satisfied, the practitioner reminds himself or herself that the offerer, the offering process, and those who have been offered to, are all "empty," and seeks to remain in the state of that understanding. The ritual ends with further teachings on the true nature of reality, and some ending prayers, for the eventual enlightenment of all beings.

Through this process, four demons are overcome. These are demons connected to the ego. It was when she understood the true nature of demons, as functions of the ego, having reread the Prajna Paramita texts, that she began to formulate the Chod. Before going on to explain the ritual instruments and so on, I would like to discuss these four demons. This explanation is based on oral explanation given by Namkhai Norbu Rinpoche.

The first demon is called "the Demon that Blocks the Senses." When we think of a demon, we generally think of an external spirit which attacks us, but Machig realized that the true nature of demons is the internal functioning of the ego. This particular demon manifests when we see or experience something with the sense, and the senses get blocked and we get fixated on the object. For example, when we see a beautiful woman or man, as soon as we see this person the perception is blocked by the desire to possess that person. The process of perception stops, and we try to meet that person, and so on. So this is one process that must be overcome by meditation. If we are in a state of true meditation, perception occurs without this fixation or attachment to the objects perceived.

The second demon is "the Demon which Cannot be Controlled." This is the thought-process which just runs on and on. The thought-process takes over, the mind wanders from one thing to another, and our awareness is completely lost in distraction.

The third demon is "the Demon of Pleasure." When we experience something pleasurable, like something delicious to eat, we become attached to it which means we want to get more, and avoid anything which stands between us and the object of pleasure. This does not mean that pleasure is in itself demonic, but rather that our attachment to it becomes a hindrance to remaining in a state of clarity. For example, a meditator might have an auspicious dream, which is a sign of progress, but then "the demon of pleasure" comes into play and he gets very attached to the dream. Or someone else might have a period when everything goes well, he feels good physically, and so he tries to continue this good period endlessly, which always ends in changing and therefore disappointing us.

The fourth demon is "the Demon of the Ego." The ego is that with which we condition our world. It rests on the principle of "self" and "other" which causes a blockage in awareness and a lot of suffering for oneself and others.

Fundamentally, all four demons are thought-processes which block a state of clear, unattached awareness, and they all grow out of the process of ego-fixation, and lack of Prajna, with the consequent misunderstanding of emptiness. The

Chod practice seeks to do away with these demons

The Chod practice employs four methods to make sound: the human voice, the drum, the bell and the human thighbone trumpet. The drum is the size of the circle created when the hand is placed on the hip; it is similar to the drum used by Siberian shamans and by the Bon priests in the native Tibetan religion. It is double-faced, symbolizing the masculine and the feminine, with two little balls hanging from strings on either side. When the drum is played, these little balls hit opposite sides of the drum, symbolizing the inseparability of absolute and relative truth. The drum makes a deep rhythmic march-like beat, and is accompanied by a bell, the symbol of the primordial space of the feminine, which is held in the left hand. At the point when the transformed flesh of the practitioner is offered to the demons, the thighbone trumpet, which is said to summon the demons, is sounded, making an eerie whining sound. The whole practice is sung, the tunes varying according to the tradition the practitioner has learned trom. Each melody has its own history, developed by Chod practitioners (called Chodpa) after many years of practice. The overall effect of these sounds combines to make a deeply sonorous, moving chant, with a beautiful melody. The use of sound is an integral part of the Chod practice, creating a vibration within the body which would not be there if the practice were merely recited silently.

The Chod was traditionally practiced in frightening places such as under lone trees (which were thought to be inhabited by demons), and in cemeteries (as we see, for example, in the biography of A-Yu Khadro). The direct encounter with one's fears and the transcending of them through the understanding of the true nature of demons is the essential point of the Chod practice. Tibetans are so afraid of demons that many are afraid of the Chod practice, and it is considered very secret. I once met a nun who, in her youth, had gone into a cave to practice the Chod. She saw something that made her so afraid that she had to do nine years of Amitabha practice (the peaceful Buddha of the Western Paradise) to recover, and when I met her she was very old and was still a bit mad.

The training for the Chod took place in colleges founded specifically for this study. It took at least five years. Towards the end of the training the students would be sent out in groups and finally alone. Chodpas were always called in when there were epidemics of infectious diseases, such as cholera. They took care of the corpses, chopping up the bones and conducting the funeral ceremony, apparently impervious to infection. Sometimes Chodpas would be called in for exorcisms.

Chod practitioners wore cast-off clothes, would eat the food of beggars, and lived in places most people disdained to go to. All of this is based on the example of Machig Lapdron, who lived in this way, paying no heed to conventional limitations of dress and behaviour. Chod practitioners would travel alone or in groups, practicing the Chod in appropriate places along the way. A-Yu Khadro followed the teachings of Machig Lapdron and lived the life of a Chod-pa for many years.

This biography is from the *Pungpo Zankur Gyi Namshe Chodkyi Don Sal*.

The story is as it was told to her disciples by Machig at their request. It was compiled by Jamgon Kongtrul Lodro Ta Ye, at the request of Choje Kunga Jamyang in the nineteenth century. Although it claims to be written by Machig herself, it is probably a composite of several biographies which Jamgon Kongtrul found in his extensive research of ancient texts.

Note

1 See Keith Dowman, *Sky Dancer*, pp. 86–7.

THE BIOGRAPHY OF MACHIG LAPDRON (1055–1145)

PART 1

Obeisance to the non-human mother,[1] the Wisdom Dakini![2] If you follow the teachings of Machig your body is offered to others. Other practices involve protecting the body, but Machig's instructions call for offering it. This biography was written by Machig herself, so there are no mistakes. Machig is the Wisdom Dakini, the heart-mind Mother of the Buddhas of the Three Times, dakini of the Vajra family.[3]

Machig's former life as Pandit Monlam Drub

For the benefit of sentient beings a son was born to the Indian king Palwang Chug. The child was named Monlam Drub (sMon.lam Grub). No one had to teach him reading and writing. By the age of five, if he just glanced at a book once, he knew it by heart. Everyone said that he must be an emanation of the Buddha.

From ten until fifteen he studied with Pandit Pitibhadra, who gave him the vows of a novice monk.[4] He was given the name Dondrub Zangpo[5] at the time of his ordination. He studied grammar, logic, the Prajna Paramita,[6] the Vinaya[7] and the Abhidharma.[8] His teacher found him to be an exceptional student and taught him the Four Tantras.[9] He became equal to his teacher in these Tantras.

Then Pitibhadra said to him: "I can no longer be your teacher. You have gone beyond me. Now you must go to Chang Chog Zangling: there you will find Guru Ratna, a great siddha who has the capacity to manifest the mandala of Cakra Sambhava. He is learned and adorned with limitless accomplishments. He will be able to guide you to accomplishment on the secret path of mantra and cut you free from doubts. Then you will be able to help sentient beings."

He went to Guru Ratna, who noticed his capacity to eventually help others. Then Guru Ratna manifested the mandala of the sixty-four aspects of Cakra Sambhava[10] in front of him and gave the four perfect empowerments.[11] After this, due to the powers he had gained, Monlam Drub was able to go to all the Buddha realms without obstacles. He stayed with Guru Ratna for three years, clearing up his doubts concerning Tantras and Sutras. He was especially accomplished in the visualization and perfection post-visualization stages.[12]

Then Guru Ratna said: "Go to Dorje Den,[13] and defeat the non-Buddhists there. You are the only one with the capacity to defeat them."

So he went to Dorje Den and defeated the non-Buddhists (in debate). As a result, 100,000 non-Buddhists became Buddhists. He stayed there for four years. Then Arya Tara advised him to go to Tibet in order to help the Tibetans. She asked him to hurry to complete his meditation, so that he would be ready to convert the Tibetans.

He had started to move north on a pilgrimage and one night he slept in a cemetery.[14] The dakini of the cemetery was disturbed by his presence.

She came to him in his sleep and said: "Don't you have anywhere else to sleep? Why do you have to sleep in my cemetery?"

She began to perform various miracles to disturb him, but he remained in an undisturbed state of meditation. The dakini was impressed and offered him her heart and promised to do whatever Monlam Drub told her to do.

At the first blue light of dawn fifteen goddesses, emanations of Damema,[15] appeared and said: "Yogi, you must go to Potari cave in south India and then go to Tibet." Having said this, they vanished into a rainbow.

He thought, "Now, I am still young enough to meditate and become accomplished in one practice, but with what method can I convert the Tibetans?"

While it was still quite dark the great female emanation Mahamaya and fifteen goddesses came and advised him: "Go to Potari and do the practice of the five black semi-wrathful Mahamaya dakinis. You must go quickly to Tibet to convert beings there. So now practice very diligently." Saying this, they vanished into a rainbow.

When it was light, the cemetery dakini said: "I will take you to Potari. We will go by means of fast walking."[16]

They arrived quickly at the cave and Monlam Drub began to do the practice of the five Mahamaya Goddesses. In fourteen days he had obtained the ordinary siddhis.[17] After a month he met the five goddesses face to face, because of his mind's accomplishment. They gave him the empowerment of the mandala of secret wisdom eye and encouraged him to go to subdue the Tibetans. Then they vanished into light and the light vanished into the body of Monlam Drub.

After another month Arya Tara appeared and instructed him to go to Tibet and then dissolved into his heart. On the third day of the waxing moon the Guardian of Long Life gave him much advice and blessings. On the eighth day Avalokitesvara, the deity of compassion, appeared and gave him advice for the future and blessing. On the tenth, the Padma Dakini[18] appeared with a retinue of dakinis and questioned him about his understanding of the Dharma, and there was nothing he did not know. Then she opened the mandala of the union of the Horse-Headed One and the Pig-Headed One.[19] From the mandala he received instructions to go to Tibet. All of the dakinis of the mandala told him to go to Tibet.

From the tenth to the fourteenth, all the dakinis appeared and told him to go to Tibet soon. On the fifteenth[20] at the break of day, a dark-blue wrathful dakini wearing bone ornaments and holding a Khatvanga staff[21] and a hooked knife[22] appeared and said wrathfully: "Now you must promise to go to Tibet. I shall kill you, and your consciousness will enter me!"

So saying, she raised her knife to kill Monlam Drub and

feigning to do so his consciousness entered her and in this way he went to Tibet without obstacles. He was twenty at this time, and his body was potentiated so that it would not decay, in order that it would eventually benefit others.

Conception and birth

In the area called Labchi Eli.Gangwar the consciousness entered the womb of the mother on the fifteenth day of the fifth month of the Horse Year. The mother and father were from this area from the town of Tso Mer, "Lake of Mer." Machig's father was the local nobleman and head of the town, and was called Chokyi Dawa, "Moon of Dharma." Her mother's name was Bum Cham, "Great Noblewoman." Both parents were kind and came from rich families. They practiced the Dharma and encouraged others to do the same. They had faith in the Jewels and served the Sangha. The nobleman and his wife were always thinking about the Three Jewels and encouraged others to see things from the point of view of the Dharma. They were like Bodhisattvas for the five hundred families under them.

When the consciousness entered the womb of the mother on the fifteenth day she dreamt that four white dakinis carrying four white vases poured water on her head and afterwards she felt purified. Then seven dakinis, red, yellow, green, etc., were around her making offerings, saying "Honor the mother, stay well our mother to be."

After that a wrathful dark-blue dakini wearing bone ornaments and carrying a hooked knife, and a retinue of four blue dakinis carrying hooked knives and skull cups,[23] surrounded her, in front of her, behind her, and to her left and right. All five were in the sky in front of Bum Cham. The central dakini was a forearm's length higher than the rest.

She raised her hooked knife and said to the mother: "Now I will take out this ignorant heart."

She took her knife and plunged it into the mother's heart,[24] took out the heart and put it into the skull cup of the dakini in front of her, and they all ate it. Then the central dakini took a conch which spiraled to the right[25] and blew it. The sound

[153]

resounded all over the world. In the middle of the conch was a luminous white "A".[26]

She said: "Now I will replace your heart with this white conch shell."

Then, as she put it into Bum Cham's body, Bum Cham experienced the five colored lights coming from the heart of the dakini and dissolving into the top of her head. Light also came from the four dakinis and dissolved into her body. Then the four retinue dakinis dissolved into light and then into the dark-blue central dakini, who seemed to dissolve into the sky, which was full of light.

During these dreams the mother felt no fear, and in fact she felt no disturbance at all, but rather she felt a blissful sensation. When her heart was taken out she felt better than before. She felt no pain and felt joyful. Her body and mind were blissful. Her consciousness was clear.

Even after she woke up she felt great bliss. The next day at sunrise a girl called Aman, "Beneficial 'A'," from nearby, came.

She said: "I have a very good dream that I am bringing you."

The mother took her into the big temple, and as they sat there the girl said: "I have a nice dream to tell you. Your noble family has been improving for generations, and now again they will have fortune as great as the sky. They have accumulated a great deal of merit and are profound people."

The mother thought: "I also had an unusual dream last night and even now I feel blissful and happy. I wonder what dream this girl has had?"

She told the servant to prepare something nice to eat and asked Aman to tell her the dream.

The girl began, saying: "Last night, in the early morning hours, I dreamt that this house was three times bigger than it really is and it had big golden crescents on the roof, where three-layered umbrellas were spinning. They were three times larger than the normal ones. Each of the four sides of the house had a silver mirror hanging from it, as big and round as the moon; they were blowing in the wind and the light reflecting from them was illuminating the countryside. Then out of the sides of the house came four young girls saying they were dakinis. They were blowing white conch shells so loud it seemed the sound would be heard on all four continents.[27] On each of the four corners were prayer flags[28] blowing each in their own direction. Under the eaves were many butter lamps burning brilliantly, illuminating everything. A red light was shining on the house from the sky in front. I was on the high part of the roof and I asked one of the dakinis what she was doing there. She said that they were preparing the house of the mother. From inside the house temple came the sounds of musical instruments. I wondered who they were calling the mother. When I thought: 'Can I enter?' I had the feeling of entering and then I woke up. Afterwards I have many other good dreams."

The mother already had a daughter of sixteen named Bumme. Bumme said: "Last night I also saw a white light in the sky and it entered into my mother illuminating the whole house. Then a girl of eight, carrying a Vajra, appeared before me and said: 'Are you well, my sister?' I asked her where she came from, and she told me it was in India. Then I asked her who she was and she said: 'I am Tara, don't you recognize me?' I wondered if this was the truth, and then I tried to catch her but she ran into mother's lap and then I woke up."

After this there were many good signs. The mother, who was forty-eight at this time, had no wrinkles and began to look younger after the conception. Everyone was saying that she must be doing some good Dharma practice and receiving blessings and this was making her look young. She looked as young as Bumme. Bum Cham had many wonderful dreams and felt very light and blissful. At night she could see as though the countryside were illuminated, as though it were daytime. She could see into people's minds and understood their suffering. Everyone thought her dream must have a very special meaning.

On the twenty-fifth day of the Rabbit Month (the second month of the Sheep Year) Bum Cham began to hear the sound of A and HA RI NI SA[29] coming from her womb. On the third day of the Dragon Month of the Year of the Sheep she heard a voice from her womb.

The voice said: "Mother, prepare some new white cotton clothes. Keep them purified with incense and perfumed with myrrh."

So Bum Cham did this, then on the third month of the Sheep

Year, at dawn, the baby was born. The house became full of incense smoke that arose spontaneously, and rainbow light, a rain of flowers, and beautiful musical sounds came from the sky. All the people of the area were saying prayers and making offerings to the family gods.[30]

As soon as she was born, the baby stood in rainbow light and took the dancing position of Vajra Yogini.

She asked: "Mother, are you well?" and then said "A."

On her tongue was a blazing red HRI[31] and it seemed to be turning. On her forehead was an eye radiating fine threads of rainbow-colored light.[32] On top of her head was a white light emanating from an "A" the size of a joint of the little finger. Bumme took the baby onto her lap in the prepared cotton clothes. After a while the HRI dissolved into her tongue. They then tried to give her white butter mixed with sugar crystals, but she spat it out.

Then she looked into the sky with her three eyes. After a while the white light on her head was absorbed into her, as was the rainbow light coming from her third eye in her forehead.

She turned her gaze from the sky and lowered her neck a little and looked at her sister directly. After a while she made sucking sounds and then she ate the butter and sugar mixture. Then she turned and smiled at her mother and went to sleep on her sister's lap.

During the birth Bum Cham had felt no pain and continued feeling well and joyful. The next morning the baby called Bumme by name.

Then she said to her mother: "Bumme is very happy to have a beautiful sister with three eyes."

When they heard that the father was coming home, Bumme was afraid that he would be displeased with a baby with three eyes and suggested that they hide her. Bumme wrapped her up in the cotton clothes and hid her behind the door.

The father, Chokyi Dawa, went into the temple to find the child because he had heard it had been born.

Bumme said to him: "Mother gave birth to a very bad girl with three eyes and we have thrown her out."

The father said: "Bring her here immediately."

So Bumme went to get the baby and gave her to him. He

examined the baby very carefully and he said: "In her third eye there is a white 'A' so fine it looks as though it were written with a single hair. She has all the signs of a dakini.[33] Her hands are webbed and her finger nails are a bit red and luminous like mother of pearl. OM AH HUM letters have appeared on them. Keep her at home, do not take her around the streets; take good care of her and do not tell anyone about her."

Childhood and education

They looked after her well and she grew rapidly. When she was three she knew many mantras like OM MANI PADME HUM and OM TARE TUTARE TORE SWA HA and TRI and OM GATE GATE PARA GATE PARA SAM GATE BODHI SWA HA and HA RI NI SA,[34] and so on.

She liked to go into the shrine room and do prostrations and make offerings. When she was five, her mother began to teach her to read and write. All she had to do was show her and she would remember everything. She became learned. Her mother got a lama to teach her the Dharma. By the time she was eight she could read two large volumes of Sutras in the time it took one adult professional reader to read half of a large volume.

Her teacher told her parents that she was no ordinary girl; in fact she seemed to be a superior dakini and she had gone beyond him.

He said: "Her prajna burns like uncontrollable fire. So I have given her the name Sherab Dronme, 'Burning torch of Prajna'."

Her mother called her Dron Tsema. The local people called her Adron, "Torch of A." Everyone heard about the miraculous little girl, daughter of the noblewoman Bum Cham, and came to see her. Those who met her loved her very much and said that she must be an emanation of the Buddha.

Then her sister Bumme cut off her hair and took the vows of a nun from Geshe Aton and was given the name Tontso Rinchen Bum, "One Hundred Thousand Jewel Lakes," and she became very learned.

Audience with the king

The king ordered Machig and her family to appear before him. Everyone was very frightened, and with great commotion the whole family, twenty-five people in all, went to see the king. He had heard stories of the miraculous child and offered them all a big feast. Then they had an audience. Noble Bum Cham was so nervous during her audience that she could barely answer the king's questions.

Then the people around the king said: "This child is not normal, she has three eyes."

He asked her if she knew how to read and write, and she said that she did, so he asked her to read a text, "The Noble Collection," in front of many learned men. After she had done so, they asked her if she understood what she was reading, and when she said that she did, they were all very impressed and said she must be an incarnation of the Wisdom Dakini. When the king looked at her closely he saw the "A" on her forehead and the other signs on her body. Then he asked her name and she said: "They call me Rinchen Dronme, 'Great Jewel Fire Torch,' or Dron Tse or Adron, 'Torch of 'A' '." He said: "If you join the name 'Dronme,' 'Fire Torch,' and the name of your birthplace, 'Lab,' it will be auspicious." The pandits, monks, and nuns, and Bumme, her sister, all agreed that it would be a good connection, so after that she was called Labdron, "Torch from Lab," and everyone far and wide had faith in her and loved her. The king took her old clothes and kept them[35] and gave her nice new ones. He gave the family three horses, food, thirty rolls of woolen cloth and many other supplies. He told her parents to keep her away from people who did bad things or she would be stained and that if they took good care of her she would be able to help the Tibetans.

Recitation of the Prajna Paramita Sutra

Then Machig and her mother and sister went to Namso Tsomer, "Upper and Lower Lakes," a place in Lhokha, in

Southwestern U Province. They stayed there five years, reciting the Prajna Paramita Sutra[36] as given by the Buddha.

By the time Machig was ten she could read four volumes a day and then her mother died. So her sister took her to see Geshe Aton and he said to her: "Your sister has all the signs of a dakini – I would like her to read one volume."

So she read a condensed version of the Prajna Paramita Sutra in the time it takes to grind four kilos of tsampa (about half an hour). Geshe Aton was shocked, as even the best scholars were much slower and they read six times as fast as ordinary people. So he said he would explain the meaning to them. They stayed there three years and he taught them about the Six Paramitas, the Ten Levels[37] of the Bodhisattva Path, and the Five Paths.[38] At the end she knew these even better than her teacher. So then Geshe Aton told her that he had taught her everything he knew and that she should go to Yoru Drathang Province to the place called Dra and there she would find a lama with omniscience[39] who was also very learned and had many monks, and she should study with him.

So when she was sixteen she went to Lama Dra with her sister and he asked Bumme: "Is this the girl who is so good at reading?" She answered: "Yes, it is." So the lama said: "Now we will compare her with my own professional reader."[40] This man read six times faster than average, but when he had finished four volumes she was on her twelfth. The lama was very surprised and said that she was at least twice as good as his reader and that now she should be his reader.

Then Bumme said to Lapdron: "Shall we attain powers and go to the heavenly realm of the dakini?"[41] She replied: "I will not go now. I have to help all sentient beings. But if you want to go you can meditate and go yourself to stay there. I will come after I have finished my work for sentient beings. So Bumme went and meditated for three years and then died leaving no body.[42]

Lama Dra, the omniscient one, saw with his omniscient vision that Machig was a disciple who could help others. He gave her the empowerment of all the Prajna Paramita teachings and explained the meaning of each word very thoroughly and profoundly. She achieved realization and offered her realization to the lama and he was delighted.

He said: "You can recite these texts by heart and you have gained mastery over the practice. I do not have this faculty, it is difficult for me." Then he gave her a red brocade hat that was white inside and had ten lotus folds and five colors of brocade at the back. He also gave her new clothes and shoes. He made a seat of three cushions[43] topped with a new carpet and told her to sit there. Then the lama and everyone praised her, calling her "Small Hat Nun."

He requested her to stay for four years and be the reader for his monastery and she agreed to do so. Though she was very well dressed, she did not like going to town and wanted to stay at the monastery with her guru. She was kind to all the monks and they had faith in her.

Initiation

People were talking about an Indian teacher called Phadampa Sangye[44] who was asking about an Indian pandit from Potari who had been born in Tibet under the name of Lapdron. He was trying to find her because he had had a vision of her.

That night she had a dream in which a white dakini appeared and said to her: "A black Indian master is coming to see you."

Lapdron asked: "Who is this Sadhu?"[45]

"His name is Phadampa," was the answer.

When she awoke she thought that even though this was a dream perhaps it was true. As soon as she went outside she met Phadampa and started to prostrate herself before him, but he stopped her and they touched foreheads instead.[46]

She said: "It is very wonderful that you are here."

He replied: "It is more wonderful that you are here, born in Tibet."

She asked: "How can I help sentient beings?"

He replied:

"Confess all your hidden faults!
Approach that which you find repulsive!
Whoever you think you cannot help, help them!

Anything you are attached to, let go of it!
Go to places that scare you, like cemeteries!
Sentient beings are as limitless as the sky,
Be aware!
Find the Buddha inside yourself!
In the future your teaching will be as bright as the sun
    shining in the sky!"

Advising her thus, he departed. She returned to the monastery
and resumed reading Sutras.

A lama called Kyo Zur Panchen Shakya Jung had a brother
called Sonam Drapa, who was a master of all the Tantras and
Sutras and who had many monks following him. Sonam Drapa
came to see Machig by himself. He was feeling sad because of
the lack of genuine Dharma practice in Tibet. He saw many
people pretending to practice the Dharma when in fact they
were thinking of worldly things.

He said to Machig: "You are very learned in the Prajna
Paramita, but do you understand the real meaning of it?"[47]

She replied: "Yes I do."

He said: "Then explain it to me."

So she explained the ten levels of the Bodhisattva path and
how to practice the five paths of the Bodhisattva, how to
practice meditation. All of this she explained in detail.

Then he said: "You are obviously very intelligent, but you do
not seem to have made the teachings part of you. Everything
you said was correct, but the most important thing to realize is:
if you do not grasp with your mind, you will find a fresh state
of being. If you let go of clinging, a state beyond all
conceptions will be born. Then the fire of great Prajna will
grow. Dark self-clinging ignorance will be conquered. The root
teaching is to examine the movement of your own mind very
carefully. Do this!"[48] Saying this, the lama went away.

She did as he had said, rereading her books in the light of
what he had said. As she was reading, she came across a
section called Du kyi Leu, about the nature of demons. She
was profoundly affected by this teaching and through it she
reached a stable understanding. She became free from petty
dualism and released the demon of self-cherishing. The sun of

Prajna arose, which stabilized the understanding that there is nothing which makes a person or thing what it is. Then she was free from even the slightest whisper of self-cherishing.[49]

As a sign of her freedom from attachment, she stopped wearing nice clothes and wore the clothes that even beggars cast off. As a sign of her freedom from attachment to friends, she stayed with beggars who were in bad shape. Previously she had associated only with her teachers and monks and nuns. As a sign of her freedom from attachment to nice comfortable places, she would stay anywhere. Previously she would stay only in monasteries or in retreat huts, but now she would stay anywhere, even in lepers' houses. Whereas previously she would go only to meaningful places like her home or where her teachers were staying, now she wandered around anywhere. This was a sign of her freedom from attachment to places.[50] Previously she had eaten only tasty food; now she would eat anything except meat. This was a sign of her freedom from attachment to food. Previously she had been happy when people complimented her, but now she was unmoved by praise. Not even a moment of unhappiness arose; she experienced pain and anxiety unflinchingly. Pain and pleasure, near and far, passion and aggression all were experienced as "one taste"[51] in the space of things as they really are.[52]

At this time she was still with Lama Drapa, with whom she had promised to stay for four years, but now the four years were up and she requested initiation.

But Lama Drapa said: "I will not give you this empowerment, you had better go to Sonam Lama[53] because in a previous life you made a prayer to meet him again and now there will be no obstacles. It has been prophesized that you will attain siddhis."

So he sent her on her way with a big piece of yak meat[54] and a large piece of dark-red cloth, for her to give as an offering to the Lama Sonam.

Before going, she went to her homeland, and her brother Sakya Gyaltsen gave her thirty bags of barley as well as meat and woolen cloth to give as her empowerment fee.[55] So she took all of this to Lama Sonam and told him Lama Dra had sent her to him for initiation.

He could see she had the potential to help others and agreed to give her the empowerments. She received them with four friends and they were from the lineage of Phadampa Sangye. They received the empowerments into the four states of meditative concentration,[56] and introduction into the fundamental voidness of all things through the example of the sky.[57] When he was giving the Mahamaya empowerment[58] it was late at night and as the stars were beginning to fade he reached the point of transference of wisdom.[59] Machig raised her body several feet from the ground and began doing the twenty-four dances of the peaceful dakini[60] and began teaching in Sanskrit. She entered the all-pervading state of the indestructible profound stabilized meditation of things as they are,[61] and passed through the wall of the shrine-room and flew into a Serlag tree over a pond containing a terrible Naga.[62] This Naga was so terrifying that no one even dared to look at the pond, but Machig stayed there in deep meditation. The Naga was angry and a little frightened and so he called up his army of demons and they made many phantoms to scare her away, but instead of being afraid she offered them her body. They could not devour her because she was egoless.[63]

They developed faith in her and offered her their hearts and protection for anyone in her lineage.

Then the Mahamaya dakini and her retinue appeared and gave her direct transmission[64] of the four empowerments while remaining in the sky before her. Mahamaya predicted that both human and non-human beings would be under her control and she would show them the path of the Bodhisattva.

Next, an ocean of Cakra Sambhava dakinis appeared and gave her much wise counsel, and then the Buddhas of the Ten Directions appeared and told her to go to the cemetery springs without fear and to generate the thought for the illumination of all sentient beings.

The next morning Arya Tara arrived and gave her one hundred empowerments to purify ignorance with heart essence.

She said to Lapdron: "Yogini, you and an emanation of the Buddha Sakyamuni called Topabhadra, who has come to Tibet, will join profound cognition and skillful means.[65] You will go to the 108 cemeteries and springs and help sentient beings.

Your teaching will shine like the sun in the sky and your followers will be non-returners." Then she spoke of many things and gave advice for the future, and then vanished in Machig's internal space.

At the first light of dawn her friends and Lama Sonam went out to look for Machig as she had left the empowerment. They found her up a tree, naked, free from karmic misery, without shame, and beyond embarrassment.[66] She did a prostration to the lama and said: "Those who make sincere prostrations[67] to the lama will be purified of karmic stains."

Then she prostrated herself again and said: "The lama is the refuge from suffering."

Then her friends said that she had missed the empowerment, but the lama said: "You all received only the relative empowerment. This young girl received the absolute dharmata empowerment."

The next morning Machig offered a mandala and requested empowerment saying:

"The outer and inner mandala are the four continents and
    Mount Meru.
The four elements and the beings of the six realms
Are the limitless jewels and treasure.
To the places of refuge the holy jewels,
Guru, Deva and Dakini,
I offer the outer and inner mandala,
Please grant your blessings.

For the secret empowerment
I offer the inner self-arising and spontaneous mandala of the
    body of aggregation[68]
As the purified ground of the mandala,
The eight consciousnesses[69] are the offerings heaped on this.
The ground of being is the jewels and treasure,
To the place of refuge, the holy jewels,
The Guru, Deva and Dakini,
I offer the mandala of the inner body,
Please grant your blessings.

For the empowerment of the Voice,

I offer the secret dharmata mandala.
The aware state of luminosity is the purified ground.
The unceasing realization of this is the heaped offerings.
When luminosity and emptiness join there is bliss.
This is the jewels and treasure.
To the places of refuge, the holy jewels,
To the Lama, Yidam, and Dakini I offer the secret dharmata
  mandala.
Please grant your blessings!"

After she had made this mandala offering,[70] Sonam Lama
gave her all four empowerments and explained everything
thoroughly. Machig absorbed and integrated everything into
her being. A great faith in the lama was born in her.

Then from Lama Sha Marpa she received the Five Dharmas
of Maitreya.[71] He taught her the whole cycle of Bodhicitta.[72]
He taught her how to change sound.[73]

From Lama Beton she received the oral teachings of Dzog
Chen.[74] She practiced these teachings and gained mastery over
them.

From a lama called Yertingpa she received the pointing-out
instruction of Mahamudra[75] and the Six Yogas of Naropa[76] as
well as the Vajra Varahi teachings and the Kalachakra
mandala,[77] and all about the songs of Mahamudra, the
dohas.[78] Then she received teachings in the three highest
yanas[79] and kept these in her heart.

Then she returned to Lama Dra and thoroughly studied the
five dharmas of Maitreya. He advised her to proceed to Central
Tibet. So she traveled to Central Tibet to Lhasa and when she
arrived she went to the temple called the Jowo.[80]

When she made offerings in the temple there were rainbows
and musical sounds in the glorious sky and a rain of flowers
and many other good signs. Everyone had great faith in
Machig and listened to her teaching. Then she went to
Dratang, and while she was there she met Phadampa, who
was in Penyul Nyiphug. He had come to see her after a dakini
told him where she was. He met her when she was making a
pilgrimage to some local sacred spots.

On seeing Phadampa she prostrated herself and then said:
"Please advise me as to how to cut sentient beings free."

Phadampa replied:

"You embody the Four Prajnas.[81]
You are the phantom body of the Great Mother Dakini!
You open the door of the three liberations![82]
She who subdues all demons!
Lapdronma, myself and all goddesses and gods prostrate to
    you!
I offer myself at your feet!
The skill of your accomplishments and compassion!
Because of you, impure sentient beings will be liberated!
Future generations will learn of these teachings thanks to
    you!"

Then Machig and her two friends Jomo Kargoma and Jomo Chotso received from Phadampa Sangye many teachings: the empowerment of the Dharma of the Wheel of the Four Meditative States,[83] the teaching on How to Open the Door to the Sky for Transference,[84] the Lapdron teachings from the Zhibyed school,[85] explanations of the six methods of offering the body,[86] the practice of the HUM in the Zhibyed tradition,[87] the Red teaching,[88] the three teachings on PHAT,[89] the Teaching of the Blue Lotus,[90] Mahamaya teachings,[91] the female deity with Two Faces,[92] the Deep Path of the Khagyu Guru Yoga, the Practice of the Great Transference,[93] the teachings on the Illusory Body, Dreams, and Bardo[94] (the time between births), the Eight Teachings on the Very Secret Chod to be done at one time in a big charnel ground.[95] They received everything; there was nothing more to give. She took it all into her heart.

Afterwards she praised Phadampa Sangye thus: "All-knowing, all-seeing father, the heart son of the Buddhas of the Three Times, Protector of all sentient beings, I prostrate myself to your phantom body." Having made this praise she stayed there for three years.

Then she went to stay in her father's district for six months. At that time Phadampa said:

"Vajra Demon Subduer,[96]

The Supreme Dakini of Great Prajna,
Mother of the Buddhas of the Three Times,
Great Wisdom Dakini,
Secret Wisdom Prajna Dakini,
Source of All Emanations of the Wisdom Dakini,
Vajra Varahi, in the State of Supreme Transcendent
   Ecstasy,[97]
The Principal Dakini of the Egoless Suchness,
Who govern the Fierce Indigo Dakini,
You are unchangeable Primordial Space,
You are as vast as the sky,
But for the benefit of all beings and due to their prayers,
You were born in India in the city of Serkya
As son of Ratsa Shri Shora Ari and called Monlam Drub."

There is a prophecy in an ancient text that during the Kali Yuga[98] following the death of the Buddha, there would be much disagreement about the teachings of the Buddha. At that time in the Northern Snow Country (Tibet) an emanation of the Mother of the Buddhas, the Dharmakaya dakini who would be called Dronme, "Fire Torch," would appear to resolve these arguments.

Another prophecy in the root Tantra of Manjushri[99] states that during a time after the death of the Buddha in the Kali Yuga when much confusion manifested, an emanation of the Great Prajna Mind called Lapdronma would appear in the Northern Snow Country. She would explain the meaning of unborn heart essence.[100]

Phadampa said that she would meditate in towns, cities, mountains and cemeteries and her teaching would spread widely. She would see that four non-Buddhist dakinis were planning to be born to take over Tibet, and therefore she would manifest four dakinis to conquer them and help sentient beings. The first of the Buddhist dakinis was Machig Zama of Latho. She benefited others through the Lam dre[101] teaching. The next was Camtro Chungma from Tritsham. She benefited others through Dzog Chen. The third was Sheldza Dromnema, who benefited others through the signs of Mahamudra.[102] The fourth was from Lablung and called Labdron and she benefited others through the teaching of offering one's flesh and blood to quell four demons.

The four non-Buddhist dakinis were Barwa Garmo of Barpu, Chomo Namkha of Tholung, Shalmo of Tsang, and Zhangmo Lhatri of Lading. The Buddhist dakinis conquered all of these and transformed them into Wisdom Dakinis who could benefit sentient beings.

When Machig was thirteen her mother passed into the dimension of the sky, and when she was sixteen her father died and was reborn in India and helped many sentient beings.

When she was twenty her sister left no body and passed into the Land of the Dakinis to join her mother. Her eldest brother, Sakya Gyaltsen, became very learned, a master in debate and mantra practice and had the signs of practice in his body.[103] Her younger brother, Pal O Tride, became an official after his father and served the causes of the Buddha.

Machig's return to Sonam Dargye marks the end of the first part of her life.

PART 2   MARRIAGE TO TOPABHADRA

The second part of Machig's life is a description of what she accomplished. Lama Drapa had two patrons, a wealthy woman, Lhamo Dronma, and her husband. They requested him to send Machig to read the Prajna Paramita Sutra at their house saying they would offer her whatever they could in return.

The lama agreed and told Lapdron: "Go and stay with them for a month and read the Prajna Paramita Sutra thirty times and they will give you riches."

She checked with Sonam Lama and he said: "You should go. You have a positive connection with these people from previous lives."

Since she had been advised to go by both of her teachers she decided to go, and then that very night she had a dream of a red dakini with only one eye in her forehead.

This dakini said: "The Indian Topabhadra and you, Yogini, should make a union of skillful means and profound cognition.

[168]

This will benefit sentient beings and stabilize your realization."[104]

Early in the morning a small blue dakini appeared and said: "You should make a union with Topabhadra – this will create a lineage and will cause the teachings to spread. You will reach beyond the ten levels of the Bodhisattva Path." Then they disappeared.

Next seven white women appeared and said: "You have a good connection with Topabhadra. Do not be ashamed, act!"

She thought in her dream: "Is this a prophecy or the trick of malevolent spirits?"

But when she tried to ask the dakini she had already vanished, and the next morning at dawn a white girl riding a white mule was seen approaching. When she arrived she said: "Machig, Great Secret Wisdom Dakini, Vajra Demon Subduer, you, Great Woman, are invited!" Machig said: "Where are you from and who are you?"

The girl dismounted and prostrated herself and said: "I have come because Topabhadra requested me to come and get you. Vajra Demon Subduer, Dorje Dudulma, leader of the Secret Wisdom Dakinis!"

Then Machig asked: "Who is this Topabhadra and what is his lineage?"

She answered: "He is from India, a place called Kosala. His father is from the Shakya family and he is called Ratna Siddhi. His mother's name is Samati. The lama himself is an emanation from the skull of the Buddha, hence his name which means just that. Externally he is learned in all the Sutras. Internally he is accomplished in all the Tantras and he has achieved the power of Chakrasambhava. He is an accomplished yogi. At the moment he is in Tibet at Ehchung and he sent me to invite you there. Please come with me riding on this mule."

They left the next day early in the morning and about noon they reached Selrong, "Cleansing Village," and met a lama there called Sherab Bum, who was very learned in the Sutras and was surrounded by three hundred monks. He was teaching the Prajna Paramita. She went to see him and the Geshe[105] and the learned people asked her: "Are you the daughter of Dawa Gyaltsen called Lapdron, who was born with three eyes?"

Machig replied: "Yes, I am."

The lama said: "Everyone says you are a great dakini and very learned in the Prajna Paramita, so let's have a debate!"

She agreed and she debated with the seven best Geshes.

No one could match her, and all of the monks agreed she must be an emanation of the Wisdom Dakini, as they had heard. They asked her to go to have an audience with Sherab Bum, but to wait while they made preparation.

Then twenty-five monks came out playing musical instruments and carrying incense and they escorted her to Sherab Bum, who appeared in the form of the red Manjushri.[106] As she began to prostrate herself before him he stopped her and stood up, saying: "Machig Lapdron, come here!"

Nearby they made a pile of three cushions and asked her to sit there. When the lama looked at her he saw the White Tara and they talked a little about the teachings of the Buddha. Then Machig asked him to give her some explanation of the teachings. The lama said: "I don't have any teachings you do not already know."

Machig replied: "It doesn't matter: to make a Dharma connection any teaching is fine."

So he taught on the twelve stages of interdependent causation,[107] for twelve days. She recognized these as pertinent teachings and all the Dharma appeared as auspicious and bore fruit.

After this she went on to Ehchung, and when she arrived she went up onto the roof of her patrons' house and from there she saw a brown-skinned yogi with bloodshot eyes, doing the self-empowerment in the mandala of Cakra Sambhava. He spoke to her, asking, in the Indian language: "Aren't you tired from your journey?"

She replied: "Yogi, when you were coming from India didn't you get confused?"

With that she turned around and went into the shrine-room and started to read the Prajna Paramita Sutra. While she was staying there they would discuss the Dharma sometimes and Topabhadra told her stories about India.

After she had been there seventeen days, on the eighth Tibetan day at about eleven o'clock in the evening, they came together, unifying profound cognition and skillful means.

Because of them the room was filled with a bright rainbow light. The woman whose house Machig was staying in, Lhamo Dron, saw the light and, fearing the butter lamps on the shrine had set the house on fire, came upstairs to see what was happening. When she opened the door she saw nothing except a room full of light and red and white spheres of light,[108] the size of the moon, stuck closely together in the middle of the room, shining. She was afraid and fell into a deep sleep. In the morning she woke up and saw Topabhadra coming out of Machig's room.

She felt unhappy and went downstairs. She brought them breakfast in Machig's room and said to them: "Last night I saw you and Topabhadra. Did he disturb you? I came into your room thinking the shrine had caught fire." Machig said, joking: "Ordinary prophecies are created by tricky demons. When a man and woman come together this is of karmic causes. You were chased by demons, how could this benefit sentient beings?"

Then after seven days Topabhadra went on a pilgrimage and Machig continued her reading of the Prajna Paramita. When she finished, the patrons offered her many things and then escorted her back to Lama Drapa.

Lhamo Dron did not tell anyone what she had seen, not even her husband. She kept it a secret, because she realized they were not two ordinary people. She had great faith in them.

Then Lapdron's lama, Drapa, told her to stay with Topabhadra because it would be beneficial to sentient beings and she had no reason to be sad. Then she went to Lama Sonam with many offerings and told him about meeting Topa at Ehchung.

He said: "You are not breaking any vows. Topabhadra is not from a bad lineage. So marry him and make a family and create your lineage. You have to stay with him: you have a karmic connection and there are good signs. It will help many sentient beings. I had a very nice dream about you last night. I saw your future. Now is a good time for you to stay together." She received more teachings and prophecies and decided to stay with Topabhadra.

So when Machig was twenty-three she went with Topabhadra to Central Tibet, and when she was twenty-four she gave birth to a son. She called him Drubpa, which means "fulfilled," because with him all the prophecies had been fulfilled.

The people of the area started gossiping about her, saying that she had been a good nun but now she had fallen. So they decided to move. They went to Dragpo and stayed in a place called Nyangpo.

Then when she was twenty-five and they were in Kongpo she had another son, called Drub Se. They also called him Kongpa Kyab, which means "Kongpo Refuge."

When Machig was thirty years old they moved to Nalai Dradolgo, "the Five Passes at the Summit of the Beautiful Dol," a place in the province of Lho.Kha, and here a daughter was born. They called her Drub Chungma, "Accomplished Little Girl," and they thought that she was a dakini and also named her after her birthplace, calling her Laduma, "She who comes from the Mountain Pass."

Return to her lamas

When Machig was thirty-four they went to Panyul Langtang, a valley just north of Lhasa, and then when she was thirty-five, after receiving prophecies from the dakinis, she appeared to be tired of Samsara and left her children there with her husband and went to Lab to see her two lamas.[109]

She asked Sonam Lama for the empowerment of the five Goddesses of the Heart of Vajra Varahi,[110] and before the ceremony sang this song to him:

"To all the Lamas who introduce the state of self-awareness
  of primordial wisdom,
I prostrate!
To the Devas and Deities who grant powers,
I prostrate!
To the Buddhas who demonstrate what should be taken up
  and what should be renounced,
I prostrate!
To the Dharma which frees from attachment;
I prostrate!

To the Sangha to whom it is beneficial to make offerings,
I prostrate!
To the Guardians of the Dharma who clear away obstacles,
I prostrate!
Until I have reached enlightenment,
I will pray to all of you!
I offer the five sense pleasures,
I renounce all negative actions,
Please turn the wheel of the Dharma!
Do not pass away,
And may any merit gained be spread to all sentient beings!"

Lama Sonam felt happy and gave her all empowerments, recognizing her to be a dakini. After that she did the visualization practice of the dakini, practiced all the Vajrayana teachings and was able to read, write and debate these teachings. Then he gave her the secret name Dorjeying Phyugma, "Woman rich in Indestructible Space."

Then she went to Lama Dra to show him her understanding of the twelve nidhanas, and the lama replied that she was a great dakini, someone hard to find and rare. He told her she was a great woman siddha.[111]

Then she asked him to confer the Bodhisattva vows on her. He said: "You do not need the Bodhisattva vows or the five precepts. You are a great woman Dharma practitioner and the Mother of all the Buddhas and Bodhisattvas. You are accomplished in your understanding of the Sutras and you have the great eye. You are the kindest mother who treats all sentient beings as your own children. You are the Great Mother, treasury of all the Dharma, you do not need teaching on Bodhicitta. I am like a star near the moon, but I am your teacher, so as an auspicious sign I will give you these vows."

When the lama was doing this she saw him as the Buddha Sakyamuni; on his right was Manjushri, and on his left Avalokitesvara, and Vajrapani[112] was in front of him. She prostrated herself and said:

"The body of the Buddha is as bright as gold.
The leader, all knowing, I bow to you.
Manjushri, you are youthful with all the signs of accomplishment.

I bow to you.
Vajrapani, you who destroy great and powerful demons.
I bow to you.
One must see the brilliant inseparability of the lama and the
    Buddha.
Avalokitesvara, with one face and two arms, with a narrow
    waist, all white, with white light continuously arising,
Your body completely full of light.
Manjushri, with a sword the color of the sky shining with
    the five colors pointed at me as if to kill me.
Vajrapani, who destroy obstructing spirits with your black
    vajra, sending forth sparks in the shape of little vajras."

Seeing this, she took the Bodhisattva and Upaseka vows and
Lama Dra advised her to go to the Copper-Colored Mountain,
Zangri Khangmar. She said: "First I want to see Phadampa and
then I will go to Zangri." The lama agreed that she should do
that.

So when she arrived in Tingri, Phadampa, intuitively
knowing she was coming, came out to meet her. When they
met she asked him for some special teaching. He replied: "I do
not have more advice than I have already given you. But the
lineage of the Prajna Paramita Sutra is powerful and can
remove hindrances in one's life and cause extraordinary
powers."

She said: "Please give me that teaching!"

So they made a big mandala and offered the outer, inner and
secret mandalas to all the lamas. They also offered incense and
music, and invoked wisdom. Then he gave her the empowerments and she kept them in her heart. Furthermore, he gave
her blessings and told her prophecies and they remained
together for a month and thirteen days. She received
many empowerments and teachings of the Upadesha series[113]
and teachings on making the prana enter the central
channel,[114] tummo,[115] Yantra Yoga,[116] and Pranayama.[117] Then
he told her to go to 108 cemeteries and to the Copper-
Colored Mountain because it would benefit sentient
beings.

Then she left Tingri and went to Tang Lha and the great
snow mountain of Jomo Jechen. She went on a pilgrimage and

then to 108 secret places and headed south to Mon where she stayed and meditated; then she descended to the Copper-Colored Mountain and the Red House, where she settled down when she was thirty-seven. The local guardian spirits came to her and asked for Bodhisattva vows and promised not to disturb sentient beings.

A nun called Chotso, a woman called Dardron and a man called Kadrag came to Machig because they had had a divination done which predicted that they would die that year. They came to Machig and asked for an empowerment. She gave them the Magyu Dhadro Negyur,[118] and then they made many feast offerings. This reversed this negative situation and everyone began to talk about the famous Lapdron. By the time she was forty her accomplishments were known all over Tibet. She helped many people. All the Dharmapalas and Lokapalas and the King of Nagas came and received Bodhisattva vows and Upaseka vows and promised to protect her lineage. For twenty-one days she taught them about taking refuge and Bodhicitta. The seven dakinis protecting her sphere surrounded her every day and most people could see them.

Then a lama, Chuba Lotsawa, arrived accompanied by eighteen people, and another, Jartiba Yartiwa, with twenty-five people, and a great teacher, Tolungpa, with thirty-five students, to challenge Machig to a debate. But no one could defeat her. They all believed in her after that and she taught them. They believed her to be Arya Tara. All the scholars had faith in her, and many monks and lamas were taught by her and she became even more famous.

A great siddha, Pamting, came to her and she explained her understanding until he no longer felt confusion arise. The siddha was very happy and said: "It is auspicious that an emanation of the goddess has been born in Tibet. Great Being, you have brought happiness to sentient beings and non-humans. I offer you my salutations, and admiration."

Then Machig asked him for a Dharma connection and he gave her a clear explanation of the Mahamudra teaching and the "Abhidharma Kosha"[119] and without resting taught "the famous Mahamudra Lineage of the Three Turnings of the Unstained Mirror,"[120] and Machig received all these teachings and kept them well in her heart.

Then the fame of the very special Dharma of the Mahamudra Chod spread,[121] and it was said that this teaching that she taught could cure 424 sicknesses and could not be obstructed by the 80,000 obstructing spirits.

Meeting with Tara

When Machig was forty-one she entered the cave of Pugzang at the end of spring. While there, she received from Tara very rare teachings and initiations into the mandala of the Five Dhyani Buddhas yab-yum. Tara manifested as the consort of the Five Buddhas and they gave this prophecy to her:

"You try to continue this teaching. It contains instructions of transforming the five passions, conquering the five Maras, entering into the five wisdoms and achieving empowerment from the Five Dhyani Buddhas.[122] This teaching has been manifested for all sentient beings so you, yogini, keep this rare teaching well. Make it the essence of your practice and enter into the stages of visualization and post-visualization with this mantra. Then, through your children, your lineage will continue like a string of pearls, one right after the other. After ten generations the lineage of your family will be interrupted. You will become the Vajra Demon Subduer Dakini, the chief of all dakinis. You hold the secret consort, the Khatavanga, you hold the secret protection mantras and the lineage."[123]

Then Machig praised the Five Dhyani Buddhas and Tara and said: "You have been very kind to me and have given me power. I am just a weak, stupid woman, but now I have become someone who can benefit others because of your grace."

Tara smiled and looked at the other dakinis and said: "Oh yogini, you have accomplished everything that you were supposed to accomplish of the teachings of Tripitaka[124] and Tantra. Now I am demonstrating to you that you are the incarnation of Prajna Paramita, Vajradhatu Consort, Source of all understanding of the Dharma. Do not be discouraged."

[176]

Then Machig said: "How can I know that we are not the same? Why am I the source of all understanding of the Dharma? Where is the Great Mother now?"[125]

Tara said: "Listen, yogini, your past is cleared from your heart but I will explain it to you. The Great Mother is the void state of all the dharmas which we call Mother of all Creation. The Mother is the Mother of the Buddhas of the Three Times, the Dharmata of the Absolute State, beyond all obstructions, the pure essence of egoless voidness-Prajna. But accordingly, the Great Mother who is the object of offerings and accumulation of merit, by the energy of the prayers and invocations of sentient beings and by means of the luminosity of the voidness of the egolessness of things as they are, became a sphere (Tig.le) of yellow-red light which manifested as the Great Mother in a palace of pure vision, surrounded by Buddhas and Bodhisattvas of the Ten Directions. She had one face and four arms and was a golden color. She sat in the lotus position and in her heart was the orange letter MUM in a bead of light.

"She had all of the signs to perfection and lived in the Tushita heaven.[126] From my heart came a dark-green light which entered into the heart of the Great Mother and made her heart function. Rays of light spread out from her heart and accumulated the wisdom and blessings of the Buddhas and Bodhisattvas in all directions, and then this empowered light was reabsorbed back into the heart of the Great Mother. Then from there a dark-blue dakini with one face and four hands came forth. From her came the Vajradhatu dakini and infinite manifestations of the body, speech and mind – accomplishments which multiplied, and the essence of her mind became Dorje Dudulma, 'the Vajra Demon Subduer,' who has one face, two hands and a pig's head coming out of the side of her head. She has power over all the dakinis, and the three worlds tremble under her. She activates all powerful beings and is the source of energy for all the dakinis. Dorje Dudulma incarnated many times to help sentient beings. She studied the Tripitaka and did much good for sentient beings. In the end she became you in Tibet!"

Then Machig said: "Great Noble Mother, everything that you have said is clear. Tell me, if I spread the Vajrayana teachings you have given me, will that benefit beings and increase?"

Tara replied: "It would not be good to teach the important points of the supreme Vajra publicly, but please feel free to teach it and practice it secretly. Teach it to suitable people, help them to develop it and reach liberation. You will be particularly benefited by uniting the Teaching of the Four Mudras[127] and the meaningful view of the Heart of the Prajna Paramita. Just as the Buddha prophesied, this is the time to conquer all humans and non-humans in Tibet. Yogini, your teachings will spread and you will attain a stable state of enlightenment."

As she said this, immeasurable light rays spread from her heart above, below and everywhere. All the lights then dissolved into Machig's heart. Then Tara and her retinue all vanished into the sky, which was full of light. At the same time dawn broke.

As Machig traveled down to the Copper-Colored Mountain she was welcomed on the road, as she arrived at "the Red House," by two black protectors wearing black capes.

Reunion with her children

When she was forty-two years old, one night she had a dream that she was in a beautiful garden full of flowers. On the ground was a huge flower with petals of many different colors. It was producing its own light rays. On top was Lama Sonam, white in color, emanating rainbow light. Above him was Phadampa Sangye, and above him was Vajradhara. On his right was Red Manjushri, on the left was Arya Deva[128] and behind was Sukha Siddhi.[129] In front was Arya Tara. They were all wearing the Sambogakaya ornaments and were untouchable because of the light they were emanating. They were all empowering her at once. She achieved great powers in her body, speech and mind, and they gave her many transmissions so that she could teach others. In the four directions four white dakinis sounded white conch shells that could be heard on the four continents. Then she woke up.

The next day when the sun had just struck the mountain

peaks her husband, Topabhadra, brought her her younger son and her daughter. Then Machig and Topabhadra compared their realizations and each told the other about their practice. They sang songs to each other and Topabhadra left for India.

The younger son, Drub Se, who was fifteen at this time, knew well his father's lineage of Cakra Sambhava, Akshobhya Vajra Vijaya,[130] the Black Horse-headed Wrathful Deity[131] practices. The daughter, a dakini, aged ten, was accomplished in the practice of the red Tara, the many armed Avalokitesvara,[132] the Sutras and the Prajna Paramita.

Then Drub Se became ill and went mad. In order to cure all the suffering and hindrances caused by the sickness, Machig advised him to do the practice of the "Precious Lamp Which Overcomes All Suffering."[133] She told him to go to stay in a cemetery for a week. After doing this he not only overcame his illness, but also gained some special understanding. Then she gave him the complete series on the "Precious Lamp Which Overcomes All Suffering" and he mastered all this knowledge. Then she invited Phadampa Sangye to Dwang Ri so that he could give vows to her son. She prepared many offerings and did him great honor.

When it came time to name him, Machig said: "I will give him the name," and she said: "His father's name is Topa, and since he became crazy and mad and then overcame his madness, and then met with you, Dampa, the essence Lama of the Three Times, from whom he received vows and gained all his wisdom, we will call him Tonyon Samdrub, which means 'Mad Son of Topabhadra, Accomplished Meditator.' He will follow my tradition and will be important. Before he came I had a dream of four dakinis blowing four conch shells and this sound spread everywhere."

Phadampa Sangye then gave Tonyon Samdrub the heart instruction of Manjushri, the five Taras and the Five Mahamaya Dakinis, all the profound Guru Yoga practices, and the method of liberation the six aggregates and not leaving a body at the time of death.[134]

Then, having made feast offerings to Phadampa Sangye she went to Lab. Tonyon Samdrub had great faith in Phadampa Rinpoche and used to say: "Phadampa Rinpoche is my father."

He praised Phadampa and Machig three times a day and three times a night for many days and so everyone called Phadampa his father.

Then the elder song, Drubpa, chose his wife from the family of Goya in the country called Ahrawa. He was not a Dharma practitioner.

Machig noticed that Tonyon Samdrub was a very good disciple and gave him complete instructions and advice in the practice of the Prajna Paramita and the Empowerment of the Dharma Wheel of the Four Samadhis, and the "Instructions on Recognizing the Consciousness through the Red Knife." He also received hundreds of empowerments of the dakini of the Mother Tantras and hundreds of initiations in thorma.[135] So he received all these teachings and initiations and trained himself and matured and practiced visualization. After four months his practice and realization became stable. Then he practiced the post-meditation practices, and after four months there were signs, and he had attained the power of the visualization and post-visualization practices. At this point she transmitted to him the understanding she had of Mahamudra and he mastered this also.

When he was sixteen Machig said: "Now go to practice on the 'Snow Mountain of Sampo' (Shangpo Gangri). You have a good connection with that place."

He left with three friends, and they walked for a month before they arrived. The morning they arrived at Shampo they were making a feast offering and Machig appeared there miraculously. She asked: "Are you tired?"

He said: "No, thank you. We are honored by your visit."

Then she gave him the greatest initiation of her lineages and the initiation of the Five Dhyani Buddhas, and the Five Secret Vajra Varahi. The initiations were perfectly performed. She stayed there in the cave for seven days. Many dakas and dakinis were present. The son saw his mother become Vajra Varahi, and there was a rain of flowers, rainbows and many miraculous signs.

Machig ordered a local guardian called Shambo not to disturb her son's practice and he promised to assist Tonyon. She ordered a Padma Dakini called Drimima, which means "Without Obstacles," to serve Tonyon and provide everything necessary for his retreat. She promised to do this.

Machig said to her son: "Practice for thirteen years and aggregations, manifestations, dimensions in space, objects and subjects of the sense will manifest as mandalas of the deity. Try to stabilize the pure vision of illumination. Don't worry about your livelihood, there are those who will serve you."

So he entered the cave and made a seat of kusha grass[136] and sat in the position of Vairocana.[137] The door was sealed and no one else entered. Then Machig disappeared into the sky with a retinue of dakinis in the direction of Zangri.

After three months he had a vision of hunger and thirst. He remembered that his mother had said that someone would feed him, but he saw no one who could help him and feed him. But he thought: "This place has been empowered by my mother. I should be able to remain with just the food of meditation empowered by my mother. It would be impossible for me to die of hunger." A while later a red lady appeared on a ray of sunlight. She was very elegantly dressed and was bringing a bowl of nectar for him to drink. She said: "Practitioner, drink this and reach the depths of your practice."

He drank the bowl full of nectar and it had a wonderful taste, and afterwards bliss spread through his whole body. He lost his desire for worldly food and he thought: "Probably this is a Wisdom Dakini. This is a sign of progress in practice."

Then the dakini said: "I was ordered by Machig to bring you what you need. I am not your teacher, so do not tell me the signs of your progress. Keep it hidden in the space of 'suchness.' You still have the desire to tell everyone the signs of your practice. Observe your mind well. When you have doubts or decisions to make, use your own innate knowledge,[138] do not go to others. Unite your way of seeing[139] with your way of behaving."

As she said this, the light stopped shining and disappeared. Every three years she came back and gave him this amrita. After five years Machig sent a yogi to check up on Tonyon and see if he was dead or alive. The yogi arrived outside the cave. "Tonyon!" he called out.

"Ah." was the response.

"Your mother sent me to see if you are hungry or cold. Do you have any difficulties you cannot overcome?"

"Aren't you tired? I am glad to know my mother is alive and well. I am living on the food of meditation – How could I be hungry? I have the clothes of the internal inner heat, and because of this I have overcome attachment to warm clothes. My visions are great companions, so I do not miss my friends. Everything that I see is full of light, so I have no attachment to places," said Tonyon from inside the cave.

Then the yogi went back and told all of this to Machig. She was happy and she said: "Oh, he has this ability."

The disciples of Machig became as limitless as the sky. They came from Central Tibet, Amdo, Kham and even Nepal. Great gurus, scholars, monks, kings, noblemen, ministers, queens, princes, ambassadors, common people, lepers and beggars, all went to Machig, bowed and received teaching from her. Eventually her fame spread to India.

Challenge from the pandits

Then pandits in Bodhgaya heard of her and they held a meeting to discuss her. They said: "All true Dharma comes from Dorje Den (Bodhagaya), but this teaching called the Mahamudra Chod did not start in Bodhagaya, even though Mahamudra does. This teaching has spread from Tibet to Nepal. Even the Nepalis are going to receive teaching from this woman with three eyes; she teaches the Chod which they claim can overcome the forty sicknesses and the 80,000 obstructions. This three-eyed woman claims to be an incarnation of the Prajna Paramita Dakini, but more likely she is an emanation of bad demons. It will probably be difficult to conquer her, and it is difficult to know by what means we should do so. But if we do not, she will destroy all of Tibet and then invade India. We must send a party to check up on her."

Everyone agreed that since she was probably a dangerous black magician they should send their most erudite and powerful siddhas. So a party of three accomplished yogis flew, like hawks in search of little birds, to Tibet. They arrived the next morning as the sun was rising. They circled the Copper-

Colored Mountain, and then Machig's cook, Sonam Gyam saw them.

She said to Machig: "There are three people on our roof terrace. They are dark and have deep-set eyes and are wearing black capes. They are not from around here, maybe they are Nepalese."

Machig said: "They are magical travelers from India, make a place for them to sit."

Seats of three cushions were prepared and then they were motioned to enter, with hand signals. They came in and sat down.

Machig spoke to them in the Indian language, saying: "Are you well? How was your trip? What's new in India these days?"

They were shocked to hear her speaking their language and asked her how it was that she knew their native tongue.

She answered: "Many of my previous lifetimes were spent in India."

They asked: "Do you remember your previous lifetimes?"

She said: "Yes I remember them all."

So they said: "Well, if you remember them, why don't you tell us about them?"

"I will, but first I will gather all my disciples from all over Tibet and Nepal and find translators. Then everyone can hear; otherwise only you will be able to understand," replied Machig.

So she sent messengers who could do magical walking, all over Tibet and Nepal to inform her disciples. Meanwhile she housed the three pandits in her guest house and had their needs looked after.

In a month people arrived bringing a month's supplies in accordance with the instructions of the messengers. There were 500,573 people and four translators who had been to India and knew several languages.

Machig taught the Dharma to everyone and provided for the 70,000 monks and nuns. The debate between Machig and the Indians was translated. No matter how hard they tried they could not defeat Machig in debate.

Finally the Indians said: "All Dharma teaching comes from

[183]

India originally; there is no Dharma teaching native to Tibet."

Machig said: "That is true. All the Buddhas and their teachings have come from India. So why don't you tell us about each one, what teachings they gave, and what kinds of disciples they had?"

Then the Indians said: "We don't know. If you do, why don't you tell us about them?"

So for seven days she spoke of all the Buddhas, their teachings and their disciples.

Then the Indians said: "All right, since you can remember all this from your previous lives, why don't you tell us about what you are teaching now?"

Machig said: "Listen to me, everyone! The Indians do not have faith in me or my teachings; that is why they have sent these three pandits here. These three could try to benefit from my teachings, but instead they just keep asking me about my past lives and my lineage. If I do not tell them my past lives, they won't believe in me, and even my own disciples will begin to have doubts. So now I will have to clear this up once and for all . . ."

Everyone listened as she explained how at the beginning of her life she had studied all the Buddhas' teachings and using that as a base she had written the Mahamudra Chod and explained the meaning of it. Then she explained what she had realized and how she had integrated these things into herself. She told of her human teachers and what she had learned from them, and her superhuman teachers like Arya Tara and what she had received from them. She also spoke of the future of her teachings, and her teacher's prophecies.

Then she told the story of her life like this:

"From the moment Arya Tara was inspired to help sentient beings and became the Prajna Paramita, until my birth as Dorjeying kyi Wang Chug, I have had 107 lives. This birth started in India where I was born as the pandit Monlam Drub. There by the blessings of Arya Tara I left that body in the cave of Potari. That body is still there! The flesh is in marvelous condition and has not decayed at all. You three should go there and burn the body. The smoke will smell like red sandalwood. It will perfume the whole area. There will be the sound of musical instruments, rainbow light and showers of many kinds of flowers.

"After the cremation you will find relief images of the Five Buddhas united with their consorts on the skull. Each vertebra will be a stupa. Each tooth will be a conch-shape spiraling to the right. A white AH will be on the chin bone. On the right shoulder blade will be the Darmakaya dakini. On the pelvic bone will be Avalokitesvara, Manjushri and Vajrapani, and the hip bones will be the green and white Tara. The heart will be a Buddha. At the center of the rib cage you will find Vajradhara. All the other bones will become numerous ringsel,[140] the size of nuts, in the five colors."

Then the pundits said: "What if it does not happen as you have said it will happen?"

Machig replied: "If it doesn't happen just as I have said, everything I have said until now, including my teachings, is false! So you pandits go now and see, the signs will be there. Now half of my benefit for sentient beings is finished. I am fifty-two years old. When I am ninety-nine I will be instantaneously born in a heavenly realm by means of transference."[141]

Everyone believed her without a doubt. She requested Phadampa Sangye to go with the pandits to India and to bring back one of the relics for the Tibetans. So they all went to Bodhgaya by means of fast walking. They arrived in Bodhgaya and told the pundits everything that had happened. They all said: "Let's go to Patari and see what happens." So fifty-two pandits went to Potari and found the body and everything happened just as Machig had said it would. So the Indians proclaimed that Machig was the incarnation of the Great Mother. They began saying that in a place like Tibet there could not be students adapted to her level, and that if she stayed there she would just fade away into a rainbow for lack of suitable students. So they decided they must invite her to India immediately.

The skull with the Five Buddhas and the five dakinis was taken to Bodhgaya. Phadampa took the heart to Tibet. The pandits all returned to Tibet.

They made offerings, circumambulated and prostrated themselves before her, and then said: "Machig, you are a phantom body from the Great Mother's heart. We have brought you this statue of the Buddha."

Everyone in the three worlds who saw it received blessings. Phadampa was told to keep it. The faith of the Indians and the Tibetans was greatly increased. The practice of Chod spread throughout Tibet and into India.

The Indians kept insisting that Machig come to India, but she said: "Going to India will not do much good. I am destined to help the Tibetans. I will not go to India in this life. India is the land of the Buddhas, and it is where the Dharma was first taught. Now it is time to bring the Dharma from India to Tibet, not from Tibet to India. I have had many lifetimes in India and have many Dharma connections there. This time I have been born in Tibet, and here I am teaching the Mahamudra Chod which has not been taught in India. This beggar woman would like to show you Indians this Tibetan way of practicing the Dharma, the Chod."

Machig sent some of her most important teachings, medium, long and short, to India. They were teachings that had come from her own heart. She taught them to the three pandits and they took them to India. All the Indians that heard about her believed in her. In this way Dharma teaching was brought from Tibet to India, for the first time.

Then the lineage of those dharmas that had been born in her heart passed to her sons and daughter. There were 116 people holding this lineage which had come from Machig. There were three main lineages. The first was called Gyud.tab, the lineage of the Sutric teachings from the Buddha, to Manjushri, to Nagarjuna, then to Aryadeva, Aryadeva Brahmin, Phadampa, Chos Shyka Yeshe, then to Sonam Lama, Uncle Khudbon and Machig. The second lineage was from Yum Chenmo (the Great Mother) to Tara, to Sukhasiddhi, to Brahmin Aryadeva, then on to the Phadampa Sangye, Sonam Lama and then to Machig. This was called Sherab Gyu and discussed the Prajna Paramita Sutra doctrine. The third lineage, called the Zungjug, descended from the Great Mother, to Buddha Sakyamuni, to Arya Tara, to Manjushri Arya Deva, Phadampa Sangye, Sonam Lama to Machig. All of the above were oral teachings.

The Vajrayana lineage passed from Vajradhara, to Tara, to Machig directly. Before her there had been no such lineage.

The oral lineage of 100 empowerments and 100 offerings went to Tonyon Samdrub, her elder son, and from him to Gangpa Mugsang, then to Drubchenpa, then to Kadrubchenpo, then to Kyeme Gamtso, and then to Manmay Rinpoche, and then to Rechen Shon, and then to Sonam Dorje.

The lineage coming from the Buddha she gave to her younger son, Gyalwa Dondrub, and he kept it in his heart.

To her own daughter, her three main women disciples and Ku gom Cho Kyi Sengye, she gave a mixture of the Sutric and the secret teachings and Dharma teachings that had been born in her heart. Also the mother tantras and the four empowerments of the dakinis, the secret path of Guru Yoga and the visualization of Avalokitesvara, Manjushri and Vajrapani, the Tantra of Mahamaya and the special teachings on how to meditate on Avalokitesvara and many other practices. They all integrated the teachings into their hearts. As if from inside a cave all these teachings issued forth from the Prajna Paramita, she advised her disciples Dode nag gi Wang chug and Grol de Gyalwa'i Jungne. She taught all this to her sixteen main disciples and she had 1,263 accomplished ones who received the fruit of the practice and helped others. About 433 lepers were cured by the practice she taught, and they became as well as before. Countless people were helped. She passed away to the land of the dakinis at the age of ninety-nine.

NOTES

1 Non-human in this case indicates someone beyond the average human, not inhuman or sub-human, but rather superhuman. Mother in this case refers to one who not only gives birth to and nourishes children, but gives birth to wisdom, supreme Matrix.

2 Wisdom Dakini: see Introduction, pp. 25–42.

3 Vajra family: see Introduction, p. 27.

4 Upaseka vows contain five precepts: (i) not to kill, (ii) not to lie, (iii) not to steal, (iv) not to take intoxicants, (v) not to commit adultery.

5 The giving of a name signifies a significant change in the identity of the person. A name change signifies the rebirth of a person into a new state. In the Tibetan tradition a new name is given whenever the disciple takes a significant step such as taking vows or receiving important initiations.

6 See n. 10, p. 130 above.

7 Vinaya: the code of behavior derived from the words of the Buddha, describing the conduct of a nun or monk. A series of rules created by the Buddha to guide the monastic community toward illumination.

8 Abhidharma (Tibetan: mNgon par mdzod): the body of the Buddha's teaching which has been described as Buddhist psychology or metaphysics or cosmogonics. The teachings which describe the nature of the mind. See Trungpa, *Glimpses of Abhidharma*.

9 The Four Tantras: (i) Bya (Sanskrit: Kriya), (ii) sPyod (Sanskrit: Carya), (iii) rNal.'byor' (Sanskrit: Yoga), (iv) Bla.na.med (Sanskrit: Anuttara). The first, Kriyayoga, is based on purification through external ritual acts such as making offerings, recitation, purificatory rituals and baths, and wearing of clean white clothes and

eating white vegatarian foods. The "Carya Yoga" is a balance of external acts with internal yoga. The third, the "Yoga Tantra," aims at the unification of bliss and emptiness, with more weight given to the internal practices. The "Anuttara Tantras" provide a method to hold the "sems" (mind) under control. (See Tucci, *Religions of Tibet*.)

10 See n. 74, p. 138 above.

11 See n. 80, p. 139 above, on the four empowerments.

12 See n. 67, p. 137 above.

13 Dorje Den: Bodhgaya, the "Vajra Throne," place of the Buddha's final illumination. Now a small village near Gaya, in the province of Bihar, India.

14 Cemeteries are places that invoke the fear of the transition from life to death. Encountering dakinis in situations which represent transition is a common motif. A fear of fixation is presented by the Dakini and it must be dealt with in order that spiritual progress can continue, and this encounter is created by the appearance of a dakini.

In this case the dakini is subdued and becomes his servant. When such an encounter has been successfully worked with, the experience serves to fuel further progress. Monlam Drub's method was not to enter into battle but to remain in an egoless state of meditation. This method is similar to that described in the hexagram "Breakthrough" in the *I Ching*: "If evil is branded it thinks of weapons, and if we do it the favour of fighting against it blow for blow, we lose in the end, because thus we ourselves get entangled in hatred and passion. Therefore it is important to begin at home, to be on our guard in our own persons against faults we have branded. In this way, finding no opponent, the sharp edges of the weapons of evil become dulled. For the same reason we should not combat our own faults directly. As long as we wrestle with them they continue to be victorious. Finally the best way to fight evil is to make energetic progress in the good" (*I Ching*, trans. Wilhelm and Baynes, p. 167).

15 Damema (bDag.med.ma): the consort of Hevajra, not to be confused with Damema the wife of Marpa the translator. Literally this means "Egoless Woman."

16 rKang mGyogs: a means of running very fast, not really touching the ground accomplished by yogic breath control. Madame Alexandra David-Neel describes this phenomenon in her book *Magic and Mystery of Tibet*, p. 146. See also "The Meeting with Dhampa Sangje," *The One Hundred Thousand Songs of Milarepa*, p. 606.

17 The ordinary siddhis include the power to pass through walls, to transform stones into gold, to walk on water without sinking, to enter fire without being burned, to melt snow with one's body heat in extreme cold, to travel to a far-distant cosmos in a few seconds, to fly in the sky and walk through rocks and mountains, extraordinary abilities to read minds and know the future, and the development of all the senses far beyond their ordinary capacities. One can also radiate beams of light from the body and stand in sunlight without casting a shadow, make one's body vanish and other so-called miracles.

18 See Introduction, p. 28 above.

19 rTa.mgrin and rDo.rje Phag.mo (Hayagriva and Vajra Varahi).

20 The Tibetan year is organized around a lunar calendar. The cycle begins with the new moon in February. Each month begins with the new moon on the first and the full moon on the fifteenth. The auspicious days vary, but the tenth is dedicated to Padma Sambhava and the twenty-fifth to the dakini and the twenty-ninth to the Protectors and the Guardians of the Teachings. The eighth is the day of Tara and Mahakala.

21 Khatvanga: see Introduction, pp. 34–6 above.

22 See Introduction, pp. 32–3 above.

23 Skull cup: see Introduction, pp. 33–4 above.

24 Here we see the dakini principle in a seemingly destructive aggressive aspect, which actually leads to greater good. It is not so much destructive as actively transformative. It is an impersonal force which strikes the recipient invasively, both here and earlier with Monlam Drub, against his or her will, forcing a transform- ation which might seem negative from the point of view of the rational consciousness, but here we see it brings forth a greater vision and bliss and makes it possible for the mother to receive the strong dakini energy of Machig Lapdron.

25 A conch which spiraled to the right: shells which spiral to the right are considered to be very sacred by Tibetans because they are unusual and Buddhists always circumambulate everything from the right (clockwise).

26 "A" is said to be the sound which expresses the primordial state of knowledge. It is the last letter of the Tibetan alphabet and the first letter of the Sanskrit alphabet. The white "A" represents primordial luminosity, that the fundamental nature of everything is light.

27 The four continents surround the central Mount Meru, which is the center of the universe. To the East is Videha, crescent-shaped; to the South is Jambuvipa, shaped like a cone, point downward;

to the West is Godaniya, circular in shape; to the North is Uttarakuru, square in shape. The central mountain (Tibetan: Rirab Lhunpo) is surrounded by seven rings of water and seven rings of golden mountains; beyond these are the four continents, and the world as we know it is Jambuvipa (Dsambu Ling). Growing up through the center of the mountain is a tree bursting into fruit and blossom at the top. The mountain is occupied by gods and demi-gods each of whom looks after the continent that he faces.

28 Prayer flags are cotton banners of all colors, hung along horizontal strings, or a long banner is hung vertically on a pole. Mantras and prayers are printed on them with ink from wood blocks. They are placed everywhere one might need encouragement and protection, such as around any sacred or religious place, springs and mountain passes, homes, etc. They are said to put prayers into the wind and carry blessings and protection.

29 HA RI NI SA: the seed syllables of the dakinis which surround Dorje Phagmo (Vajra Varahi).

30 As the Tibetans see themselves as being under constant threat from possible spirit-attacks, they have various and multiple gods and methods to protect them. See Tucci, *Religions of Tibet*, pp. 187–90.

31 The "bija" or seed syllable of Vajra Yogini and Avalokitesvara. See n. 5, p. 129 above.

32 The third eye is that which sees beyond two, i.e. beyond dualistic vision. The third eye lies between the two eyes in the middle of the forehead. It is associated with psychic powers and greater vision. All esoteric traditions recognize the existence of this center, which must be opened through various meditation practices.

33 The signs of a dakini are considered secret and are not to be vulgarized by publication. However, they are actual signs on the body of a woman, for example moles in certain places. In *The Blue Annals*, trans. Roerich, pp. 220–1, there is a description of the signs of a Padma dakini, which I will include here as they give an idea of the kinds of signs there are: "On her navel there was the image of the red lotus with three roots; between her breasts, an image of rosaries of precious stone, reaching down the navel, and on each of her shoulders – images of the swastika. At the back of her ears she had coils similar to those of a conch or lotus. Under the tongue there was the image of a sword of the colour of the utpala flower marked with the letter TAM (symbolizing the first syllable of Tara's name). Between her eyebrows she had the image of a banner with the Sun and the Moon on it." See also

Introduction, p. 25 above.

34 OM MANI PADME HUM is the mantra of Avalokitesvara, OM TARE TURARE TURE SWA HA is the mantra of Arya Tara, OM GATE GATE PARA GATE PARA SAM GATE BODHI SWA HA is the Buddha's mantra.

35 Tibetans believe that clothes pick up the vibrations of the wearer and places they are worn and so the clothes of any great person are revered. This is also why you see Tibetans wearing huge woolen coats and winter robes in their pilgrimages to India. The clothes are thought to pick up the blessings of the place and therefore they want to wear in India what they wear at home in the mountains.

36 Teachings on the nature of the Prajna Paramita. See n. 10, p. 130 above.

37 Ten levels of the Bodhisattva path: the Joyful One, the Stainless One, the Illumining One, the Flaming One, the One Difficult to Conquer, the One Who Is Present, the One Who Goes Far, the Unshakeable One, Good Intellect, Cloud of Dharma. These are levels through which the Boddhisattva passes before reaching complete illumination. See sGampopa, *The Jewel Ornament of Liberation*, ch. 19.

38 The Five Paths: (i) preparation, (ii) application, (iii) seeing, (iv) practice, (v) fulfilment. (See sGampopa, *The Jewel Ornament of Liberation*, pp. 232–8.)

39 Tibetan: ngo-shes.

40 Professional reader: there is a tradition in Buddhism whereby the laity or a monastery invite a monk or group of monks to their house or monastery to read a certain text, once or a number of times. The purpose is to remind the householder of the teachings so that he accumulates merit.

41 *Heavenly realm of the dakini*: a dimension which incorporates the dakini energy into which embodied dakinis pass at the time of death, and from which they come when they are born.

42 There are two ways that the body can disappear at the time of death: the sGyu.lus (Body of Illusion) and the 'Ja'.lus (the Rainbow Body). Considering the lineage in which Bumme studied, it is most likely that she took the Body of Illusion. In this case luminosity and prana are united in Ye.shes (wisdom), and while the being is still in the defiled karmic body, this body can perform many kinds of miracles for the good of others. Finally at the moment of death the subtle prana of wisdom joins with luminosity ('Od.gsal), and the vajra body (rDo.rje sKu) is achieved. At this point the karmic body, made of gross elements,

disappears and the corpse disappears into what might be called "cosmic particles." The Rainbow Body, on the other hand, is accomplished by means of the "great transference." The practices of 'Khregs.chod followed by Thod.rgyal, precede this transference. At the fourth and ultimate stage of Thod.rgyal the substance of the body, which is a combination of the elements, is refined and transferred into the subtle form of these elements, which is luminous colored light. Only the hair and fingernails, which are the impurities of the body, remain behind. However, the person doesn't actually die, but transfers into a body of light, or rainbow form. This body is active and can be seen by those with clarity of vision. The rainbow body is only manifested by practitioners of Dzog Chen schools (both rNyingma and Bonpo traditions), whereas the sGyu.lus is manifested in other lineages. For further explanation see Tucci, *The Religions of Tibet*.

43 The status of a person in Tibet was indicated by the number of cushions they were given to sit on. The more important the person the higher the seat or throne. This is why the thrones of "high" lamas were literally very high, sometimes well over the heads of persons standing on the floor. A seat of three cushions is considered to be very respectful.

44 Pha.dam.pa Sangs.rgyas: see n. 24, p. 132 above.

45 Sadhu: an Indian word for a religious ascetic or yogi, someone who has left behind the concerns of a householder's life in order to follow the spiritual path. Usually sadhus have no fixed abode and wear rags or robes of saffron color, or they may even be naked.

46 This is how equals greet each other to express mutual respect and affection.

47 The esoteric teachings constantly stress the difference between intellectual understanding and personal integration with the meaning of the teachings. (See *The Life and Teachings of Naropa*, trans. Guenther, pp. 24–5, for a very similar passage except that the challenger is a dakini.)

48 This passage incorporates the fundamentals of the philosophy behind the Chod practice, the idea being that if we stop grasping, then from under the neurotic clinging the already existing joyful refreshed state of mind emerges.

49 Dag.med rTogs.pa, the stabilized realization that there is not a permanent soul or self.

50 This passage indicates the principles behind the lifestyles of the followers of Machig Lapdron, the "chodpas" who were wandering practitioners, and who lived in cemeteries and frightening

places. Chodpas were not afraid of contamination from what society considered "bad." Nor were they attached to the things which everyone else considered "desirable." They were called in to handle the dead bodies when there were epidemics in Tibet because they were immune to contamination.

51 See n. 60, p. 137 above.

52 Chos Nyid kyi dByings: altogether this phrase means: "The space of dharmas as they are," or "the space of suchness." The space (dByings) of moment points in the process of perception (dharmas) as they are (ta).

53 Sonam Lama: see n. 24, p. 132 above.

54 A big piece of yak meat. Because Tibet is at such a high altitude, the growing season is very short and there are few legumes or vegetables that grow there, so the diet of the Tibetans has always been very dependent on meat as a source of protein. Also the Buddha did not teach strict vegetarianism, but rather that all meat one eats should have passed through at least three hands before a Buddhist should consume it. A Buddhist should never eat anything that has been killed for him or her, or encourage anything to be killed. The Tantric approach, which is what is being referred to here, is that, if a Tantric practitioner eats the meat of an animal with awareness and transcendent insight into the true nature of reality, this creates a connection between the animal and the yogi, and therefore the animal will have a much better chance of reaching a higher rebirth than if it had not been killed and offered to the yogi or yogini. Also the consuming of meat and wine is, and always has been, since the days of Indian Tantra, an integral part of the Tantric Buddhist feast offering. It symbolizes going beyond the limitations of vows and conventional "goodness," and transformation of poison and dangerous substances into a means for enlightenment. Therefore a big piece of meat would be an appropriate offering for a Tantric initiation.

55 The empowerment fee is a traditional way of expressing gratitude to one's teacher. It is not traditionally a stated amount, but there is the assumption that a fairly sizable offering will be made as a gesture of recognizing the immeasurable value of the teachings. Theoretically it is given not because the teacher desires material wealth, but as an act which benefits the giver. For example, when Marpa offered Naropa his hard-earned gold, Naropa said, " 'I do not need it; all that is here is gold', and touching the ground with his big toe, turned it all to gold" (p. 105, *The Life and Teachings of Naropa*, trans. Guenther).

56 Chos.dbang Sems la bsKur.ba ba'i Zab.pa'i Ting.nge.'dzin.gyis

dBang.bzhi: the initiation into the four states of meditative concentration that bring one to the state of Dharma dhatu (Chos.dByings). The space (dhatu) of moment points in the process of perception (dharmas).

57 Nam.mKha' sGo.'byed bya ba'i Shin tu Byin.rLabs che ba'i Byin.rLabs.kyis dBang.bskur: literally, "Initiation into the Door to the Sky, Blessing of the great Blessing."

58 sGyu.'Phrul Chen.mo.dBang.

59 Ye.shes.dBab.

60 According to Professor Namkhai Norbu this actually sometimes happens at this point in the initiation because the energy which enters from the guru and the Buddhas and Bodhisattvas activates the internal energy of the initiate. These dances are the movements of enlightened energy in its pacific form.

61 Chos.nyid la rTogs.pa Med.pa rDo.rje lTa.bu'i Ting nge 'dzin.

62 If we understand the serpentine underwater Nagas as a manifestation of Machig's unconscious, as part of her own mind, this assumption being based on the idea that our environment is a manifestation of our karma and our own projection, this encounter with the underworld character of the Naga is very interesting. The reaction of the Naga, who is both afraid and angry, is like the reaction of the unconscious to an unwelcome visitation. The unconscious, full of powerful fury and fear of loss, attacks the intruding consciousness. The archetypal tree, guarded by monsters, is described as follows by Esther Harding in *Woman's Mysteries*: "The moon tree is frequently represented as guarded or attacked by animals or monsters . . . The serpent, however, is associated with the moon for another reason. Snakes live in dark holes, they are cold-blooded and inaccessible to human feeling. For these reasons they have always been considered to be related to the underworld, and to the shades of the dead" (p. 63). The tree is a symbol of individuation in Jungian psychology, and since she flies (transcendence) to the top of the tree, if interpreted psychologically it could mean that at this point she has completed her individuation process. The direct transmission in the tree is a turning point in her life, her spiritual coming of age. Up until this point she has been in training but after this she becomes aware of her future as a teacher and that she will not remain alone, but will meet a consort and have children. (See n. 13, p. 130 above.)

63 Since demons (a projection of the ego) can only harm someone with something to defend, they cannot disturb someone who has no territory (i.e. ego) to defend. This is the philosophical basis of

the Chod teachings.

64 These deities exist independently of our beliefs, and therefore, when a person is properly prepared and open, a direct transmission may occur instead of through a guru. (See n. 80, p. 139 above.)

65 This is the way of referring to the marriage of a yogini and a yogi. Profound cognition (prajna) represents the female, and skillful means (upaya) the male.

66 The naked state of the mind in its awareness of itself, not clothed with confusion, is sometimes expressed by a yogini's or yogi's literal nakedness. This also expresses going beyond conventional limitations into spontaneous wisdom with actions beyond repetitive patterns and therefore sometimes called crazy wisdom, an epithet of many maha siddhas (sDrub Tobs). This craziness is not, however, to be confused with the craziness of suffering, confused and deluded people, as it is an expression of clarity: "The naked body represents truth, the truth that goes deeper than social custom. Witches worship naked for several reasons: as a way of establishing closeness and dropping social masks, because power is most easily raised that way, and because the human body is itself sacred. Nakedness is a sign that a Witch's loyalty is to the truth, before any ideology or any comforting illusion" (Starhawk, *The Spiral Dance*, p. 83). Machig has progressed from a child prodigy nun to a naked yogini, who has gone beyond the constrictions of the collective imperatives.

67 Prostrations, whether full-length, or only the head, hands and knees touching the floor, are a way of expressing devotion and overcoming pride.

68 Skandas (Phung.po) make up the body of aggregation, or literally "heaps." There are five: (i) form (gZugs), (ii) sensory perception (Tshor), (iii) conceptualization ('Du.shes), (iv) habitual impulses ('Du.byed), (v) consciousness (rNam.shes).

69 Eight consciousnesses: (i) the storehouse consciousness which is the instigator of all mental activities, Alaya Vijnana (Kun.gzhi); (ii) Nyon.yid, the subconscious which has a more active involvement than Alaya; (iii) the other six are the five senses plus the consciousness which is aware of the five senses.

70 A mandala offering is a symbolic offering of a mandala of the universe. It can be made through symbolic objects or just through the imagination. Here three levels of mandalas have been offered: outer, inner and secret.

71 The five Dharmas of Maitreya were written by Asanga ("Mind Only" Yogacara School).

72 Bodhicitta – the thought of enlightenment for all sentient beings, basis of the Mahayana teachings.

73 sGra 'gyur sKor: a practice using sound as its method.

74 rDzog.chen.po'i sKor: see n. 28, p. 132 above, and Introduction.

75 Phyag.rgya Chen.po brDa. In order that the disciple may understand the true natural mind after preparation, the guru grants the disciple a pointing-out instruction, or demonstration. This may be a blow, a smile, a remark, the showing of an object, a gesture, etc. In this way the natural state of the mind is understood.

76 The Six Yogas of Naropa: a doctrine significant especially to the bKa'bryud school, from the Indian yogi Naropa. These doctrines entered Tibet through his Tibetan disciple Marpa. They are: (i) gTum.mo; the yoga which manifests its results in a rise of body temperature so significant that practitioners can live at high altitudes in winter with no clothes or heat, (ii) rGyu.lus, illusory body, (iii) rMi.lam, dream yoga, (iv) 'Od.gsal, clear light, (v) 'Pho.ba, transference to other forms of existence, (vi) Bar.do, after-death yoga.

77 The Kalachakra is literally the "Wheel of Time," a famous Tantra first revealed at dPal.ldan 'Bras Spungs (Sri Dhanyakataka in East India) and emphasized by Jo.nang.pa school. It is a mystical teaching kept in Shambhala, a spiritual kingdom to the northeast of India, which treats the dimension of time as a Tantric practice, and which was allegedly taught by the Buddha in Kalapa, the capital of Shambhala.

78 A doha is a kind of song or mystical poetry originating with the Indian siddhas. They are cryptic verses often difficult to understand, describing the doctrines and meditation experiences. (See *The Royal Song of Saraha*, trans. Guenther, containing many dohas and Guenther's explanations, and translated commentaries.)

79 Maha Yoga Tantra, Anu Yoga Tantra and Ati Yoga Tantra. (See Tucci, *The Religions of Tibet*.)

80 This temple houses the image of Sakyamuni Buddha, said to have been brought to Tibet by the Chinese wife of Songtsen Gampo (Srong.btsan sGam.po), at the time of the first diffusion of Buddhism in Tibet (seventh century). It is held in great reverence by Tibetans and many miraculous occurrences are attributed to it.

81 Four Prajnas, the profound cognition from (i) listening, (ii) thinking about, (iii) meditating on, (iv) understanding.

82 Three doors to liberations: (i) Voidness, Sunyata (sTong.pa.nyid), (ii) Unconditionedness (mTshan.ma.Med.pa), (iii) Passionlessness

(sMon.pa Med.pa).

83 Chos dbang Sems, the oral explanation of the preliminary experiences (Nyams) of the true sense of the Empowerment of Dharma (Chos.dbang).

84 The method of leaving the body through the top of the head at the time of death (Nam.mkha'sGo.'byed kyi Ngo.sprod 'Pho.ba).

85 Lap.sgron.Ma'i Zhi byed.

86 gCod.tshogs.drug.gi gDams.pa.rnams.

87 Zhi.byed Hum sKor.

88 dMar.khrid sKor.gsum.

89 Phat.chos sKor.gsum.

90 Authapall'i brda. chos.

91 sGyu. 'phrul Chen.mo.

92 Jo.mo Zhal. gnyid.ma.

93 bKa'.brgyud Bla.ma'i rNal.'byor Zab.lam'Pho.ba Grong. 'jug.gi gDams.pa rLung.sems 'Dren pa'i.gnad.kyi. Lhag.pa'i.lam.

94 sGyu.lus rMi.lam.dang Bar.do 'Byongs Cig.char.du sTon pa'i Phra.thig.gis Man.nag.gi.gNad.

95 'Phrul.gcod bKa'.rgya.ma'iMan.ngag Dur.khrod Chen.mo'i dMigs Bya gDan.thog gCig.hu gCod pa'i gDams.pa b'rGyad.

96 'rDo.rje bDud.'dul Chen.mo.

97 Maha Sukha.

98 Kali Yuga: this present degenerate age or epoch. We have degenerated from the Golden Age through the Silver Age and the Copper Age, and are now in our most degenerate (spiritually and morally) Iron Age, which will become worse and worse with things getting faster and faster until the end of the Yuga when evil will have spread to such an extent that it will reach the sacred kingdom of Shambhala, at which time the kings of Shambhala will muster an army and the tides will be reversed. This is to happen about three hundred years from now.

99 Youthful or wrathful deities; 'Jam.dpal 'rTsa.ba'rGyud.kyi rGyal.po.

100 sKye.med sNying.po.

101 Lam.'bras: based on the teachings of Virupa, a collection of Annutara Tantras, particularly connected to the Tantric deity Hevajra, called rDo.rje Tshig.rkang. Lamdre is a commentary on this and this teaching, which literally means "the path and fruit," is the basis of the Sakya lineage.

102 Phag.rgya Chen.po'i brDa. The natural state is often spoken of in the Mahamudra teaching. As is stated in the "Song of Maha-mudra" by Tilopa:

The Void needs no reliance,
Mahamudra rests on nought.
Without making an effort,
But remaining loose and natural,
One can break the yoke,
Thus gaining Liberation.
(C.C. Chang, *Teachings of Tibetan Yoga*, p. 25.)

103 When the practices are effective there are certain signs that appear in the body, such as inner heat, blissful sensations, feeling very light.

104 A way of referring to sexual intercourse between a yogini (Profound Cognition) and a yogi (Skillful Means). This is sexual contact, considered a powerful part of the path. It is the energy which circulates because of the sexual intercourse, especially the activation of the rTsa, rLung and Thig.le (the subtle nerves, life force vibration and the essences of male (semen) and female (menstrual blood)) which opens areas of consciousness previously closed off to the practitioner. In the biography of Yeshe Tsogyel the necessity of finding a suitable partner is explained in this way: "Now, girl without a consort, a partner of skillful means, there is no way that you can experience the mysteries of Tantra. It is rather like this: if a pot is unfired it will not bear usage; in an area without wood a fire will not burn; if there is no moisture to sustain growth it is useless to plant a seedling" (Keith Dowman *Sky Dancer*).

In order to activate our energy and test our development we sometimes need to enter into relationship with an external partner. This is quite the reverse of the usual process wherein we enter into a marriage before we have a chance to prepare ourselves spiritually, as was the case for Nangsa Obum. Machig has such doubts that she seeks several confirmations from her teachers before she is sure she will enter into this partnership. Machig also bore children and she went through a series of pregnancies in rapid succession in very primitive conditions. Her intellectual understanding of surrendering one's selfish desires for the benefit of others, as one must do as a mother, must have been severely tested in this time. (This is also the basis of the offering of the body in Chod.) Without this experience she probably would not have become as mature or as compassionate a woman as she was.

105 dGe.shes is a title for the highest degree of learning in Tibet. It is the Tibetan equivalent of a Doctor of Divinity. Literally it means

"virtue knowledge," and it takes from ten to twenty-five years of study to attain this degree.

106 The Deity of Intellect and Learning, who carries a sword which cuts off the root of wrong view and unstable emotionality.

107 rThen.'Brel Yan.lag bCu.gnyis, the twelve stages in the process of a karmic act, begining with its conception and going through the process of solidifying the thought and action and finally its death. This process is often pictured around the edge of the Tibetan Wheel of Life. The twelve stages are (i) ignorance, (ii) associations or imprints, (iii) consciousness, (iv) name and form, (v) the six sense organs (five senses and the consciousness of the senses), (vi) contact, (vii) feeling, (viii) desire, (ix) sensual enthrallment, (x) procreation, (xi) birth, (xii) old age and death.

108 This is the joining of the white drop (Thig.le) (masculine) and the red blood drop (Thig.le) (feminine) at the heart. Progressive meditation on these follows a similar pattern to that of the Four Empowerments: at the end the two points join together, which is the most important moment, the activation or 'Od.gsal (light), which radiates by itself and is beyond duality, an infinite radiance, radiant voidness. Obviously through yogic practices they had transformed their energy into the red and the white essence and manifested luminosity through their development of the Four Empowerments.

109 The text is painfully brief in explaining this important decision but here again we see that she is guided by the dakinis in making the transition from one phase of her life to the next. It appears that she was not meant to continue her role as mother beyond the time her children absolutely needed her (she left when her youngest was four, after ten years with Topabhadra). Later on when she connects with them again it is in the role of a teacher not a mother. Perhaps it was necessary for these children to be born so that her lineage could be continued by them as her guru told her, but it was not necessary for her to raise them otherwise she would not have had this guidance from the dakini. It is moving to see Topabhadra's understanding of the situation. When he brings them back, rather than recriminations, he offers her his understanding gained in the years they have been apart and she takes over the role of giving them a spiritual education.

Another interesting expression here is that she "appeared" to be tired of the cycles of transmigration (Samsara). This implies that she was not actually tired but gave that as her excuse, because her real reason, i.e. communication with the dakini, either could not be revealed or understood, or should not be revealed. This brings up the whole question of secrecy involved with the dakini principle. The vogue in our society is now "honesty," meaning telling everything that you are thinking or experiencing, to almost anyone. This is not the case in the relationship to the dakini, or when dealing with spiritual practices. Many profound spiritual changes can only be developed in silence. This is the reason why almost all literature based on the dakinis' communication is secret. To reveal the secrets is to cause the wrath of the dakinis, which manifests as obstacles in spiritual development. This principle is echoed by M.L. Von Franz in her lectures on *The Feminine in Fairytales*: "There are things not even discussed by oneself – they must be left in the twilight and must not be looked at too exactly. There are secret things of the soul that can only grow in the dark – the clear sun of consciousness burns the life away. In mythology there are such fairies, trolls, etc., even good ones, who have been struck by a ray from the sun and petrified. They have to live in the twilight, and if they are struck by the sun's rays, they turn into stone" (p. 90).

The reason for the secrecy of the Vajrayana teachings is not to try to make a "secret society" but because, if the lid is left off, the perfume escapes. It is for this reason that the dakini escapes definition, appears in many forms and must remain in the twilight zone along with the "secret" teachings that the dakinis preside over.

110 Phag.mo Thugs.sgrub Lha.lnga.

111 Siddha (Drub.Thob): one who has achieved both the ordinary and extraordinary powers, an accomplished yogi or yogini.

112 Vajrapani is a Tantric Protector.

113 Upadesha (Man.ngag.sde): the most advanced of the Dzog Chen teachings. It is divided into Khregs.chod, wherein the individual recognizes innate awareness (Rig.pa), followed by Thod.rgal, which uses specific postures and meditation techniques, and only Thog.rgal practices develop the capacity to experience wisdom (Ye.shes) and pure light. The ultimate result of these practices is the manifestation of the body of light at the time of death, when the physical and mental spaces dissolve into light. See Tucci, *Religions of Tibet*, pp. 85–7.

114 If the Yogi succeeds in getting the prana into the central channel, discursive thought stops, and he or she enters the meditative state. (See n. 6, p. 129.)

115 gTum.mo: the inner heat practice based on control of the prana, which allows one to stay in very cold places with little or no clothing.

116 Yantra Yoga: the physical movements with co-ordinated breathing which untie the knots in the subtle nerves, make the prana flow smoothly, and most importantly create deep even breathing which leads into meditation. It also contains exercises for the development of inner heat and can be used for healing imbalances which cause illness. Namkhai Norbu has published a text of Vairocana on this subject accompanied by a commentary called *Khrul.'khor Nyi.zla Kha.sbyor*.

117 Pranayama: breathing practices which bring the prana and therefore the mind (which is greatly influenced by the prana) under control.

118 Ma.rgyud mKha'.'gro gNas.'gyur, a dakini sadhana of the Mother Tantra lineage.

119 Mngon.pa'i bZhad.pa rCyas.pa mDzad.

120 Phyag.rgya Chen.po sNyen.rgyud Dri.med Me.long sKor.gsum.

121 Chos Phyag.rgya Chen.po'i gCod.

122 See Introduction, pp. 27–8 above.

123 See Introduction, pp. 21–4 above.

124 Tripitaka – the Sutras, the Vinaya and the Abhidharma (Buddhist psychology), the Hinayana teachings.

125 See Introduction, pp. 27–9 above.

126 A heavenly realm where the Buddha was allegedly dwelling before his birth in Lumbini, India.

127 The Four Mudras are a progressive path toward the fourth mudra called Mahamudra (Phyag.rgya Chen.bo) the Great Seal of the Great Movement. The first is the "Mudra of Dharma," which is the understanding of what a teacher is saying when the Dharma is explained, the understanding of the nature of reality (dharmas). The second, the "Karmamudra," has to do with the practices involving physical contact, the sexual practices. (See *The Life and Teachings of Naropa*, trans. Guenther.) The third, the "Samayamudra," involves keeping the promises, or vows, of doing the visualizations and mantras given during empowerments. Then finally there is the "Mahamudra," the unification of everything in a state of Sunyata (Phyag) and freedom from worldliness (rGya); Chen.po means the unification in one state of these two functions. (See *The Teachings of Tibetan Yoga*, trans. C.C. Chang; Wang Chug Dorje, *The Mahamudra Experience: Eliminating the Darkness of Ignorance*.)

128 Arya Deva – disciple of Nagajuna, founder of the Madyamika school of Mahayana philosophy.

129 "Dewa Ngodrub," a dakini.

130 rDo.rje rNam.rgyal.

131 A wrathful purification deity.

132 Thugs.rje Chen.po Kha.sal.pa. When the Bodhisattva Ava-
lokiteshvara reached enlightenment and was leaving the world,
he turned to look down and saw so much suffering that his head
split into many pieces and he grew a thousand arms and used
these heads and arms to help sentient beings.

133 Rin.po.che'i.sGron.me.

134 sGrol tshogs Drug gDams.pa Lhag Lus.med.pa.

135 gTor.ma – these are offerings made of roasted barley flour or rice
mixed with butter moulded into shapes symbolizing jewels or
elixir. They are used in rituals to appease opposing energies and
please invoked deities. The art of gTorma making and the rituals
accompanying their offering comprise a central part of Tibetan
rituals, and there are hundreds of kinds of torma and rituals
involved with offering them.

136 Kusha grass: the kind of grass that the Buddha sat on when he
achieved illumination. This grass is also given the night before
certain initiations and placed under the pillow and the dreams of
the initiate are told to the lama the next day before the initiation.

137 See n. 38, p. 134 above.

138 Rigpa is the pure intelligence which is actualization of the
uncreated luminous void which is without origin and yet exists.

139 The way of seeing Tawa (lTa.ba) is very important in the Dzog
Chen teachings. The lTa.ba is the most important aspect of the
teaching, because to do practice without correct view is a meaningless activity. When the view is put into action this is the way
of behaving (sPyod).

140 Ringsel are small spherical relics, usually white, though sometimes manifesting the five colors, which emerge from the ashes of
great teachers after their death or from sacred places such as
Buddha statues or stupas. It is said that they are brought forth by
the devotion of the disciples, and that even when a very very
advanced practitioner dies, if there are no devoted disciples, there
will be no ringsel. There are also cases of ringsel appearing after
the ashes or bits of bones have been collected and kept for some
time. Someone might have some remnants and keep them very
devotedly and carefully, and after some time, look at them and
they may have turned into ringsel. Ringsel also have the ability to
reproduce. One of them gets bigger and bumps appear on the
side and then the bumps become small ringsel. In 1970 the stupa
of Swayambhu in Kathmandu produced ringsel on the eastern
side of the stupa. There were thousands all over the ground and
all the monastery, including the highest lama, who almost never

left his room, were outside picking them up.

141 Pho.ba; this practice involves shooting the consciousness out of the top of the head at the time of death and directing it to where you want it to go – to a Buddhafield or the Darmakaya, etc.

3
JOMO MEMO

PROLOGUE

This is a very abbreviated version of the life of one of the best-known women tertons (see Introduction, pp. 42-3). It is an example of a terton Namthar (liberation story). It differs from other kinds of Namthar in that it is not so much the story of an ordinary person who reaches enlightenment through her or his own efforts, but rather the story of a destined woman who receives knowledge through a revelation. After her experience in the cave of Padma Sambhava, she is transformed so completely that she frightens those who knew her before and they accuse her of being a demoness. This story is oriented around this revelation and the teachings which are revealed to her by Vajra Yogini, as is the case with all terton Namthar.

This biography also has elements of the descent motif found in that of Nangsa Obum. Jomo Memo's descent, however, is into a cave where she receives initiation. It is not a voluntary choice, nor is it a negative experience, as in the case of a depression. However, because of the suddenness of the realization gained, she has to leave where she has been living and go to find someone who can help her to use the knowledge she has received. In her teacher Guru Chowang not only does she find someone who can guide her, but he finds in her a dakini who helps him to reveal a terma which he has been unable to decipher previously. Through his sexual contact with her a block in his subtle energy is released, enabling him to decipher the terma.

Jomo Memo is famous less for the terma she received, which was a "yang ter" (see Introduction, p. 44) than for her "death," when both she and two companion yoginis entered the body of light after doing a feast offering. Her "death day" is still celebrated, as we see in the life of A-Yu Khadro (p. 244). She was still very young and must have known that her mission was completed, and therefore she returned to the land of the dakinis.

There is another biography of Jomo Memo, translated by Eva Dargyay in *The Rise of Esoteric Buddhism in Tibet*, pp. 119–23, which states that she was an emanation of Yeshe Tsogyel, the consort and assistant of Padma Sambhava who was responsible for concealing many terma. Here it also states that her instantaneous illumination was caused by the blessing of the dakini. This story is more detailed than my version and has slight differences. For example, it states that she fell asleep near the cave, rather than that she slipped and fell. It also gives further details about her relationship with Guru Chowang.

Yeshe Tsogyel mentions Jomo Memo in her biography thus: "An activity emanation of my speech will appear in Tsang. And known as Jomo she will found a Phakmo Meditation Centre. And the Rites of the Pig-face will embrace the world."[1] Phakmo refers to Vajra Varahi, the dakini with a sow's head coming out of her head.

Note

1 Keith Dowman, *Sky Dancer*, p. 174.

THE LIBERATION STORY
OF JOMO MEMO
(1248–83)

Among the 108 tertons, there were two dakinis. Jomo Memo was one of them, she was considered to be an emanation of Padma Sambhava's consort, Yeshe Tsogyel. She was born in Dagpo, in a place called E, where there was a cave made sacred by Padma Sambhava called the Zarmo Lung cave.

Her father was an accomplished Tantric practitioner by the name of Dorje Gyalpo. Her mother was a dakini called Padma Paltsum. Jomo Memo was born in the fourth Rabjung,[1] in the Year of the Monkey. Her parents called her Padma Tsokye, "Joyful Lotus Lake."

Until she was four her parents kept her at home in quiet, comfortable surroundings. Then her mother died and her father remarried. Her stepmother forced her to do a great deal of heavy work, such as carrying wood and taking care of the animals.

When she was thirteen years old, one day, at noon, she was minding the cattle near the sacred cave, when she slipped and fell. Then she heard a sweet voice calling her from the cave. She was awakened by this very pleasing voice and she looked into the cave and saw a door at the back. She opened the door and saw a heavenly cremation ground, with Vajra Varahi in the center, surrounded by many other dakinis. They were making a feast offering.[2]

Vajra Varahi said to her: "So, my girl, you have arrived?" She took a text and placed it on Jomo Memo's head, blessing her with it. Then she gave her the text. She said: "This is the teachings of the dakinis, 'Sangwa Kundu';[3] if you do this meditation you will reach liberation." As soon as she received the book she knew immediately all that it contained.

After she had feasted with the dakinis and eaten the feast offerings, she awoke and found herself in the place where she had fallen. After this experience she became suddenly all-knowing and very learned. Teachings she had never studied came into her mind spontaneously. She could leave footprints and handprints in stone.

Most people said this was because when she had gone to the mountains she had fallen asleep and a demoness (sMan.mo) had come to bless her. This is how she got her name, which means "Demoness Nun." Because local people, suspicious of her powers, considered her a demoness, she moved to a place about twenty-five days' journey away. The place was called Lodrak.[4] In Lodrak was a famous terton called Guru Chowang. In his prophecies there were to be five dakinis in his life, and he recognized Jomo Memo as one of them.

When Jomo Memo and Guru Chowang were united, he was able to reveal a terma that he could not decipher previously. Whatever she knew she told him, and he told her everything that he knew.

After some time he said to her: "The book given to you by Vajra Varahi is a teaching from Yeshe Tsogyel. Go and meditate on it very secretly. Do not tell anyone that you are going. Then go to Central Tibet, with your two women disciples."

At one point, she met a siddha called Lingje Repa. Through his contact with her he was able to open the channel of profound cognition. He gained the highest realization of anyone between the River Ganges in India, and Tibet.

From the age of fourteen to the age of thirty-six she traveled around, never staying anywhere very long. When she was thirty-six, on the tenth day of the eighth month, she went up to the top of Lhari Mountain in Central Tibet with her two disciples and they made a big feast offering. At the end of the feast she and two attendants flew away to Guru Rinpoche's Copper-Colored Mountain and left no bodies behind.[5] The leftover food, blessed from the feast offering, had the power to bring realization as vast as the sky; the herdsman that ate what was left gained instant realization.

NOTES

1 Fourth Rabjung: just as we measure time by counting in centuries from the time of Christ, the Tibetans count by sixty-year cycles, called Rabjung, dated from the time the Kalachakra was first taught in Tibet, in AD 946. So this would be between 180 and 240 years after the first Kalachakra initiation in Tibet. The eighteenth Rabjung began on Tibetan New Year 1984.

2 A feast offering (Sanskrit: Ganachakra) is an essential part of the life of a Tantrika. A group of Tantrikas get together on auspicious days, usually either five days before the full moon (Padma Sambhava day), or ten days after (dakini day), and practice together and then afterward eat the food and liquor which has been consecrated by the ritual, then they may dance, sing and generally celebrate, offering poems of realization to the gurus, etc. The difference between this kind of feast and an ordinary one is that the practitioners have mentally transformed everything into the sphere of the Tantric deity, and when they eat and drink they work with their awareness and try to remain free from dualistic fixation about "good" and "bad."

3 This text is mentioned in the biography of A-Yu Khadro. It is the terma of Jomo Memo which was rehidden and rediscovered (Yang.gter) by Jamyang Khyentse Wongpo.

4 The area of Southern Central Tibet where Marpa and Milarepa also lived.

5 Body of light: see n. 42, p. 192 above.

4
MACHIG ONGJO

PROLOGUE

Here we have a very interesting example of how a sacred biography can be used as a vehicle to convey teachings. In this story the actual tale of her life is a mere skeleton on which is hung a discourse on the Six Paramitas. One might ask why it would not be sufficient to just give a straightforward teaching on the Six Paramitas. This question contains the crux or the *raison d'être* of the sacred biography. When the teachings are incorporated into a life story as the gradual attainments gained by a practitioner, suddenly they come to life. They are no longer theoretical virtues one could develop but one is shown in which way someone else actually did live these "perfections". Theory is brought into actuality. The use of the direct quotation enhances this device and makes the potentially dry subject-matter even more immediate.

This story is from the *bDem.mchog mKha.'gro sNyen.rgyud* compiled by Byang.chub bZang.po, in the sixteenth century approximately. It was found at the monastery of Abo Rinpoche, in Manali, India. The text was a reprint of a rare text reprinted in New Delhi in 1983. The book is a compilation of oral precepts transmitted by the early masters of the Kargyu (bKa.'rgyud) lineage. There is a similar biography of Machig Ongjo in *The Blue Annals*, but it is even briefer than this one. Apparently she followed quite soon after Rechung, the favored disciple of Milarepa, and was a lineage holder in this Kagyu lineage in the twelfth century.

THE BIOGRAPHY OF
MACHIG ONGJO
(Twelfth Century)

Part 1 Life Story

Machig Ongjo was born in Tsang in the area of Yug. In her
father's family there had been one hundred generations of
Bodhisattvas.

He called her Ongjo. When she was young she had great
faith and devotion. She loved to say prayers and felt sad when
seeing the suffering in the world. She was studious and
listened intently whenever teachings were given. She heard
and understood everything that was said. Her teacher was
Gyalwa Kyang Tsangpa, a disciple of Rechung Dorje Dragpa.
As soon as she met him, she had great faith in him. On seeing
her faith and devotion, he accepted her as his disciple and gave
her the secret ear-whispered teachings, which are given by a
guru to the one who will carry on his lineage. In this case the
lineage had passed from Marpa to Milarepa to Rechungpa to
Kyung Tsangpa and then to Machig Ongjo. She spent much of
her life in retreat and purified all her negative karma.[1] Then
her meditation became clear and she attained many accomplishments.

Part 2 Accomplishments

She became accomplished (yon-then) in: generosity, discipline,
patience, the ability to keep her mind on the path and not
waste time, the ability to keep her mind calm, and the

[216]

realization that no entity has an individual nature, or ego. This last one was realized through the use of the faculty of "Profound Cognition Which has no Beginning."[2]

Machig Ongjo's accomplishments

Generosity (Dana)
First she gave all her belongings to her guru. When he asked her if she might not need this wealth later she responded: "You are my guru and the Buddha incarnate. I have complete faith in you. All these things are impermanent and have no essence. I have no attachment to them. The teachings of the Buddha are so much more precious than this wealth. It would not make sense to be practicing the teachings of the Buddha and at the same time cling to material things. The time of death is not known. It is much better not to procrastinate, but practice the teachings now."

Discipline (Sila)
In the retreat of Ga Gong she attained the second accomplishment. Here she was the leader of all the monks and nuns. Once at a feast offering she said to her disciples: "I have been accumulating merit[3] for many lifetimes, and because of this I have been able to meet my great guru. I have attained the precious human body and have not wasted this body. I have used it to practice the Dharma. I have kept all my vows, so even if I died now I would have no regrets."

Patience (kShanti)
In Ngo.pa Na Shugpa she spoke of patience. She said: "The Dharmata is as pure as the sky. The mind itself is unstained and luminous. The root of the ego is not connected to the natural state. This is my stabilized understanding of the essential instructions. This is the jewel of the ear-whispered lineage.[4] I have been cut free from all doubts through the transmission of these teachings. I have not wasted my time and have understood everything."

Energy (Virya)
When she was at Bul Ngag she did four meditation periods a day, of visualization practice, and her worldly body, speech and mind, became the transformed and purified body, speech, and mind of the visualized deity. She said of this time: "When I practiced the meditation with prana and nadis,[5] my mind did not wander. I realized the Great Bliss of the undefiled natural state. Knowing this, my mind flows like water."

Meditation
When she was in retreat at Dzarana she said: "Knowing the essence of my own mind; whatever discursive thoughts arise, I am not distracted and remain in a state of awareness."

Profound cognition (Prajna)
When she was at Kyung Tsang she said: "The distinguishing factor of all phenomena, is emptiness. Spontaneous liberation is the Great Bliss itself. It is Dharmakaya, beginningless, beyond name and words. I know this only because of the guru's kindness. The natural state, spontaneity, arises by itself. This is the bliss of knowing myself as not separate."

This is the short explanation of the accomplishments and realization of Machig Ongjo.

NOTES

1 The results of actions naturally occur in a state of ignorance, when we act and react continually and impulsively. Causes lead to effects, every action has an equal reaction just as in physics, but if we stop making impulsive actions then we can begin to work with all the impulses and "karmic traces" that have already built up within us. In retreat not only are we removed from the world where we create so much ignorant karma, but we also have time to apply efficacious methods in clearing out the karmic traces which we have imprinted in our psyches.

2 sKye.med Shes.rab: literally skye med means "no birth." This indicates that a Prajna, profound cognition, is outside conditioned existence. That which has birth also will die, and that which is "not born" is therefore not within these limits. That "which has no beginning" is also different from being eternal, because eternal also indicates something within certain limits.

3 Accumulation of merit: see n. 33, p. 133 above.

4 The ear-whispered lineage: Kagyu lineage.

5 Tsa.rlung: the subtle nerves and energy controlled through yogic practices.

5
DRENCHEN REMA

PROLOGUE

We can ascertain that Drenchen Rema lived in the middle of the fourteenth century if we judge from the dates of someone she met during her lifetime, Guru Urgyenpa. She is one of the few women in the Kagyu lineage descending from Rechung, and Milarepa.

This biography is a typical short rNam.thar in that all the events in her life are recounted only as they relate to the spiritual path. This biography also contains the tales told by her disciples about her miraculous powers. The stories of her miracles are tacked on to the end like a kind of list, obviously collected from her disciples. This is the only example of this kind of biography in the collection. Others that might have fallen into this category, such as A-Yu Khadro, did not because the biography was taken only from A-Yu Khadro herself, not her disciples, except the very end when her disciple reports how she died. The tales of miraculous episodes are frequently attractive for disciples as they seem to represent a proof of the extraordinary ability of their guru.

The story is from the *bDem.mchog mKha'.'gro sNyen rgyud*, compiled by By.ang.chub bZang.po in the sixteenth century. It was found at a monastery of Abo Rinpoche.

THE LIBERATION STORY OF DRENCHEN REMA

Drenchen Rema Shegmo ("Cotton Clad Woman of Great Mindfulness") was born in Tsang in the area of Gurmo in the monastery called Ri chung.

Her father was of the very eminent lineage of Ba. His name was Geshe Nyen Jansem Sogyal, and her mother's name was Semo Chodar. They had three sons and two daughters. One of these daughters was called Rema, though her real name was Yeshe Kunden. Because she had accumulated stores of merit in previous lifetimes, she often considered the imminence of death and experienced sadness and compassion when she saw the suffering of the world. She saw all worldly existence as suffering and decided that she would never want to marry and become trapped in the suffering of worldly life, even on the threat of death. She was determined to pass her life practicing the Dharma.

When she was thirteen she began to study reading and writing. She learned all of her prayers by heart. When she was fourteen she decided to leave the world and live the rest of her life in a hermitage. She dismissed the problem of food with the thought that if she did not get food she would subsist on water.[1] She decided that if she did not have clothes she would wear discarded rags.

When she told her father of her decision and asked him for some teachings, he said: "You are too young for this and will find it too difficult to practice in this way. But I know you are not an ordinary girl. You are a dakini blessed by Vajra Varahi. I know this because before you were born I had a dream that you had a pig's head coming out of the side of your head.[2] When this head made noises everyone was frightened."

Her mother said: "My dear, girls cannot practice the Dharma. It would be far better for you to marry now that you have many suitors."

Rema thought to herself: "I will prove to her that girls can practice the Dharma."

Then she had a dream of a Dharma Protector and in the dream he said to her: "You should go to practice the Dharma."

Shortly afterward she read a book called *Ser O Dampai Do*, "The Sutra of the Holy Golden Light," which said: "The relative truth is that everything you see externally is as substantial as a dream. The absolute truth is that the essence of mind does not exist. It has no shape or color that is stable. The primordial awareness of the mind is unconditioned."

Inspired by this she wrote another book herself on black paper in gold letters. Afterward she said: "My Lama is the Buddha. The Dharma is this book I read."

One day she read another book called *Gye Tong*, an abridged Mahayana scripture. After reading it she understood that Samsara and Nirvana, and all dharmas, are unreal and like a dream. After this she wrote many songs. Then her father, who was also her guru, said to her: "You should study with some other gurus." She replied: "There is no need to study any more, I need to meditate. Studying is only useful in this life. People do it to gain respect, which brings food and lodging. They do not think of future lives and they do not practice meditation."

Her father said: "How can you meditate if you do not study first? If you only meditate, people will have faith in you and come to you and ask for teachings. Then you will be unable to teach them because you will not have studied. If someone asks you for an empowerment you will not have any idea how to give it. If your disciples die, you will not know how to help them in the Bardo state."

Rema replied: "Even if I do not study, if I meditate I will get results. The fruits of the meditation will be enough. I do not want to study. I will teach only what I have understood from my own practice. If people want empowerments, I will not be able to give them. I have no desire to learn rituals. I only want to meditate."

[225]

Her father said: "Even though what you say is true, I still want you to study." So he taught her various practices, rituals and philosophy.[3] Then she received the inner teaching of the wish-fulfilling gem of Rechungpa, and many other practices.[4]

Then he taught her the meditation of holding the mind steady and she decided to go far away to practice in retreat. She sold all of her possessions, including her personal jewelry, and with the money she made, she made a big feast offering and prepared to leave. Then all of her family started to cry and begged her not to go.

Her father said: "If you want to go far away it must mean you are looking for a husband. You will not be able to study if you go away, and anyway it is not good for girls to travel alone. You can do your three-year retreat near here. If what you want to do is to practice, you can do it here as well as anywhere."

So she stayed in retreat for a year above her village, but she found it very noisy as it was too close to the town. Then she heard of a place further away which had been blessed by Padma Sambhava. She thought she would go there and even if she could not find food, she could live on water. She intended to become enlightened in one lifetime.

She left her retreat and went to this place called Shang. After she had been in retreat for some time she was very happy with the results, and one day she went down to a field where some people were working. She asked them to bring her rice, beer and food. They did so and among these people was a woman who had great faith in Rema and asked if she could follow her. Rema said: "If you come with me you have to give up everything and live on water."

The woman agreed and they left for Zabbu. They meditated there, living on water. They had many obstacles and were both sick and attacked by spirits, but they continued meditating and eventually pacified the spirits. When they went begging they inspired many people. The villagers used to ask them to come and heal their animals and to give teachings. Rema gave them instructions and sang them Dharma songs. As her fame began to spread, many people came to see her. Once a group came and asked her if she was a dakini. She replied that she was, and then they said: "If you are a dakini, show us your powers!"

She said: "I have no powers!" She got angry and threw stones at them. The stones, instead of hurting them, cured all of their illnesses. Many people gained faith in her and offered her their hair and many substantial offerings, but she gave everything away to her gurus.

She traveled to various places to do retreats, and she began to see deities in her sleep and while awake. Then she returned to the place where she had done a year's retreat, in order to do the practice of Cakra Sambhava. She began to dream of places she had never been, and in one dream she saw three thrones. She asked: "For whom are these thrones?" The response was: "The Buddhas of the Three Times." At that moment she saw the Buddhas on their thrones. After receiving Dharma teachings and Bodhisattva vows from them she woke up.

Another night she had a dream that she went to a place where Guru Rinpoche and four dakinis were living.

In another dream, she was in robes and carrying many weapons and was surrounded by dakinis who were fighting savage Non-Buddhists with matted hair. She was victorious. This indicated that she had conquered her obscurations and hindrances.

Another time she dreamt that she was holding a crystal stupa. There was a rainbow over the stupa and inside was a luminous Buddha.

Once she traveled to Lhasa with fifteen disciples and visited the famous Buddha in the center of the city. As she prayed there, five kinds of flowers fell from the sky. The temple keeper and many others saw this with their own eyes.

Another time she was in a closed cave, which was sealed except for a small air hole. On the night of the lunar eclipse she slipped through the hole carrying her small drum and bell. She went up above and behind the roof of the nearby house, and climbed the cliff behind the house without using her hands. Then she returned to her cave without making her body any smaller or the hole bigger. Many of her disciples saw this, but she told them not to tell others because they would not believe it in any case.

Once she had to go up a high mountain so her disciples gave her a yak to ride. The yak slipped and she fell into an abyss and a lot of rocks fell with her. Everyone was sure she was dead, but when they found her she was sitting quietly on some rocks. Everyone was very surprised and very thankful. She sang them a song and then got up, uninjured. She told everyone to keep this a secret for one year.

On another occasion she was giving teachings on the ordinary Dharma to a group of people. While making a feast offering with about fifty disciples she manifested a red and blue dorje, and a skull in her hands. Around the dorje was a circular rainbow. All those present saw this. One of her disciples, Deleg Rinchen, asked her to give him the skull, which she did. Then he asked her to show him some miracles.

She replied: "From the age of eighteen until the age of seventy-one, I have been staying in retreat and meditating. I have not been roaming around aimlessly and I am not dependent on anyone. These are my miracles, but probably you will not understand them."

Once she was chanting the mantra of a wrathful protector, and a long piece of flesh in the shape of an eye-tooth grew out of her mouth. Then she subdued all the non-human spirits and they began to have faith in her and bowed to her. She had great psychic powers but did not show them often to worldly people. Whatever she predicted came to be; for example, if she said the crops would not be good one year, the crops would fail.

Whatever problems she had would never deter her; she always continued to practice with an unwavering mind. She treated everyone equally. She was not especially ingratiating to rich patrons or impatient with the poor. Although her realization was far beyond external and preparatory practices, she never neglected forms such as keeping a shrine, doing prostrations, and making offerings. She was correct on every level. Whatever wealth she accrued from offerings of devotees, she gave for Dharma activities.

Once she said:

"Meaningless talk is parrot's chatter, even if we believe in it,
It will not create any positive results.
If merit has been accumulated,
Even a little talk will cause positive results.
If you have no inner accomplishments,

But act like you are a big yogi,
You are really useless.
Even if you have been taught the Great View,
Do not think you are so advanced,
Or you are in danger."

Toward the end of his life Rema's father was contemplating and praying. He was concerned above choosing the successor for his lineage and thinking about whom he would give his most secret teachings to. From the sky came a voice that said these words: "The lineage of the Victorious Ones of the Three Times."

He thought: "What does this mean? Who does this refer to?" Then later, with his psychic powers, he saw that it was to Rema that he must pass his lineage. At the same time he remembered his dream of Vajra Varahi before her birth.

Once when she was young the Great Siddha Urgyenpa (1323–60), disciple of Gyalwa Gutsang, came to see her on his way to China.

He asked: "Are you thirty-five?"

She said: "Yes, I am."

He replied: "Yes, I know you must be."

Then he told her special disciple: "When Gutsang was alive he said that his disciple Machig Drowa Zangmo would become the special disciple of Rema, and if Machig cured a particular impurity, she could become very useful to sentient beings."

Rema lived to be eighty years old and at that time one of her disciples, the monk Dzijid Gyaltsen, wrote this biography. He collected the stories herein, from Rema herself and her disciples.

NOTES

1 There are various yogic practices that help one to remain in isolated places for retreat. One of these is called bCud.len, and is a method of extracting essences from minerals, water, tree saps, and even air, which can be used by the meditator to sustain life instead of gross food. Yogic practices of inner heat, gTum.mo, are also useful, because if one becomes an adept one no longer needs to worry about staying warm in the winter or procuring clothing.

2 Pig's head: see Introduction, pp. 31–2.

3 rGyud gSang.ba sNying.po: Secret Heart Tantra. A.roa'i Theg chen rNal.'Byor: the Mahayana yoga of Ahro. Yang.dag Grub.mchog Che.chung: the Great and Small Through Accomplishment. Ma.mo dang Phur.pa dang Ngan.song dang Sprug.rnams kyi sGrub Thabs 'Phrin.las: the Actions and the Power over Mamos (female spirits, Mystical daggers, the Damned and Phantoms). rNam.'joms: Subduing. Phyag.rdor: Vajrapani. rTa.mgrin: horse-headed Tantric deity. Thugs.rje Chen.po: Avalokitesvara. Gu.ru'i.sKor: the circle of the Gurus. mGon.po Legs.ldan: the protector Legden. rNam.sres Zhi.drag Sogs.pa'i sGrub.Thabs Phyag.len rNams bslabs: Teachings and ceremonies of the Siddhas of the Major and Minor Peaceful and Wrathful Deities.

4 rDo.rje Tshig rkang: the indestructible essence words. rDo.rje gZhung.chung: the Indestructible Small Middle. rJe Mi La'i Khrid. yig sBas.pa: the Hidden Letters in the Instruction of Milarepa. Yab.bKa Yum bka'i dBang.dang Byin rLambs.kyi bKa'.ma Lus. rDzogs bar gSang: the Secret Body of the Dzog Chen Oral Transmission of the Blessing and Empowerment of the Yab and Yum. bLa.ma Khro Phur.ba la sMen.bla dang Don.zhags: the Wrathful Avalokitesvara and the Supreme Medicine of the Wrathful Guru Phur.ba, A Collection of Tara Practices; Ye.shes Kun.lden la

mDo gCod sKor.gsum: the Three Cyles of Chod Discourse on All-Truthful Wisdom. bLa.ma Kar.ma.pa dang 'Dzam.gLing rGyan. ang Grub.thob mGon.po Ye.shes: the Wisdom Protector Siddha Ornament of the Earth Lama Karmapa. Tar.pa Lo.tsa.ba.dang mKhas-Grub Chos.rje la.sog.pa bLa.ma bCu.tsamMang.du.gsan: the Translation of Tar.pa (a Sanskrit scholar from the area of Tar in Tibet) and the Secret Teachings and Verbal Instructions of Lama Chutsam, the learned Accomplished Lord of Dharma.

6
A-YU KHADRO

PROLOGUE

This is the most contemporary biography in this collection. It is interesting and special for several reasons apart from being a wonderful story. First through Norbu Rinpoche's description of how the biography came into being we can see the process of the making of a Namthar very vividly. We can see that what she selected was what would be relevant for another practitioner to know.

This story also represents the lives of many great yoginis who lived and died in relative obscurity. The other biographies in this collection are all of women who achieved great fame in their time. We can also see how the tradition Machig Lapdron handed down through generations from the eleventh century remains intact up into modern times. Most of A-Yu Khadro's life before she went into retreat consisted in living the life of a Chodpa, wandering from one pilgrimage place to another practicing the Chod. We know that there were others like her: for example, her lifelong friend Pema Yangkyi, with whom she traveled for years, achieved the rainbow body at the time of her death. From this story we get the feeling of the freedom and independence of a Tibetan yogini.

THE BIOGRAPHY OF
A-YU KHADRO,
DORJE PALDRON

Homage to Dorje Paldron and Vajra Yogini!

This biography is only a drop of the nectar of A-Yu Khadro's life. As I write of her I will try to remember her presence. I am the insignificant disciple Namkhai Norbu,[1] and this is the story of how I met A-Yu Khadro and how I came to write her life story.

When I was fourteen in the Year of the Iron Rabbit, 1951, I was studying at Sakya college.[2] My teacher there, Kenrab Odzer, had twice given me the complete teachings of Vajra Yogini in the Norpa and Sharpa[3] Sakya tradition.

One day he said to me: "In the region of Tagzi, not far from your family's home, lives an accomplished woman, a great dakini, A-Yu Khadro. You should go to her and request the Vajra Yogini initiation from her."

That year he let me leave a month early for the autumn holidays with the understanding that I would be going to see A-Yu Khadro. So first I returned home and prepared to go with my mother Yeshe Chodron, and my sister Sonam Pundzom.

We set off, and after a journey of three days we arrived at A-Yu Khadro's place in Dzongsa. She lived in a little stone hut near a river in a meadow under the cliff face of a mountain to the east of a small Sakya monastery. The hut was tiny, with no windows.[4] She had two assistants, an old man, Palden, and an old nun, Zangmo. They were also strong practitioners of yoga and meditation.

We were very happy and amazed to see this situation. When we entered the Khadro's room for the first time only one butter lamp was lit. She was 113 at that time, but she did not look particularly ancient. She had very long hair that reached her knees. It was black at the tips and white at the roots. Her hands looked like the hands of a young woman. She wore a dark-red dress and a meditation belt over her left shoulder. During our visit we requested teachings, but she kept saying that she was no one special and had no qualifications to teach.

When I asked her to give me the Vajra Yogini teachings she said: "I am just a simple old woman, how can I give teachings to you?"

The more compliments we offered her, the more deferential she became toward us. I was discouraged and feared she might not give us any teachings.

That night we camped near the river and the next morning, as we were making breakfast, Ani Zangmo, the old nun, arrived with her niece bringing butter, cheese and yogurt. These, she said, were for the breakfast of my mother and sister, and I was to come to see Khadro.

I went immediately, and as I entered I noted that many more butter lamps were lit and she touched her forehead to mine, a great courtesy. She gave me a nice breakfast of yogurt and milk and told me that she had had an auspicious dream that night of her teacher, Jamyang Khentse Wangpo.[5] He had advised her to give me the teachings of Khadro Sangwa Kundu,[6] his Gongter. This was not the teaching I had asked for, but was a teaching she had received from him directly which she had practiced extensively. While we were having breakfast she was examining the Tibetan calendar. Then she said: "Since tomorrow is the day of the dakini we will begin then. Today go to visit the Sakya monastery and in the meantime we will make preparations."

So we went off to visit the monastery and made some offerings there. They had statues of the Buddhas of the Three Times and a stupa five arm lengths high made of gilded bronze and studded with many jewels. It had been made according to the Khadro's instructions. Inside it was empty.

The next day around eleven we began with the initiation of Khadro Sangdu. From that day on, every morning she gave teachings including the practices of the subtle nerves and the subtle breath. In the afternoon at the end of her meditation session[7] she gave further explanation of the Khadro Sangdu and the Chod of Machig Lapdron, the Zinba Rangdrol.[8] This was the Chod practice she had done for many years when she was younger. There were five of us receiving these teachings: Khenpo Tragyal,[9] the abbot of the monastery; Yangkyi, a nun; my mother; my sister; and I. Her hut was so small that not everyone could fit in and Yangkyi had to sit outside the doorway. The Khenpo assisted with the shrine and the mandalas.

A month later she began the Yang-Ti,[10] one of the most important of the Dzog Chen teachings in the most advanced Upadesha series, having to do with the practice in the dark.[11] This teaching took five days. Then she began teaching on the Longchen Nying Thig.[12] This ended on the 24th. In the seventh month on the tenth day she gave the Vajra Yogini in the Sharpa tradition, the instruction I had requested, followed by a complete explanation. This was linked to the Kha Khyab Rangdrol[13] teachings of Nala Pema Dundrub. Then she gave the complete teachings of her Singhamukha Gongter[14] which took until the tenth of the following month. At the end she gave the long life White Tara practice. Not only did we receive formal teaching, but in addition she made time for informal conversations and personal advice. I was not with her a long time, a little more than two months. During that time she had given eight kinds of teachings and was really so kind and gentle. We were very content with the generous gift of these precious teachings.

The Khenpo, one of her principal disciples, told us that he had, from time to time, received teachings from her, but the kind and extent of the teachings she had given us were rare indeed. She normally did not give much teaching and had never given so much in such a short time. He was afraid this meant that she might pass away very soon. Then Palden, the old man, said that several months before we came she had a dream indicating that she should give certain teachings soon. Before we arrived they had begun the preparations. So there was definitely a motive for giving these teachings.

Sometimes, at my request, after the afternoon teachings, she would tell me about her life. I had the peculiar habit of writing everything down, unusual for Tibetans, so I wrote down everything she told me. From these notes I constructed this biography. What follows is what she herself told me.

I would ask her a question, for example about her birth and childhood, and she replied: "I was born in the Fourteenth Rabjung in the Year of the Earth Boar, 1839, during the winter, on the day of the dakini. The Togden[15] who lived on the nearby mountain, Togden Rangrig, was at our house when I was born. He named me Dechen Khadro, which means Great Bliss Dakini.

"Some people also reported some auspicious signs on the day of my birth. I was born in Tagzi in the village of Dzong Trang in the family of Ah-Tu Tahang. In ancient times this had been a very rich family, but when I was born we were neither rich nor miserably poor. My father's name was Tamdrin Gon, but he was called Arta. My mother's name was Tsokyi, but she was called Atso, and they had three sons and four daughters. All the sons became traders and all the daughters did nomad's work, looking after animals. Since I was the youngest and the weakest I was sent to look after the small animals and given the worst clothes. This is the story of my birth and childhood."

Then I asked her how she had met a teacher and begun to practice meditation. She said: "My aunt Dronkyi was a strong practitioner and lived near the cave of Togden Rangrig in another cave. From childhood she had been interested in meditation, and I, too, was strongly drawn to the teachings. I went to this place, Drag ka Yang Dzong, by my own choice when I was seven. I stayed there until I was eighteen, in 1856. I assisted my aunt, bringing her water and fire wood. I also assisted a disciple of the Togden, Kunzang Longyang, and he taught me and his nephew Rinchen Namgyal to read and write Tibetan. I began to become quite good at reading because the disciples of the Togden decided to read the Kangyur[16] twice to extend the Togden's life and I participated in this. When I was thirteen I received initiation and teaching on the Longsal Dorje Nyingpo.[17] I also received the explanation and did my best to participate fully; although I had no understanding of the teaching really, I had much faith.

"A man called Apho Tsenga came to receive this teaching. He was from the rich family of Gara Tsong in the region of Nya Shi. They were friends of my aunt. My parents also attended the teachings but their minds were not on the teachings, rather on my future. By the end of the teaching I had been betrothed against my will to Apho Tsenga's son. I had no idea, really, what it meant, but I understood an interruption to my practice was being planned. My aunt did her best to intervene but my parents were interested in the wealth of the Gara Tsong family. They only consented that the wedding be delayed a few years.

"When I was fourteen I went with my aunt and Togden Rangrig to see Jamyang Khentse Wongpo, Jamyang Kongtrul, and ChoGyur Lingpa, three great lamas, gathered together to consecrate a special place. It was a seven-day journey to this place, Dzong Tsho, and there we also met a lot of other teachers and great masters and received much instruction. My desire to participate more fully in the teachings increased at this time, particularly when we stopped to see Situ Rinpoche at Pema Nyingkye on our way back. From him we received teaching on the White Tara. After this we returned to the Togden's retreat place and he and my aunt went straight into retreat. I began doing the preliminary practices[18] of the Longchen Nying Thig in my spare time. I was instructed by Kunzang Longyang.

"When I was sixteen, in the Year of the Wood Tiger, 1854, my aunt and I went to see Jamyang Khentse Wongpo. When we arrived we heard that he was in very strict retreat, but we sent him a message saying we had come from Togden Rangrig.

"Since we had come from so far away with great self-sacrifice he agreed to see us. When we met him, he told us that the preceding night he had had a dream which indicated he should teach us. He had decided to initiate us into the Pema Nying Thig, his White Tara Gongter. During the initiation he gave me the name Tsewang Paldron. For more than a month every time he finished a session he gave us teachings. I began to get some idea of the meaning of the teachings at this time and when we returned to Togden's place I made a White Tara retreat.

"When I was nineteen, in the Year of the Fire Serpent, 1857, my parents and my brothers and sisters all decided it was high time I got married. They began to make great preparations for my marriage and my aunt was very worried. She felt responsible for introducing the Gara Tsong family to my parents. It was against her advice that they proceeded with my marriage. She pleaded that I should be left to do what I wanted to do and that my practice should not be interrupted. But my parents insisted on marriage – not for my happiness, rather for their gain.

"Towards the middle of the summer the wedding took place. It was a very happy occasion: even Togden Rangrig came to the wedding and showered blessings on us. It seemed as if we would be happy.

"I stayed for three years with the Gara Tsong family, and my husband, Apho Wangdo, was very kind and generous. Then I fell ill and slowly weakened for two years. The sickness could not even be diagnosed. Sometimes it seemed like a prana disease,[19] at other times I had convulsions like epilepsy; sometimes it seemed like a circulation problem. In short none of the doctors could help or even distinguish what the problem was. Whatever ritual or medicine was advised had little effect. I became worse and worse and was near to death when they finally asked Togden Rangrig to come to see me.

"He gave me a long-life initiation and performed a ceremony to call the spirit back into the body and many other rituals. Both he and my aunt insisted that the real cause was that I was being forced to lead a worldly life and stay in that household which was not what I really wanted to do. They told my husband and his family that I must be allowed to leave and follow my heart. They told them about the signs at my birth and my encounters with Jamyang Khentse Wongpo. Finally they convinced them that marriage was a blockage of innate propensities to the extent that it was endangering my life force.

"My husband was a very kind man and agreed that if married life was endangering my life, it must be stopped. I told him that if he genuinely understood and loved me he would want to follow the Togden's advice and let me be free to go and do as I pleased. I also told him that I would welcome his assistance in my retreat and hoped we could have a relationship of spiritual brothers and sisters, and if he agreed perhaps I would get better.

"He promised to do this, and who knows whether it was because of giving his word or the rituals of the Togden, but after a while I began to get better. As soon as I was strong enough, he accompanied me to the caves of the Togden and my aunt. It took me a year to recuperate. I was helped very much because he made offerings to a nun there with the understanding that she would serve me and help me with the necessities. He and his sister also brought me food and supplies, acting as my patrons. During this year I received the termas of Guru Chowang.[20]

"During this time I had a dream indicating that the passing away of Togden Rangrig was imminent. When I told him this dream he said: 'I have already given you all the teachings I received from my gurus Motrul Choying Dorje, Migyur Namkhai Dorje and Rigdzin Pema Dupa Tsel.'

"I asked him to give me a practice to extend his life; I did this and he lived another three years. During this time I received teachings from him of Guru Nyang Ralpa[21] on the Dzog Chen of Nyima Dragpa and many other teachings. Then with the experienced guidance of my aunt I began to do a lot of practice. When I was twenty-seven in the Year of the Iron Bull, 1865, and Togden Rangrig was seventy-seven, he fell ill, and one morning we found he had left his body. He remained in the meditation posture[22] for more than seven days. We made many offerings and many people came to see him. After the seventh day we found that his body had shrunk to the size of an eight-year-old child. He was still in position and everyone continued to pray.

"As we were making the funeral pyre and preparing the body to be burned everyone heard a loud noise, like a thunderclap. A strange half-snow half-rain fell. During the cremation we sat around the fire chanting and doing the One 'A' Guru Yoga practice from the Yang-ti teachings. At the end there is a long period of unification with the state. When this was over we discovered that my aunt had left her body. She was sixty-two at the time, and when everyone else got up she didn't, she was dead. She was in perfect position and remained in the seated posture more than three days. We covered her with a tent and remained in a circle around that tent day and night, practicing.

"Everyone was saying what an important yogini she was. Previously no one had said this. After three days she was cremated on the same spot where the Togden had been cremated. Although everyone spoke well of my aunt I was terribly sad. I felt so lonely after the death of both the Togden and my aunt, even though it was a good lesson in transience and the suffering of transmigration. Many people continued to hear sounds from the funeral pyre for many nights. I decided to do a three-year retreat in my aunt's cave. I was assisted by the Togden's disciples and thus had good results from the retreat.[23]

"When I was thirty, in the Year of the Earth Dragon, Kunzang Longyang and the nun that had been serving me and I began to travel around practicing Chod. We decided to visit Nala Pema Dundrub, also called Chang Chub Lingpa, as had been indicated by Togden Rangrig.

"We visited many sacred places and various monasteries on the way, so the journey took more than a month and a half. When we arrived at Adzom Gar we met Adzom Drukpa and his uncle Namkhai Dorje. They told us that Nala Pema Dundrub was expected shortly. Since Namkhai Dorje was giving teachings on Longde[24] to Adzom Drukpa and a group of about thirty of his disciples, we joined the group and received these teachings. The young Adzom Drukpa reviewed the teachings we had missed before we arrived.

"Toward the beginning of the sixth month Nala Pema Dundrub arrived. When he gave the great initiation on the Tshog Chen Dupa,[25] including Adzom Drukpa and Namkhai Dorje we were about one thousand people. He also gave teachings on Tara Gonpa Rangdrol[26] the root text about the practice at the time of death, and finally the Kha Khyab Rangdrol his own Gongter. Namkhai Dorje and Adzom Drukpa gave more detailed explanations of the essential teachings of Dzog Chen. Thus we received not only initiations, but practical explanations of how to do the practices.

"Kunzang Longyang and the nun I had come with decided to return to Togden Rangrig's place and I decided to go to visit Dzog Chen monastery and Sechen monastery with some of Adzom Drukpa's disciples. One of the people I traveled with, Lhawang Gonpo, was a very experienced Chodpa[27] and I learned a lot from him.

"When we arrived at Dzo Chen monastery, winter was approaching and it was becoming colder every day. Lhawang Gonpo taught me the inner heat practice, and the practice of living on air and mineral substances, and so, thanks to his skillful instructions, I was able to live there quite comfortably in bitter cold winter.[28] We visited many lamas and other teachers at Dzog Chen monastery and it was during this winter that I met my friend who was the same age as me, a nun called Pema Yangkyi. We became close friends and traveled together for years.

"When we were thirty-one, in 1869, Lhawang Gonpo, Pema Yangkyi and I went to try to see Dzongsar Khentse Rinpoche with a khenpo of Dzog Chen monastery called Jigme and ten of his disciples.

"Along the way we visited Dege Gonchen monastery, where they had the woodblocks for the Kangyur. We also visited other interesting places and slowly made our way to see Dzongsar. When we got there, to the place called Tashi Lhatse, we discovered that Dzongsar was in Marsho in strict retreat. So Khenpo Jigme and his disciples went off to visit Katu Payal monastery.

"Lhawang Gonpo, Pema Yangkyi and I decided to go to Marsho with the intention of either seeing Dzongsar Jamyang Khentse Rinpoche or remaining in retreat near his retreat place. We made our way there begging, and when we arrived found he was, in fact, in strict seclusion. We could not even send him a message, so we camped among some rocks below his retreat and began to do some intensive practice ourselves.

"We were there for more than a month before a monk called Sonam Wongpo came by one day to see what we were doing there. We told him where we were from and what we had been doing and that we had hoped to see Khentse Rinpoche. This became an indirect message to Dzongsar Khentse Rinpoche.

"One day, a while later, that monk came back and told us that Khentse Rinpoche would see us following his meditation period that morning. We were elated and when we entered his room he called me by the name Tsewang Paldron that he had given me. He had decided to give us teachings on the Khadro Sangdu between his meditation sessions, since he knew us to be serious practitioners of meditation, but we were not to utter a word of this to anyone or it would become an obstacle for us.

"Since in two days' time it would be the anniversary of Jomo

Memo's entrance into "the body of light," he thought that that day we should begin the teachings. So in the meantime we went out begging to get enough supplies for ouselves and to offer feasts when it was appropriate.

"We took much teaching from him and still had plenty of time to practice. Then we returned with him to Dzongsar, and along with hundreds of other monks, nuns and yogis we received the Nying Thig Yabzhi,[29] which took more than three months. It seemed to me that during that period I really understood something about Dzog Chen.

"He also gave us teachings from all the schools, the Kama Terma, Sarma and Nyingma schools,[30] for more than four months. We attended these teachings and met teachers from all over Tibet and received teachings from them as well. Afterwards we felt it was time to do some practice.

"When we were thirty-two, in 1870, we went to see Nala Pema Dundrub in Nyarong; we went with some disciples of Dzongsar Khentse who were from Nyarong. Traveling slowly we eventually arrived in the region of Narlong in a town called Karko, where Nala Pema Dundrub was giving the Longsal Dorje Nyingpo initiation. We received the rest of this teaching and the Yang-ti Nagpo. We were there more than three months.

"After this we went with Nala Pema Dundrub to Nying Lung to the area of Tsela Wongdo, where he gave the Kha Khyab Rangdrol. When this teaching had come to an end he called for Pema Yangkyi and me. He had named my friend Osel Palkyi, 'Glorious Clear Light,' and me Dorje Paldron, 'Glorious Indestructible Vajra.' During this teaching, and addressing us with these names, he said: 'Go to practice in cemeteries and sacred places. Follow the method of Machig Lapdron and overcome hope and fear. If you do this you will attain stable realization. During your travel you will encounter two yogis who will be important for you. One will be met in the country of Tsawa and the other in Loka, Southern Tibet. If you meet them it will definitely help your development. So go now and practice as I have instructed.'

"He presented us each with a Chod drum, and after further advice and encouragement we saw no reason to delay and set off like two beggar girls. Our only possessions were our drum and a stick.

"We visited Kathog and Peyul monasteries and many sacred places, encountering many teachers. Eventually we arrived at the caves of Togden Rangrig, where I had lived as a girl. I had been gone three years and it certainly gave us a desolate feeling. We found only an old disciple, Togden Pagpa, an old nun, and Chang Chub, a younger nun that I'd known, and Kunzang Longyang. It made me very sad to be there. When we said we were going to Central Tibet, Kunzang Longyang said that he would like to come with us. So we stayed for two weeks. As he made his preparations, we practiced Guru Yoga, made feast offerings, did practice of the guardians and so on with the old disciples of Togden.

"We were thirty-three in 1871, and it was the third month on the tenth day of the Year of the Iron Sheep that we made a fire puja and set off for Central Tibet. We traveled with about twenty other people on their way to Central Tibet. We followed them for about a month until we arrived in the region of Tsawa.

"When we reached Tsawa we slowed down and began our pilgrimage, begging here and there. One day we arrived at a big plateau called Gurchen Thang. We approached a large encampment of nomads to ask them for food. We stood at the edge of the camp and began to sing Chod. A young robust woman came toward us and as she approached we could see she was crying.

"She rushed to us and said: 'Thank goodness you Chodpas have come! Please help me! The day before yesterday my husband was killed for revenge in a feud. He is still lying in the tent. It is not easy to find a Chodpa in this part of the country. Please help me take care of his body.'

"We were rather at a loss as none of us were really experts at funerals, but she was so desperate we agreed to do our best.

"We asked her: 'Is there a good cemetery around here?'

"She replied: 'Toward the south, about half a day's journey from here, there is an important cemetery. If that is too far there are other, smaller ones closer.'

"We decided to go to the larger one, and the next day in the morning we set off with someone carrying the corpse.

"As we were approaching the cemetery we heard the sound of a drum and bell. As we got closer we heard the sound of a

[246]

beautiful voice singing the Chod. As we entered we saw a Chodpa at the center of the cemetery. He was quite young, with a dark complexion and a big turban of matted hair,[31] wrapped around his head. He wore a dark-red robe and was singing the feast offering of the Chod.

"At that moment we were reminded of Nala Pema Dundrub's prophecy that we would meet a Chodpa who would help us in Tsawa. When we arrived at the center of the cemetery with the corpse he stopped singing.

"He asked: 'Who among you is Dorje Paldron? Where have you come from? What are you doing here?'

"I said: 'I am called Dorje Paldron. These are my friends, Osel Wongmo (previously called Pema Yangkyi) and Kunzang Longyang. We are disciples of Nala Pema Dundrub. We are going to Central Tibet practicing the Chod in various charnel grounds on the way. We happened upon this situation and the family requested that we take care of this murdered man, so we brought him here. Who are you?'

"He replied: 'I am a disciple of Khentse Yeshe Dorje, my name is Semnyi Dorje and I was born in Kungpo. I have no fixed abode. I have been practicing here for the last few days. Several days ago when I was between sleeping and waking I received a communication that someone called Dorje Paldron was coming. Since then I have been waiting for you and that's why I asked which one of you is Dorje Paldron. Welcome! But a murdered corpse is not a simple matter to offer to the vultures. If you are not sure how to do it, maybe we can do it together.'

"We were very happy and set to work immediately on the funeral. We practiced together for seven days, and the relatives of the dead man brought us food. Togden Semnyi gave us teachings on the Zinba Rangdrol Chod and we became a party of four.

"We traveled at a relaxed pace begging on the way, stopping a few days here and there to practice at special cemeteries, sometimes stopping at length. After a few months we arrived at Dzayul, near Assam, and went to Tsari, where there was a temple called Phagmo Lhakang in the area of Chicha. We traveled up and down in that area for a year and three months. We went to many important places to practice.

[247]

"Then in the sixth month of the Monkey Year, 1872, Kunzang Longyang fell ill with a terrible fever. We called doctors and did many practices, but he did not get better and towards the end of the sixth month he left his body. He was fifty-six years old. When we performed the funeral there were many interesting signs, like a huge rainbow so large everyone for miles around saw it and it remained for the whole funeral. The local people were convinced a Maha Siddha[32] had died. They honored us very much and we stayed there more than three months doing practice for Kunzang Longyang.

"After this we went to Jar and then on to Lodrag and visited all the sacred places there. This is the country of Marpa the translator, where Milarepa's trials took place.[33]

"On the tenth day of the tenth month we reached Pema Ling and did a feast offering. There is a huge lake at Pema Ling and many saints and yogis have lived around it, including Guru Chowang. That night we decided each to practice separately in different places around the lake.

"Pema Yangkyi went to a place called Rona and when she arrived she saw a yogi practicing there.

"He said to her: 'Three months ago I was practicing in Ralung, the original seat of the Drukpa Kagyu lineage, and I had a vision of Dorje Yudronma.[34] She gave me a little roll of paper about as long as my finger. I quickly unrolled it and it said 'In the tenth month on the tenth day go in practice at a place called Rona'.'

"She realized this was the yogi Nala Pema Dundrub had predicted we would meet in Southern Tibet. After the evening practice he came back to the main temple with her and thus we became four again.

"This yogi's name was Gargyi Wanchug, but he was called Trulzhi Garwang Rinpoche and he was a disciple of the famous woman Mindroling Jetsun Rinpoche who taught on the Dzog Chen Terma of Mindroling. He had a large following around Pema Ling. His disciples requested Chod teachings and so we also became his disciples and stayed to hear his teachings.

"We stayed there until the tenth of the third month practicing intensively. We did 100,000 feast offerings from the Chod practice, and there were many patrons to help us.

"Although we had previously planned to go to Samye, we

decided to go with Trulzhi Garwang to Western Tibet to see Gang Rinpoche. So we traveled at a leisurely pace toward Yardro, where there is a huge lake, and then on to Ralung. We stayed there more than a month while he gave some of his disciples teaching in the Ati Zadon[35] in the tradition of Mindroling. We were happy to receive such a precise explanation and were treated very well.

"Then we set out for Gyaltse, Shigatse, Sralu, and Sakya, and all the principal places in Tsang. We did purification and Chod practice in all these places and then in the summer arrived in Tingri where Phadampa Sangye had lived. After staying there for a while we went to a place called Nyalam and then with great difficulty we went into Nepal.

"We stayed at Maratika doing White Tara practice for long life and Pema Nying Thig[36] of Jamyang Khentse Wongpo. Togden Trulzhi asked Pema Yangkyi and me to give him the transmission of this, and since we had it we did our best to give it to him.

"Then we went on to Kathmandu and toured the Great Stupa[37] and other pilgrimage places in Kathmandu valley for a month or so, practicing and making offerings. Then we did another month of Chod, which fascinated the people, and we began to receive many invitations and became a bit better off.

"Trulzhi Garwang Rinpoche said that this fame was an obstacle to the practice, a demonic interruption. So we left for Yanglesho[38] and visited a Vajra Yogini temple[39] in nearby Parping.[40] Next to this is the temple of Dakshinkali,[41] down by the river. Here there is an important Hindu temple, and we went to the nearby cemetery, which was an excellent one for Chod. But after a few days and nights we were disturbed by people, not spirits.

"So we went back to Yanglesho and stayed there near the cave and Todgen Semnyi gave Togden Trulzhi the transmission of a particular Vajra Kilaya practice[42] he had. We practiced it for several days and then decided to leave Nepal.

"We headed for Dolpo, and through Purang we arrived at Kyung Lung, where there was a cave in which Togden Trulzhi had stayed before. We stayed there and in the first month of the first year we received the Kadro Nying Thig[43] from Trulzhi Rinpoche. We received a very elaborate complete version and stayed there for more than three months. It was a beautiful retreat. At Trulzhi Rinpoche's request we did our best to give the transmission of the Khadro Sangdu we had received from Jamyang Khentse Wongpo.

"At the beginning of the fifth month we were guided to Mount Kailash[44] by Trulzhi Rinpoche. We stayed in many caves and sacred places around and on the mountain for over three years, always practicing everywhere.

"Then Trulzhi Rinpoche and Pema Yangkyi decided to stay on there and I decided to return to Central Tibet with Togden Semnyi.

"In the second month of the Year of the Fire Bull we said good-bye and we left, making our way slowly to Maryul doing Chod at all the interesting places along the way. We stopped at Jomo Nagpa, the former residence of Taranatha,[45] and many other places beneficial for practice.

"In the fourth month we stopped at Tanag and Ngang Cho, where there lived a great Dzog Chen master, Gyurme Pema Tenzin,[46] who was giving teaching on Dzog Chen Semde[47] his speciality. We stayed there more than nine months and received complete teachings in the eighteen series of Dzog Chen, including initiations and explanations.

"Then we met some pilgrims who had come from Kham, and they told us that, several years before, Nala Pema Dundrub had taken the Body of Light,[48] and this had made him very famous. We were both joyful and sad on receiving this news. When I was forty, in 1878, Togden Semnyi and I left for Central Tibet. We went through Ushang, where there is a famous shrine of the Blue Vajra Sadhu, protector of Dzog Chen. We traveled all over that area on pilgrimage practicing a bit everywhere. During the fourth month we sighted Lhasa. We visited all the holy places of Lhasa and met many famous people. Then we visited the nearby monasteries of Sera, Drepung, and Trayepa, Gaden, Katsal, Zvalakang. Then we went on to Yangri, Drigung, and Tigrom. We always did a bit of practice everywhere we went.

"Then we returned to Lhasa, where I became very seriously ill. For nearly two months I was severely sick with a very high fever which became paralysis. The doctors succeeded in lowering the fever but the paralysis continued to worsen.

Togden Semnyi did special Chod practices to clear up the paralysis, and finally I started to get better after two months. It took another month to start moving and recuperate. In the eleventh month we decided to go to Samye for the New Year celebration. We did many days of feast offering of the Ringdzin Drupa.[49]

"In the first month we left for Zurang and visited Gamalung, a Padma Sambhava spot, and Wongyul, and then we sighted the Red House at the Copper Mountain, and stayed in the cemetery there. This was the former residence of Machig Lapdron. We stayed there for three months practicing the Chod.

"After this we went to Tsethang and Tradru, and from there we went to Yarlung Shedra, another place that Padma Sambhava empowered. Then we went on to Tsering Jung, where Jigme Lingpa[50] had had his residence. We went on up and down for more than eight months.

"When I was forty-two, in 1880, in the second month, we arrived at Mindroling. We visited Zurkar and Drayang Dzong, and the Nyingma monastery Dorje Dra, as well as Ushang Do and Nyethang and Talung, and also Tsurpu, where the Karmapa[51] resided. We met many teachers and received many teachings during our travels.

"In the fourth month of 1880 we arrived at Payul and Nalandara and Lang Thang, one of the residences of the Khadampa[52] school. Then we arrived at Na Chu Ka[53] and headed towards Eastern Tibet.

"In the seventh month we arrived at Kungpo, where Togden Semnyi had been in retreat in the region of Kari at Deyang. In those caves there was another yogi, a monk and some nuns. When they saw Togden Semnyi they were very happy. I stayed there more than a year practicing and deepened my understanding of the Zinba Rangdrol Chod. Togden Semnyi gave me teachings in the Yang Sang Tug Thig, the most secret Dzog Chen Gongter.

"In the Year of the Iron Serpent, 1881, I decided to travel on to my home country. I met some traders on their way to China who were to pass through my country, so I decided to travel with them.

"When we got to the place I had lived when I was married I

said my farewells to the traders and did some invocations to protect them on their ventures and set out in the direction of Togden Rangrig's retreat center. When I approached the spot I made some inquiries as to what had happened there, but most people had never heard of the place. A few remembered that a yogi had lived there years before, but, they said, he had died and the few who remained had either left or died.

"I decided to go there anyway. The place was in ruins. The wooden doors and window sills had been pulled out by the local people to be used elsewhere and I could not even recognize the caves of my aunt and Togden Rangrig.

"I stayed the night there. I felt very sad and did some practice. The next day I went down the mountain a bit to the cemetery to stay and do Chod. The following morning I had a vision when I was between sleeping and waking of an egg-shaped rock in Dzongtsa, which I could enter through a cave. When I got inside there was a very intense darkness which suddenly was illuminated by multi-colored light streaming out of it. This illuminated the cave and pierced the walls so that I could see through to the outside.

"Then I awoke, and seeing this as a good indication and since I'd heard there was in fact such a place, I left for Dzongtsa. When I arrived I found the place. It was near Dzongtsa, but was on the opposite side of the river from where I was. I decided to camp on a nearby hill and wait for some help or for the river to go down so I could cross. But it was autumn and the river was very high.

"I practiced day and night, and during the third night after midnight something inexplicable happened to me. I had fallen asleep and a long bridge appeared. It was white and reached the other shore near the rock I had dreamed of. I thought, 'Good, finally I can cross the river.' So I crossed, and when I awoke I was actually on the other side of the river.

"I had arrived but I did not know how.

"I put my tent on the spot where I had landed and stayed there practicing Chod for more than a month. I was assisted by a nomad, Palden, who lived nearby. He supplied me with cheese and yogurt, etc., and from time to time people came by. But even if they had known me before they did not recognize me.

"In late autumn an epidemic broke out among the nomad's animals. I was asked to intervene, which I did with the Chod and fire practice. The epidemic stopped and everyone began to say I was a great practitioner. As they began to honor me I was worried remembering that Trulzhi Rinpoche had said this was a demonic interruption. So I entered a stricter retreat. After a month or so my former husband arrived with his second wife and daughter. He had heard of my arrival and brought me many supplies. We had a very good rapport; I gave him teachings and he asked if he might build me a house.

"I told him I would like it to be right on the same spot and explained to him how I wanted it built. They invited me to their house for the winter. As it was very cold that year and his parents had died I went to their house and meditated for the benefit of the deceased for about three months. My father and siblings with many nieces and nephews came to see me and I helped them as much as possible by teaching them.

"When I was forty-four, in the Year of the Water Horse, 1882, in the third month my husband and others began my hut. I decided to go to see my master Khentse Rinpoche. I arrived on the tenth day of the fourth month and received many teachings and he clarified all my doubts.

"Then I left for Adzom Gar and met Adzom Drukpa and Drodul Pawo Dorje. I received his Gongter, and all the 'Nying Thig' transmissions. Adzom Drukpa asked me to stay and do a retreat at Puntsom Gatsal near Adzom Gar where he had been in retreat, which I did.

"In the second month of the Year of the Wood Monkey, 1884, Adzom Drukpa and his disciples went to see Jamyang Khentse Wongpo at Dzongsar and I went with them. Because Adzom Drukpa had requested it he gave us the Gongpa Zangthal. Both Adzom Drukpa and Khentse Wongpo told me to return to Tagzi, where I had landed after crossing the river in my dream.

"So I left immediately, stopping only to see Kongtrul Rinpoche and receive teachings on the Six Yogas of Naropa[54] and to learn from the others who were there taking teachings. On the eighth I returned to Tagzi, and my former husband and other faithful people had built me a hut precisely according to my instructions.

"At this point I lacked nothing and decided to go into retreat. My eldest sister's daughter had become a nun a few years before and she wished to act as my assistant. As she was also very committed to practice, I accepted her offer.

"So in the Year of the Wood Bird, 1885, in the first month on the day of the dakini I began a seven-year retreat. From the beginning I spent most of my time doing the practice of the dark. At first this was sometimes difficult so I alternated the dark and light,[55] but the majority of the time was spent in complete darkness.

"When I was fifty-three, in the Year of the Iron Rabbit, 1891, in the fifth month on the day of Padma Sambhava, when I was doing practice in the dark I had a vision. I saw a very clear sphere; inside it were many dakinis carrying another sphere with the form of Jamyang Khentse Wongpo inside. I was sure this meant that he had been invited by the dakinis to leave this world of suffering.

"Although I still had seven months before the end of the seven years I had promised myself to complete, I decided it was more important to see him before he left his body. So I left my hut and a few days later went directly to him in Dzongsar, accompanied by my niece.

"We reached him without obstacles, and he was very kind and taught me a lot; most importantly, he clarified my practice by answering all of my questions. When I told him the vision I had had of him being carried away, I requested that he remain longer. He said that all that is born must die and that his death could not be delayed. He told me it would be best for me to return to my retreat hut and continue my practice in the dark.

"With great sadness I left him and returned to my hut. When I was fifty-four, in the Year of the Water Serpent, 1892, I received the news of his death. At that moment I decided to stay in retreat for the rest of my life. So I alternated the practice in the dark with the practice in the light. When I was fifty-six, in the Year of the Wood Horse, 1894, both my mother and the wife of the nomad Palden who had been serving me died. I did the practice of the Korwa Dongtru[56] for them for several months. Then Palden came to serve me here.

"When I was sixty in the Year of the Earth Dog, 1897, my husband Apho Wangdo died, so I did purification for him and his family for an extended period of time.

"At the end of autumn in the Year of the Iron Mouse, 1900, my old friend Pema Yangkyi appeared unexpectedly. She brought the news that in the third month of the previous year, 1899, Trulzhi Rinpoche, at the age of eighty-three, had passed away taking the body of light and leaving no corpse. She told me the whole story of how this had happened in his cave on Mount Kailash.

"She stayed in my tiny hut with me for a year and we did retreat together. This was a big boon for me; it really helped the development of my practices.

"After a year she left for Kawa Karpo, a mountain in Southern Tibet which had been indicated by Trulzhi Rinpoche as the place she should go to. I later heard that she lived there for many years and had many students. Then in the Year of the Iron Boar, 1911, she took the body of light at the age of seventy-four.

"After her departure her students came to me for teachings and told me stories from her life and about her death. Then in the Year of the Wood Tiger at the end of summer some disciples of Togden Semnyi came and told me he had sent them to me specifically. They told me that he had not remained in Chumbo but had traveled toward Amdo on pilgrimage, practicing everywhere.

"At the end of his life they went towards China to Ribotse Na. He stayed there teaching for three years and had many disciples, both Chinese and Tibetan. At the age of eighty-five he passed away and there were many auspicious signs and many ringsel in his ashes.

"Realising that all of my friends had left the world made me very conscious of impermanence, and I was inspired to practice as much as possible with the time I had left. I taught Togden Semnyi's disciples for several months and then sent them off to various places to practice meditation."

That is the end of what A-Yu Khadro told me herself. The rest is the story of the passing away as I heard it.

She told me these stories, gave me much wise counsel and then I returned to my master at the Sakya College. That year I finished college.

In the Year of the Water Dragon, 1952, in the eighth month, I went to Sengchen Namdrag, where my uncle had been in retreat. I did a Simhamukha retreat and various other practices there.

I had a dream while I was there of a brilliant crystal Stupa which appeared to be being pushed toward the West. Slowly it disappeared in space and at that moment I heard a voice saying: "This is the tomb of Dorje Paldron."

The voice woke me up and I felt really very empty inside, and even doing some breathing practices did not make me feel better. I felt I had lost something very important inside myself.

A few days later the son of Adzom Drukpa came by on his way back from Central Tibet. I told him about this dream, and he said that, in fact, he had stopped to see her on his way and she had indicated by the way she spoke of time and so on that she would not live much longer. He thought probably my dream indicated that she would die soon. So we did some Khadro Sangdu practice for three days to try to extend her life.

In the Year of the Water Serpent, 1953, I was with my uncle on the mountain and taking Nying Thig teachings when I received word she had left her body. I said a few prayers, as I did not know what else to do.

In the sixth month I went to Dzongtsa, where she had died in her hut, and discovered that the servant Palden had died the same year. They said there were many auspicious signs at the time of his death.

I met the Khenpo and the nun Zangmo who had served her, and Zangmo told me this story of her death:

"In the Year of the Water Serpent Khadro said to us: 'Now I feel really old. I think in a little while I shall go!' She was 115 at the time.

"We begged her not to go, but she said: 'Now bad times are coming and everything is going to change. There will be terrible problems and it's better I go now. In about three weeks I won't be here anymore. Start preparing for the funeral.'

"She instructed us precisely on how to conduct ourselves during the funeral and in preparation for it. She had an important statue of Padma Sambhava which she sent to Gyur Rinpoche, son of Adzom Drukpa. She left a little statue of Jamyang Khentse for Namkhai Norbu and various other things for Khenpo and her other disciples.

"At the end she opened herself completely to everyone who wanted to see her. During the last twenty days she stopped doing regular meditation periods and just saw people, giving advice and counsel to anyone who wanted it.

"Near the twenty-fifth without any sign of illness we found that she had left her body one day at the time she would normally be finishing her meditation session. She remained in meditation posture for two weeks and when she had finished her Tugdam her body had become very small. We put some ornaments on it and many many people came to witness it.

"In the second month on the tenth day we cremated her. There were many interesting signs at the time of her death. There was a sudden thaw and everything burst into bloom. It was the middle of winter. There was much ringsel and as she had instructed all this and her clothes where put into the stupa that she had prepared at the Sakya monastery."

I, Namkhai Norbu, was given the little statue of Jamyang Khentse Wongpo and a volume of the Sehmukha Gongter and her writings and advice and spiritual songs. Among her disciples there were few rich and important people; her disciples were yogis and yoginis and practitioners from all over Tibet. There are many tales told about her, but I have written only what she herself told me. This is just a little biography of A-Yu Khadro written for her disciples and those who are interested.

This text was written and verbally translated from Tibetan to Italian by Namkhai Norbu Rinpoche, and simultaneously translated orally into English by Barrie Simmons in Conway, Massachusetts, on the day of the dakini, 8 January 1983. It was taped in Conway, then transcribed, edited, and footnoted by Tsultrim Allione, finished in Rome, Italy on the day of the dakini, 7 February 1983.

NOTES

1 Namkhai Norbu: a Tibetan lama born in 1937 in Kham, the recognized incarnation of Adzom Drukpa and formerly tulku (lineage of reincarnating lamas) of the Gonchen monastery. He is particularly closely familiar with the doctrines of the Dzog Chen school and is also the major expert on Bon, the native Tibetan religion predating Buddhism. He has lived in Italy for more than twenty years and currently teaches Tibetan and Mongolian at Naples University.

2 Sakya: one of the four great sects of Tibetan Buddhism. The Sakya gained political pre-eminence in Tibet by winning the favour of Genghis Khan during the creation of the first Mongol empire. 'Phags pa, leader of the Sakya, granted the initiation of Hevajra (Kye rDo,rje) to Genghis Khan in exchange for sovereignty over Tibet which lasted a bit less than one hundred years. The current leader of the sect is Sakya Pandita (Sakya Tendzin).

3 Ngor.pa and Tshar.pa: two subdivisions of the teachings of the Sakya school signifying the monasteries they emerged from. These schools are normally included in the Sakya teachings.

4 A windowless structure is the ideal for a retreat in the dark, an important part of the Upadesha practices in the Dzog Chen tradition. A-Yu Khadro specialized in this kind of practice.

5 Jamyang Khentse Wongpo (1820–92), the fifth discoverer king, allegedly the incarnation of Vimalamitra. He studied widely, far beyond sectarian limits, and was known as a great scholar and meditator. Also called Jamyang Kyentse the Great. Since his death there have been various lineages of Khentse Rinpoche's who are said to be aspects of this original one. He compiled the *Rinchen Terdzod*, an anthology of Dzog Chen termas which includes the "mKha'.'gro gSang.ba Kun.'dus."

6 The teaching given to Jomo Memo (1248–83) by Dorje Phagmo in the cave of Padma Sambhava. (See Dargyay, *The Rise of Esoteric Buddhism in Tibet*, p. 119, and biography of Jomo Memo, pp. 207–11 above.) This text was lost and it was not until Jamyang Khentse Wongpo in the nineteenth century discovered it as a Gongter that the teaching was available again. The text is referred to from here on in its abbreviated form, Khadro Sangdu (mKha'.'gro gSang. 'dus). It is a great series of teachings on Vajra Varahi, some say a Mother Tantra, associated with the four trinlay ('prin.las) or actions: calming, enriching, overawing, and destroying.

7 Tun is the Tibetan name for a meditation session. Usually there are four tun in a day – early morning, mid-morning, afternoon and evening.

8 See Prologue to Machig Lapdron, pp. 144–9 above.

9 Khenpo is Tibetan for abbot.

10 Yang-ti: essential teachings of Dzog Chen (Sanskrit: Maha Ati).

11 The practice in the dark (Mun.mtshams): this practice is part of to-gyal (Thod-rgal) teaching in the Upadesha series which aims at the dissolution of the physical and mental world into the body of light or the rainbow body. This is done through physical positions and breathing techniques which activate the internal vision and space (dByings) to be externalized as tigle (Thig.le), a circular apparition which embodies the absolute awake state, a combination of luminosity, voidness and infinite potential. The practice of the dark shows clearly the non-duality of internal and external space because of the manifestation of light from the mind in complete external darkness. There is a development of these lights and tigle, which often have images in them, which culminates in the internal space (dByings) manifesting externally as vision and then the physical elements being transformed into their pure essence, light. At the time of death the accomplished practitioner of Thod.rgal manifests the rainbow body having absorbed all the energized transformable cells into a body of light leaving only the hair and fingernails behind. This is the fruit of the Thod.rgal practice. When we hear of someone's body shrinking to the size of an eight-year-old child or smaller, this is the process which is being referred to, which is another manifestation of Thod.rgal practice of rgyu lus (see n. 42, p. 192 above).

12 kLong.chen sNying.thig: 'Jigs.med gLing.pa (1729–98) had spiritual contacts with Kun.mKyen kLong.chen Rab.byams.pa, usually called Long Chenpa (1308–63), and thereby wrote this text, synthesizing into a cohesive system the divergent strains of the Nyingma teachings current in the fourteenth century. The Nying

Thig describes the outer, inner and secret meanings of Sadhana practice, the oral tradition, and initiation. This text was allegedly originally revealed at the time of Triston Desson (Khri.srong lDeu.btsan) (756–977) to Vimalamitra.

13 mKha.khyab Rang.grol: a text on the Upadesha series (Man.ngag. sde) in the Dzog Chen teachings.

14 Simhamukha: a lion-headed semi-wrathful dakini, dark-blue in color, carrying a skull cup in her left hand and a hooked knife in her right, often used in the Dzog Chen practices.

15 Togden (sTogs.ldan) is a way of describing a yogi. It is a title signifying one with long matted hair usually wrapped around the head to become like a turban. Sometimes a togden also takes monks' vows but more often than not they are not monks but have a self-discipline far beyond that of many monks. They usually wear the white cotton clothes and a red and white shawl. There is a group of these togdens living at Tashi Jong, Palampur, Kangra Valley, Himachal Pradesh, India.

16 The Kangyur (bKa'.'gyur) is a massive encyclopedia of the Buddha's teaching in 108 large volumes. These doctrines were edited by Rinchen Zangpo (Rin.chen bZang.po) during the "Second Diffusion of the Doctrine" during the ninth and tenth centuries (AD) and put into their final form by Bu.ston (d.1364). The Kangyur is followed by the Tangyur (bsTan.'gyur): commentaries, glosses, and secondary works. These are the Buddhist canon in Tibet.

17 Longsal Dorje Nyingpo: a terma of Longsal Nyingpo. A disciple or terton of bDud.'dul rDor.je (1615–72), Longsal Dorje Nyingpo wrote this terma on Upadesha. His son, rGyal.sras bSod.nams lDe.btsan, possessed the throne of Ka.thog monastery as did his descendants. He also wrote the terma of sKu.gsum kLong.gsal sNying.po.

18 The preliminary practices (sNgon.'Gros) consist of the four 100,000s: prostrations, recitations of the Vajrasattva mantra and visualization, mandala offering, and invocations of the lineage (Guru Yoga). This is a very strenuous, time-consuming series of practices usually undertaken at the beginning of any major practice or retreat, and is almost always performed once in the lifetime of a practitioner.

19 Prana (rLung) disease is caused by an upset in one of the five rLungs of the body: (1) Srog.zhin rLung, at the crown of the head controls swallowing, breathing, clearing sense organs and concentration; (2) Gyen.rgyu rLung, in the thorax, responsible for speech, good complexion, body weight, memory, and energy to work; (3)

Khyab.byed rLung, resides in the heart area and controls muscle function, lifting, walking, stretching, opening and closing of mouth, eyes, etc. (4) Me.mnyam rLung is in the abdomen area, responsible for the functioning of the organs and the metabolism; (5) Thur.sel rLung resides in the perineal region and is responsible for the bowels, semen, menstrual blood and uterine contractions.

20 Guru Chowang (1212–73): Guru Chos.kyi dBang.phyug was the second of the great tertons following Nyi.ma 'Od.zer. His biography is published in Dargyay, *The Rise of Esoteric Buddhism in Tibet*. He was the guru of Jomo Memo.

21 Guru Nyang Ralpa: a terton from ancient times, also called Nyima 'Od.zer (1124–92), the first of the Discoverer kings and considered to be one of the greatest tertons who ever lived. (See Dargyay, *The Rise of Esoteric Buddhism in Tibet*.)

22 The period of time that the body holds the meditation posture and shows no signs of life is called the Thugs.dam. During this time the being is in profound meditation and giving out her or his final energy before taking another form. It is very important to leave the practitioner undisturbed during this time. It is also a good time for disciples to practice Guru Yoga, i.e. unifying with the mind of the guru.

23 The role of the assistant to a person on a long retreat should not be underestimated. They become the lifeline for food and water, and the karmic connection formed here is very strong and beneficial to the server. Not only do they act as a major cause for the realization of the hermit, they create a karmic bond with the teachings as well.

24 kLong.sDe: lies between Sems.sDe and Man.Ngag.sDe in the three series (sDe.gSum) of Dzog Chen teachings. The practice utilizes a belt and a stick with the hand cupped under the chin as one sees in some Milarepa tankas in order to control the flow of prana in the body and to develop visions in the process of stabilizing the state of contemplation. The practitioner using the above-mentioned aids fixes the gaze in space in the morning and late afternoon. Of course kLong.sDe can also be practiced without these aids, but they are distinguishing external features of kLong.sDe practice. kLong.sDe is characterized by the four Da (brDa): (1) clarity (gSal); (2) no thought (Mi.rtog.pa); (3) sensation of bliss (bDe.ba); (4) union (dByer.med).

25 Tshogs.chen 'Dus.pa: a series of teachings on Anu Yoga.

26 dGongs.pa Rang.grol: the root text for the after death practice in the Dzog.chen tradition.

27 Accomplished practitioners of the practice of Machig Lapdron, Chod (gcod).

28 See n. 1, p. 230 above.

29 sNying.thig Ya.bzhi: the four series on Man.Ngag.sDe (Upadesha), the quintessence of the Dzog Chen teachings which lead to the development of the Thod.rgal practice. See n. 14, above.

30 bKa'ma: those teachings which have been passed down through oral transmission. gTer.ma: see Introduction, pp. 43–4. gSar.ma: the new or reformed Tantras taught after the "Second Diffusion" in the ninth and tenth centuries, that is following Rinchen Zangpo and Atisa. (See also n. 22 in Tucci, *The Religions of Tibet*.) Nying.ma: the oldest school in Tibet, based on the Dzog Chen teaching coming from Padma Sambhava and Garab Dorje, called the old ones to distinguish them from the new school (gSar.ma).

31 Matted hair is an ancient way for ascetics to wear the hair. The hair forms matted strands about the width of a pencil and requires no care. In Tibet togdens were very often seen with these mats, similar to the dreadlocks of the Rastafarians in Jamaica and the hair of the sadhus in India. If the locks are very long, they are wrapped around the head in a turban-like form.

32 Maha Siddha is a realized being from the history of Buddhism (a tradition which began in India), who usually continued her or his mundane work in the world, like washing clothes or selling wine, but reached realization through that work and attained magical powers.

33 For further information read: W.Y. Evans-Wentz, *Tibet's Great Yogi Milarepa; Drinking the Mountain Stream*, trans. Cutillo and Kunga, 1978.

34 rDo.rje gYus.Gron.ma: Female divinity used for prophecy.

35 Ati Zab.don: Dzog Chen teaching in the Upadesha series, written by Zig.po gLing.pa (1829–70), a terton, after seeing Padma Sambhava in a vision. (See Dargyay, *The Rise of Esoteric Buddhism in Tibet*.)

36 Pema Nying Thig: one of the eight sections of the sGrub.sde, the texts with practical instructions for meditation by Padma Sambhava himself.

37 The Great Stupa: called Baudhanath by the Nepalis, in Tibetan mChod.rten bya rung Kha shor. It was built in ancient times by a woman, Bya.rDzi.mo, and her four sons. It is said that when it was consecrated one hundred million Buddhas dissolved into it and it is said to be full of relics (Ring.bsrel). "Whatever prayer is offered to it is fulfilled, and if you meditate upon your personal deity (yi-dam) here, at the time of your death you will be reborn in Skhavati. Here is the cremation ground Spontaneously Amassed (Lhun.grub brTsegs.pa), one of the eight great cremation grounds.

See Keith Dowman, "A Buddhist Guide to the Power Places of the Kathmandu Valley," *Kailash: A Journal of Himalayan Studies*, pp. 259–63.

38 Yanglesho: this cave and the cave of Asura above it are both sacred to Padma Sambhava. "In Guru Padma's biographical bKha.thangs it is not made exactly clear how he divided his practice between the cave at Yanglesho and the Asura Cave; but it may be inferred that his Mahamudra Practice is associated with the former, and the Yang-dag and Phur-ba practice with the latter" ("A Buddhist Guide," p. 251).

39 Vajra Yogini temple: "this image of Vajra Yogini is the embodiment of pure awareness (jnana, Ye.shes) and is a speaking Yogini. She is an image of the heart-vision of Phamthingpa and others" ("A Buddhist Guide," pp. 254–5).

40 Parping: this is a small village near Yanglesho and Dakshinkali. The name of the town may be a corruption of the Naga Shesa's epithet Phanathinggu, "the Nine Hooded Cobra," and the great yogin Pham-thingpa who studied nine years with Naropa took his name from this place where he was born.

41 Dakshinkali: a fearful cremation ground close to Parping and a good place to practice the Chod. It is the most popular temple in the Kathmandu valley for blood sacrifice.

42 rDo.rje Phur.ba.

43 Khadro Nying Thig: Padma Sambhava gave the initiation for this teaching to Yeshe Tsogyel and Lacam Pema Sal but hid the text as a terma, and the teachings were reabsorbed by dakinis until Terton Padma Las 'brel unearthed the teachings, but since he was not ordained in the tradition of concealed treasures, he was unable to explain it. Longchen Rabjam (1308–63) revealed its contents only after a dakini, an emanation of Vajra Varahi, had initiated him. So Longchen Rabjam became the first to teach this teaching in this world hundreds of years after Padma Sambhava. (See Dargyay, *The Rise of Esoteric Buddhism in Tibet*, p. 56.)

44 See n. 54, p. 136 above.

45 Taranatha was the most important of the Jonangpa school founded by Sherab Gyaltsen (1292–1361) whose teacher's teacher was a Saivite pandit from Kashmir. The Gelugpa school considers the Jonangpa school almost heretical as they believe that what can be cognized is non-existent and only Tathagata or the absolute essence really exists. (See Tucci, *The Religions of Tibet*.)

46 'Gyur.med Pad.ma bsTan'dzin: master of Peyul monastery.

47 Sems.sde: the Dzog Chen teachings which culminate in the Maha Yoga Tantra and have to do with the calming of the mind using

specific fixation points and moving toward not using the support of a visualization or object such as the breath. The Sems.sde series includes teachings on Zhi.gnas and Lhak.mthong. (See Tucci, *The Religions of Tibet*.)

48 See n. 42, p. 192 above. "Rainbow Body" and "Body of Light" are the same thing.

49 Rig.'dzin 'Druspa: another name for Nala Pema Dundrub.

50 Jigme Lingpa (1729–98): a great terton who, from a very young age, began to have visions. After seeing Longchen Rabjam he wrote his famous treatise on the Longchen Nying Thig, plus he collected and republished many Dzog Chen texts including those of Mindroling and the Nyingma Gyudbum.

51 The head of the Karma Kagyu monastic sect descending from Tilopa, Naropa, Marpa the Translator, Milarepa and Gampopa. This sect combines deep contemplation and asceticism with monastic life and philosophical studies.

52 The Khadampa school traces itself back to Atisa, who lived at the same time as Machig Lapdron (died at sNye.thang in 1054) and to Rin.chen bZang.po (see n. 16, p. 260). This "second diffusion" of Buddhism in Tibet aimed at purifying Tantrism of its aberrations and its proponents practiced particularly the Tantra of the form of Vairocana called Kun.rig. They enjoyed prestige among other sects and many monks were sent to study with them. This movement evolved into the Gelugpa sect synthesized by Tsong Khapa (1357–1419).

53 There is a nuclear power installation here now, built by the Chinese.

54 The Six Yogas of Naropa: see n. 76, p. 197 above.

55 See n. 11 on Mun.mtshams.

56 'Khor.ba Dong.sprugs is an Avalokitesvara practice for those who have recently died.

GLOSSARY

Adron	A.sgron
Adzom Drukpa	A.'dzom 'Brug.pa
Adzom Gar	A. 'dzom Gar
Ah Lang Go	A.'a Glang.mgo
Aman	A.sman
Ani Nyemo	A.nyes sNyed.mo
Apho Tsenga	A.pho Tsen.dga
Apho Wangdo	A.pho dBang.rdo
Ati.Zadon	A.ti Zab.don
Atso	A.mtsho
Barpu	sPar.pu
Barwa Garmo	sPar.ba dGar.mo
Bul Ngag	Bul.sngags
Bum.Cham	'Bum.lcam
Bumme	'Bum.me
Camtro Chungma	lCam.brod Chung.ma
Chang Chub	Byang.chub
Changchub Lingpa	Byang.chub Gling.pa
Chang chug Zangling	Byang.phyogs Zangs.gling
Chicha	gCig.char
Chod	gCod
Chodpa	gCod.pa
Chogyur Lingpa	mChog.gyur Gling.pa
Choje Kunga Jamyang	Chos.rje Kun.dga' 'Jam.dbyangs
Chokyi Dawa	Chos.kyi Zla.ba
Chomo NamKha	Chod.mo Nam.mkha'
Chotso	Chos.mtsho
Chowang	Chos.dbang
Chuba Lotsawa	Shud.bu Lo.tsha.ba

Dag.po	Dwags.po
Damema	dDag.med.ma
Dardron	Dar.sgron
Dawa Gyaltsen	Zla.ba rGyal.mtsham
Dechen Khadro	bDe.chen mKha'.'gro
Delog	'Das.log
Dodenag Gyi Wangchug	sTo.sde Ngag.gi dBang.phyug
Dondrub Zangpo	Don.grub bZang.po
Dorje Den	rDo.rje gDan
Dorje Dudulma	rDo.rje bDud.'dul.ma
Dorje Gyalpo	rDo.rje rGyal.po
Dorje Paldron	rDo.rje dPal.sgron
Dorjeying Kyi Wangchug	rDo.rje dByings.kyi dBang.phyug
Dorjeying Phyugma	rDo.rje dByings. Phyug.ma
Dorje Yudronma	rDo.rje gYus.gron.ma
Drachen	Grags.pa
Dragka Yang Dzong	Brag.dkar Yang.rdzong
Dragpa Samdrub	Grags.pa bSam.'grub
Dratang	Gra.thang
Drechan Rema Shegmo	Dren.chen Res.ma Sheg.mo
Drepung	'Bras.spungs
Drigung	Bri.gung
Drimima	Dri.mi.ma
Drodul Pawo Dorje	'Gro.'dul dPa'.bo rDo.rje
Dronkyi	sGron.skyid
Drontse	sGron.tse
Dron Tsema	sGron.tse.ma
Drub Chungma	Grub Chung.ma
Drubpa	Grub.pa
Drubse	Grub.se
Dudkyi	bDud.Kyi Le'u
Dzayul	rDza.yul
Dzijid Gyaltsen	gZi.brjid rGyal.mtshan
Dzogpa Chenpo	rDzogs.pa Chen.po
Dzompa kye	'Dzom.pa sKyid
Dzongsa	rDzong.sa
Dzongtsa	rDzong.rtsa
Dzong Tsho	rDzong.tshod
Ehchung	E.chung
Gaden	dGa'.dan
Gamalung	gYa'.ma.lung
Gang	Gangs
Gara Tsang	rGa.ra Tshang
Gargyi Wangchug	Gargyi dBang.phyug
Geshe Aton	dGe.bshes A.ston

Geshe Nyen Jangsem Sogyal	dGe.bshes gNyen Byang.sems bSod.rgyal
Gongpa Zangthal	dGongs.pa Zang.thal
Gonpa Rangdrol	dGongs.pa Rang.grol
Grolde Gyalwai Jungne	Grol.sde rGyal.ba'i 'Byung.gnas
Gurchen Thang	Gur.chen Thang
Gyaltse	rGyal.rtse
Gyalwa Gotsangpa	rGyal.ba rGo.tshang.pa
Gyalwa Khyung Tsangpa	rGyal.ba Khyung Tshang.pa
Gye Tong	brGyad.stong
Gyur	'Gyur
Gyurme Pema Tenzin	Gyur.med Pad.ma bsTan.'dzin
Jamgon Kongtrul Lodro Taye	'Jam.mgon Kong.sprul bLo.gros mTha'.yas
Jamyang Khentse Wangpo	'Jam.dbyangs mKhyen.brtse'i dBang.po
Jamyang Kongtrul	'Jam.dbyangs Kong.sprul
Jangpang Kur Nangpa	lJang.phang Khur Nang.pa
Jar	Byar
Jomo Chotso	Jo.mo Chos.mtsho
Jomo Karguma	Jo.mo mKhar.sgo.ma
Jomo Nagpa	Jo.mo Nag.pa
Kagyu	bKa'.brgyud
Kama	bKa'.ma
Kangyur	bKa'.'gyur
Kardrag	Kar.grags
Karko	mKhar.Khog
Kathog	Ka.thog
Katsal	sKa.tshal
Kawa Karpo	Kha.ba dKar.po
Khadampa	bKa'.gdams.pa
Khakyab Rangdrol	mKha.kyab Rang.grol
Khandro	mKha'.'dro
Khenpo Tragyal	mKhan.po Grags.gyal
Khentse Yeshe Dorje	mKhyen.brtse Ye.shes rDo.rje
Khung Tsang	Khyung.tshang
Khyenrab Odzer	mKhyen.rab 'Od.zer
Kongpo Kyab	Kong.po sKyabs
Korwa Dongtru	'Khor.ba Dong-sprug
Kunzang Dechen	Kun.bzang bDe.chen
Kyepo Yarlung	sKyid.po Yar.klungs
Kyozur Panchen Shakya Jung	sKyo.zur Pan.chen Sha.kya 'Byung
Kyungpo	Kyung.po
Kyung Tsang	Khyung.tshang

Glossary

Labchi ei Gangwar	lHa.phyi'i Gang.bar
Labdron	Lab.sgron
Lachi	lHa.phyi
Lading	Lha.lding
Laduma	La 'Dus.ma
Lamdre	Lam.'bras
Lang Thong	Glang.thong
Latho	La.thod
Lato	La.stod
Lawang Gonpo	Lha.dbang mGon.po
Lhamo Dronma	Lha.mo sGron.ma
Lhau Darpo	Lha'u Dar.po
Lhodrag Marpa Lotsa	Lho.brag Mar.pa Lo.tsa
Lhoka	Lho.kha
Lingje Repa	Gling.rje Ras.pa
Lodrak	Lho.brag
Longchen Nyingthig	Klong.chen sNying.thig
Longde	Klong.sde
Longsal Dorje Nyingpo	Klong.gsal rDo.rje'i sNying.po
Machig Lapdron	Ma.gcig Lab.sgron
Machig Ongjo	Ma.gcig Ong.jo
Machig Zama	Ma.gcig Zha.ma
Margyu Khandro Negyur	Ma.rgyu mKha'.gro gNas.'gyur
Marsho	sMar.shod
Milarepa	Mi.la Ras.pa
Minroling	sMin.grol Gling
Monlam Drub	sMon.lam Grub
Motrul Choying Dorje	rMog.sprul Chos.dbyings rDo.rje
Nachuka	Nga Chu Kha
Nalai Dradolgo	Nga.la'i bKras.dol.mgo
Namkhai Dorje	Nam.mkha'i rDo.rje
Namkhai Norbu	Nam.mkha'i Nor.bu
Namsho Tsomer	Ngam.shod mTso.mer
Nang Cho	Ngang.chos
Nangsa Obum	sNang.sa 'Od.'bum
Nopa Na Shugpa	rNgos.pa Na.shugs.pa
Norpa	Ngor.pa
Nungdro	sNgon.'gros
Nyagla Pema Dudul	Nyag.bla Pad.ma bDud.'dul
Nyalam	gNya'.lam
Nyang	Myang
Nyangla Ralpa	Nyang.la Ral.pa
Nyangtsa Seldron	Myang.tsha gSal.sgron
Nyashi	Nyag.gshis
Nyethang	rNye.thang
Nyingthig Yabzhi	sNying.thig Ya.bzhi

Osel Dorje Nyingpo	'Od.gsal rDo.rje sNying.po
Osel Palkyi	'Od.gsal dPal.skyid
Pal O Tride	dPal.'od Khri.sde
Palwangchug	dPal dBang.phyug
Pamting	Pham.mthing
Panyul	'Phan.yul
Panyul Langthang	'Phan.yul Lang.thang
Pema Nying Kye	Pad.ma Nying bkyed
Pema Paldzam	Pad.ma dPal.rdzom
Pema Tsokye	Pad.ma mTsho.skyid
Pema Yangkyi	Pad.ma Yang.skyid
Penyul Niphug	'Phen.yul Ni.phug
Peyul	dPal.yul
Phadampa Sangye	Pha.dam.pa Sangs.rgyas
Phagmo Lhakang	Phag.mo'i Lha.khang
Pitabatdra	Pi.ti.bha.tra
Pugzang	Phug.bzang
Pungpo Zankur Gyi Namshe Chod kyi Don Sal	Phung.po gZan.skyur gyi rNam.bZhad gCod.kyi Don.gsal
Puntso Gatshal	Phun.tshogs dGa'.tshal
Purang	Pun.rang
Rechung Dordag	Ras.chung rDor.grags
Rechung Dorje Dragpa	Ras.chung rDo.rje Grags.pa
Rigdzin Drupa	Rig.'dzin Grub.pa
Rinang	Ri.nang
Rinchen Dronme	Rin.chen sGron.me
Rinchen Zangpo	Rin.chen bZang.po
Ringsel	Ring.bsrel
Rinpoche	Rin.po.che
Rolang	Ro.langs
Sakya	Sa.skya
Sakya Gyaltsen	Sha.kya'i rGyal.mtshan
Samye	bSam.yas
Sangwa Kundu	gSang.ba Kun.'dus
Sarma	gSar.ma
Sechen	Zhe.chen
Selrong	Sel.grong
Semde	Sems.sde
Semnyi Dorje	Sems.nyid rDo.rje
Semo Chodar	Sre.mo Chos.dar
Sengchen Namdrag	Seng.chen gNam.brag
Sera	Se.ra
Serlag	rSer.glag
Sero Dampai Do	Ser.'od Dam.pa'i mDo
Sero Yarlung	Se.ra Yar.klung

Shalmo	Zhal.mo
Shamarpa	Zhwa dMar.pa
Shampo Gangri	Sham.po Gangs.ri
Sharpa	Tshar.pa
Sheldza Dromnema	Shel.zla sGron.ne.ma
Sherab Bum	Shes.rab 'Bum
Sherab Gyu	Shes.rab brGyud
Shigatse	gZhis.ka.rtse
Sonam Drapa	bSod.nams Grags.pa
Sonam Gyam	bSod.nams rGyam
Sonam Lama	bSod.nams Bla.ma
Sonam Palkye	bSod.nams dPal.skyid
Sonam Pundzom	bSod.nams dPal.'dzoms
Sonam Wongpo	bSod.nams dBang.po
Sralu	Zhra.lu
Tagzi	sTag.gzig
Talung	sTag.lung
Tamdrin Gon	rTam.mgrin mGon
Tanag	rTa.nag
Tashi Lhatse	bKra.shis Lha.rtse
Terma	gTer.ma
Thagma	sThag.ma
Tholung	Tod.lung
Tigle	Thig.le
Tigrom	Tis.grom
Tingri	Ding.ri
Togden Rangrig	rTogs.ldan Rang.rig
Tontso Rinchen Bum	sTon.mtsho Rin.chen 'Bum
Tonyon Samdrub	Thod.smyon bSam.grub
Tradru	Khra.'brug
Trayepa	Bra.yer.pa
Tritsham	'Bring.'tshams
Tsang	gTsang
Tsawa	Tsha.ba
Tse Chen	rTse.chen
Tsela Wongdo	Tshe.lha dBang.mdo
Tsering Jing	Tshe.ring 'Jongs
Tsethang	rTse.thang
Tsewang Paldon	Tshe.dbang dPal.sdron
Tshog Chen Dupa	Tshogs.chen 'Dus.pa
Tsokyi	mTsho.skyid
Tsomer	mTsho.mer
Tsurpu	mTshur.phu
Tugsdam	Thugs.dam
Tulku	sPrul.sku
Tummo	gTum.mo

Ushang Do	Ushang.rdo
Yangri	Yang.ri
Yang.sang Tug.thig	Yang.gsang Thugs.thig
Yardro	Yar.brog
Yarlung Shedra	Yar.klung Shel.brag
Yarthingpa	Yar.thing.pa
Yartiwa	Yar.this.ba
Yeshe Chodron	Ye.shes Chos.sgron
Yeshe Tsogyel	Ye.shes mTso.rgyal
Yoru Grawa Thang	gYo.ru Gra.wa Thang
Yug	Yug
Zangmo	bZang.mo
Zangmo Lhatri	Zhang.mo Lha.krid
Zangri Khangmar	Zangs.ri Khang.dmar
Zarmo Lung	gZar.mo Lung
Zinpa Rangdrol	'Dzin.pa Rang.grol
Zralakang	Zhrai Lha.khang
Zungjug	Zung.'jug
Zurkar	Zur.mkar

BIBLIOGRAPHY

Tibetan Sources

The History of All Buddhist Dharma, The Mirror Which Reflects All Things, by dPalden Tsul.khrims bDem.chog mKha'.'gro sNyen.rgyud mKhas.pa'i dGal.ston Pat III sNang.sa 'Od.kyi rNam.thar Phung.po gDzan skyur.gyi rNam.bzhad gCod.kyi Don.gsal.byed 'Khrul.'Khur Nyi.zla Kha.sbyor

Books

Aziz, B., *Tibetan Frontier Families*, Vikas, New Delhi, 1978.

Bachofen, J.J., *Myth, Religion and Mother Right*, Bollingen/Princeton University Press, 1973.

Bell, C.A., *The Religion of Tibet*, Clarendon Press, Oxford, 1924.

Bernbaum, E., *The Way to Shambala*, Doubleday, New York, 1980.

Beyer, S., *The Cult of Tara*, University of California Press, Berkeley, 1978.

Bharati, A., *The Tantric Tradition*, Samuel Weiser, New York, 1975.

Blofeld, J., *Bodhisattva of Compassion*, Shambhala, Boulder, 1977.

Chang, C.C., *The One Hundred Thousand Songs of Milarepa*, Vols. I and II, University Books, New York, 1962.

Chang, C.C., *Teachings of Tibetan Yoga*, University Books, New York, 1963.

Christ, C., *Diving Deep and Surfacing: Women Writers on a Spiritual Quest*, Beacon Press, Boston, 1980.

Christ, C., and Plaskow, J. (eds.), *Womanspirit Rising: A Feminist Reader in Religion*, Harper & Row, New York, 1979.

Conze, E., *Nineteen Selected Sayings from the Perfection of Wisdom*, Prajna Press, Boulder, 1978.

Cooper, J.C., *An Illustrated Encyclopedia of Traditional Symbols*, Thames & Hudson, London, 1978.

Dargyay, E., *The Rise of Esoteric Buddhism in Tibet*, Samuel Weiser, New York, 1978.

Das, C., *Tibetan English Dictionary*, Rinsen Book Company, Kyoto, 1979.

David-Neel, A., *Magic and Mystery of Tibet*, Abacus, London, 1977.

de Castillejo, I.C., *Knowing Woman*, Harper & Row, New York, 1973.

Dowman, K., *Sky Dancer: The Secret Life and Songs of the Lady Yeshe Tsogyel*, Routledge & Kegan Paul, London, 1984.

Dowman, K., *Songs of the Dakini*, Diamond Sow Publications, Kathmandu, 1980.

Eliade, M., *Birth and Rebirth: The Religious Meanings of Initiation*, trans. Willard Trask, New York, 1958.

Eliade, M., *Myths, Dreams and Mysteries: The Encounter between Contemporary Faiths and Archaic Realities*, London, 1960.

Eliade, M., *The Myth of Eternal Return*, trans. Willard Trask, Harper Torchbooks, New York, 1960.

Eliade, M., *Shamanism*, trans. Willard Trask, Bollingen/Princeton University Press, 1972.

Evans-Wentz, W.Y., *Tibet's Great Yogi Milarepa*, Oxford University Press, 1928.

Evans-Wentz, W.Y. (ed.), *The Tibetan Book of the Dead*, Oxford University Press, 1960.

Evans-Wentz, W.Y. (ed.), *Tibetan Yoga and Secret Doctrines*, Oxford University Press, 1958.

Falk, N.A., and Gross, R.M., *Unspoken Worlds: Women's Religious Lives in Non-Western Cultures*, Harper & Row, New York, 1980.

Ferrari, A., *Mk'yen Brtse's Holy Place in Central Tibet*, ISMEO, Rome, 1958.

Freemantle, F., and Trungpa, C., *The Tibetan Book of the Dead*, Shambhala, Berkeley, 1975.

sGampopa, *The Jewel Ornament of Liberation*, trans. H. Guenther, Shambhala, Berkeley, 1971.

Guenther, H., *The Life and Teachings of Naropa*, Clarendon Press, Oxford, 1963.

Guenther, H. (ed. and trans.), *The Royal Song of Saraha: A Study in the History of Buddhist Thought*, University of Washington Press, Seattle, 1969.

Guenther, H.V., *The Tantric View of Life*, Shambhala, Boulder, 1976.

Guenther, H., and Trungpa, C., *The Dawn of Tantra*, Shambhala, Berkeley, 1975.

Hall, N., *The Moon and the Virgin*, Harper & Row, New York, 1980.

Harding, E., *Woman's Mysteries*, Bantam, New York, 1971.

Harding, E., *The Way of All Women*, Harper Colophon Books, New York, 1970.

Horner, I.B., *Women under Primitive Buddhism*, Motilal Banarsidass, New Delhi, 1930.

Inayat, T., *The Crystal Chalice*, Sufi Order Pub., Lebanon Springs, New York, 1980.

Kunga, Lama, and Cutillo, B., *Drinking the Mountain Stream*, Lotsawa, New York, 1978.

Lederer, W., *The Fear of Woman*, Harcourt Brace Jovanovich, New York, 1968.

Lhalungpa, Lobsang, *The Life of Milarepa*, Prajna Press, Boulder, 1977.

Mander, A.V., and Rush, A.K., *Feminism as Therapy*, Random House, New York, 1980.

Mariechild, D., *Mother Wit: A Feminist Guide to Psychic Development*, The Crossing Press, Trumansburg, New York, 1981.

Miller, J.B., *Toward a New Psychology of Woman*, Beacon Press, Boston, 1971.

Nalanda Translation Committee (under the direction of Chögyam Trungpa), *The Life of Marpa the Translator*, Shambhala, Boulder, 1982.

Neuman, E., *Amor and Psyche*, Bollingen/Princeton University Press, 1971.

Neuman, E., *The Great Mother*, Bollingen/Princeton University Press, 1972.

Norbu, N., *Magic Dance: The Display of the Self-Nature of the Five Wisdom Dakinis*, P.O. Box 146, New York, 10062, 1981.

Norbu, N., *On Birth and Life: A Treatise on Tibetan Medicine*, Shang-Shung Edizioni, Grosseto, 1982.

Norbu, N., and Turnbull, *Tibet*, Simon & Schuster, New York, 1968.

Ortner, S., and Whitehead, H., *Sexual Meanings: The Cultural Construction of Gender and Sexuality*, Cambridge University Press, 1981.

Paul, D., *Women in Buddhism*, Asian Humanities Press, Berkeley, 1979.

Perera, S.B., *Descent to the Goddess: A way of Initiation for Women*, Inner City Books, Toronto, 1981.

Reynolds, F., and Capps, D. (eds.), *The Biographical Process: Studies in the History and Psychology of Religion*, Mouton, The Hague, 1976.

Roerich, G., *The Blue Annals*, Motilal Banarsidass, Calcutta, 1949.

Snellgrove, D., and Richardson, H., *A Cultural History of Tibet*, Prajna Press, Boulder, 1980.

Spretnak, C., *The Politics of Women's Spirituality*, Anchor Books, New York, 1982.

Starhawk, *The Spiral Dance*, Harper & Row, New York, 1979.

Sullerot, E., *Women on Love*, Doubleday, New York, 1974.

Suzuki, Shunryu, *Zen Mind, Beginner's Mind*, Weatherhill, New York and Tokyo, 1970.

Taring, R.D., *Daughter of Tibet*, Allied Publishers, New Delhi, 1970.

Therigata, *Psalms of the Early Buddhists*, trans. C.A. Rhys Davids, London, 1964.

Trungpa, C., *Cutting Through Spiritual Materialism*, Shambhala, Berkeley, 1973.

Trungpa, C., *Glimpses of Abhidrama*, Vajradhutu, Boulder, 1975.

Trungpa, C., *Meditation in Action*, Shambhala, Berkeley, 1969.

Bibliography

Trungpa, C., *The Myth of Freedom*, Shambhala, Berkeley, 1976.

Tucci, G., *The Religions of Tibet*, Routledge & Kegan Paul, London, 1980.

Von Franz, M.L., *The Feminine in Fairytales*, Dallas, Spring Publications, 1972.

Waddell, L.A., *Lamaism*, W. Heffer & Sons, Cambridge, 1939.

Waelti-Walters, J., *Fairy Tales and the Female Imagination*, Eden Press, Montreal, 1972.

Wang-Chug Dorje, *The Madhamudra Experience: Eliminating the Darkness of Ignorance*, trans. Alexander Berzin, Library of Tibetan works and Archives, Dharamsala, 1978.

Wayman, Alex, *The Buddhist Tantras*, Samuel Weiser, New York, 1973.

Wilhem and Baynes, *The I-Ching or the Book of Changes*, Bollingen/Princeton University Press, 1950.

Magazine articles

Dowman, K., "A Buddhist Guide to the Power Places of the Kathmandu Valley," *Kailash: A Journal of Himalayan Studies*, vol. VIII, no. 3, 1981, Ratna Pustak Bhandar, Kathmandu.

Govinda, L.A., "Pilgrims and Monasteries in the Himalayas," *Crystal Mirror*, vol. IV, Dharma Publishing, Berkeley, 1975.

Katz, N., "Anima and nKa'-'gro-ma: A Critical Comparative Study of Jung and Tibetan Buddhism," *Tibet Journal*, vol. II, no. 3, The Library of Tibetan works and Archives, Dharamsala, 1977.

Saklani, C., "A Hierarchical Pattern of Tibetan Society," *Tibetan Journal*, Winter 1978, Dharamsala.

Trungpa, C., "Femininity," *Maitreya* IV, "Woman," Shambhala, Berkeley, 1973.

Unpublished sources

Norbu, N., "Dzog Chen," A series of talks by Namkhai Norbu Rinpoche, Copyright Dzog Chen Community, San Francisco, 1980.

Sarfaty, C., "Towards Autonomous Affiliation: Issues of Dependence and Autonomy for Women in Love Relationship Crisis," Goddard College, Vermont, 1981.

Trungpa, C., "The Feminine Principle," Copyright Chögyam Trungpa Rinpoche, Boulder, Colorado.

Trungpa, C., "Hinayana Mahayana Seminary Transcripts," Vajradhata, Boulder, 1974.

Trungpa, C., "Mandala Sourcebook," Copyright Chögyam Trungpa Rinpoche, Boulder, Colorado.

Trungpa, C., "Visual Dharma Sourcebook II," Copyright Chögyam Trungpa Rinpoche, Boulder, Colorado.

INDEX

Index

Ceridwen (goddess), 33
chang, 70, 80, 110
Chang Chog Zangling, 151
Chang Chub, 246
Chicha, 247
children: Machig Lapdron's, 171–3, 178–80; Nangsa's, 96–102, 117, 128; spiritual path and, 18, 77
Chod, 15, 53, 145, 146, 148, 186, 235, 238, 239, 243, 245, 246, 247, 248, 249, 250, 251, 252, 253; *see also* Mahamudra Chod
Chodpa, 148, 149, 243, 246
Cho Gyur Lingpa, 240
Choje Kunga Jamyang, 149
Chokyi Dawa, 153, 156
Chos' byung, 22
Chowang (guru), 55, 207, 208, 210, 242, 248
Christ, Carol, 2
Christianity, 3, 13, 15, 56
Chuba, 83
Chuba Lotsawa, 175
Chumbo, 255
conch, 153, 154
confession, 126

Dakini, 24–38, 66–7, 76, 85–151; language of, 13, 42–6; *see also* Wisdom Dakini
Dakshinkali, 249
Damaru, 92, 93
Damema, 3, 151
Dargyay, Eva, 208
Dawa Gyaltsen, 169
death: as descent and re-emergence, 49–54; Lord of, 91, 116, 126, 127
Dege Gonchen, 244
Deleg Rinchen, 228
Delog, 47, 65, 98, 109, 110
Demeter, 31
demoness, 55, 82–3, 121
depression: descent and, 53; Nangsa's, 73–7, 103
descent, 2, 46–57; Nangsa's, 90–2; Jomo Memo's, 207
Deva, 37, 76, 92, 103, 110, 164
Dharmakaya, 35, 102, 167, 218
Dharma of the Wheel of the Four Meditative States, 166
Dharmapalas, 175
Dharma Protector, 225
dharmata mandala, 165

Dhatisvari (dakini), 27
Diamond Sow, 31, 32
divination, 90
Diving Deep and Surfacing (C. Christ), 2
dohas, 39, 165
Dondrub Zangpo, 150
Dorje Den, 151, 182
Dorje Dudulma, 169, 177
Dorje Gyalpo, 209
Dorje Paldron, 236, 242, 247, 256
Dorjeying Phyugma, 173
Dorje Yudronma, 248
Dra, 159
Dra (Drapa) (Lama), 159, 162, 165, 168, 171, 173, 174
Dragka Yang Dzong, 239
Dratang, 165
dreams: A-Yu Khadro's, 237, 253; dakinis in, 37, 151–5; Drenchen Rema's, 227; Machig Lapdron's birth and, 151–5, her children and, 178, her marriage and, 169; Namkhai Norbu's, 256; prophetic, 46, 66–7, 225, 237, 240, 242, 246
Drimima, 180
Drodul Pawo Dorje, 253
Dron Tsema, 157, 171
Drubchenpa, 187
Drub Chungma, 172
Drubpa, 172, 180
Drub Se, 172, 179
Du Kyi Leu, 161
Dzarana, 218
Dzijid Gyaltsen, 229
Dzog Chen, 43, 54, 89, 165–7, 238, 242–3, 244, 245; women in, 13–14, 18
Dzogpa Chenpo, 85
Dzom Kye (Dzompa Kyi), 75, 95, 104, 108
Dzongsar, 245, 253
Dzongsar Khentse Rinpoche, 244–5, 253
Dzong Trang, 239
Dzongtsa, 252, 256
Dzong Tsho, 240

ego, formation of, 26, 217
Ehchung, 170
Eliade, Mircea, 56
energy, dakini and, 37
Ereshkigal, 35, 36

Index

Khentse Wongpo, 44, 250, 253, 254
knife, hooked, 32–3
Kongpo, 172
Korwa Dongtru, 254
Kunzang Dechen, 66, 68, 71, 73, 105, 108, 118
Kunzang Longyang, 239, 240, 243, 246, 247, 248
Kusha grass, 181
Kyeme Gamtso, 187
Kyepo Yarlung, 85
Kyo Zur Panchen Shakya Jung, 161
Kyung Lung, 249

Labchi Eli Gangwar, 153
Labdron, 158
Lablung, 168
Laduma, 172
Lama, 76, 225
Langdharma, 64
Lapdronma, 166
lapis lazuli, 93
laywoman, Buddhist, 8
Lhamo Dronma, 168, 171
Lhasa, 165, 227, 250
Lhawang Gonpo, 243, 244
Lhokha, 158
Lingje Repa, 210
Lodrag Marpa Lotsa, 85
Lodrak, 210
Lokapalas, 175
Longchen Nying Thig, 238, 240
Longsal Dorje Nyingpo, 239, 245

Machig Drowa Zangmo, 229
Machig Ongmo, 53
Machig Zama of Latho, 167
McLaughlin, Eleanor, 15
madness, Machig Lapdron's son and, 179
Magyu Dhadro Negyur, 175
Mahamaya, 152
Mahamudra Chod, 144, 165, 176, 182, 184, 186
Mahapbajapati, 3, 6, 7
Mahayana, 127, 163
Maitreya, 165
Mala, 107
Mamaki (dakini), 28
Mandala, 107, 151, 152, 164, 174, 176; of Tsendura, 121
Mani, 98

Manjushri, 173, 174, 187; Red, 178, 179, 185
Manmay Rinpoche, 187
Mantras, 107, 228
Maras (Five), 176
Marpa the Translator, 64, 216
masculine, in Tibetan Buddhism, 10, 17, 24, 35
matriarchy, and Dzog Chen, 14
meat: symbolism of, 37–8; as offering, 162
Meru, Mount, 164
Migyur Namkhai Dorje, 242, 243
Milarepa, 37, 42, 64, 81, 82, 85, 88, 117, 125
milk: symbolism of, 33; first, 67; of Dharma, 121
Mindroling, 251
Mindroling Jetsun Rinpoche, 248
Monlam Drub, 150, 151, 152, 167
monkey, 85
moon, crescent symbol of, 33
"Moon of Wisdom," 63
mother, reinforcing collective standards, 50, 109–16
Mother Hulba, 46
mother-in-law, 51–2
Motrul Choying Dorje, 242

Na Chu Ka, 251
nadis, 218
Naga, 70, 163
Nalai Dradolgo, 172
Nalandara, 251
Nalanda University, 40
Nala Pema Dundrub, 238, 243, 245, 247, 248, 250
Namkhai Norbu Rinpoche, 13, 14, 16, 146, 236, 256, 257
Namso Tsomer, 158
Namthar, 207, 235
Naropa, 38, 40, 41, 42
nidhanas, 173
Nirmanakaya, 35, 102
Nirvana, 127, 225
Norpa and Sharpa Sakya, 236
nothingness, experience of, 2
nungdro, xxi
nuns: Buddhist, 3, 7–8, 39, 107, 160; Jain, 3, 7
Nyangpo, 172
Nyang Ralpa (guru), 242
Nyang To, 118

[279]

Index